Fire, Blood and the Alphabet:
one hundred years of Lorca

edited by Sebastian Doggart
and Michael Thompson

Manchester University Press
Manchester and New York

Distributed in the United States exclusively by Palgrave Macmillan

© Individual Authors

Llagas de amor and *La doncella, el marinero y el estudiante* by Federico García Lorca copyright © Herederos de Federico García Lorca. Translations copyright © Candida Clark, John Clifford, Sebastian Doggart, John Edmunds, Gwynne Edwards, James Flint, Paula Guarderas, Brendan Kenelley, John Kerr, Al Robertson, Nicholas Round, Caridad Svich, Colin Teevan, Mark Westcott, Merryn Williams, and Herederos de Federico García Lorca. Drawings by Federico García Lorca copyright © Herederos de Federico García Lorca.

Herederos de Federico García Lorca is hereby identified as the author of the Spanish-language works and drawings in accordance with applicable law throughout the world, and the translators are hereby identified as authors of the translations in accordance with applicable law throughout the world.

All rights are reserved throughout the world by Herederos de Federico García Lorca and Translators. All enquiries should be addressed to William Peter Kosmas: E-mail:_wpk_artslaw@compuserve.com; 8 Franklin Square, London W14 9UU, England.

Copyright © Manchester University Press 2010

While copyright in the volume as a whole is vested in Manchester University Press, copyright in individual chapters belongs to their respective authors, and no chapter may be reproduced in whole or in part without the express permission in writing of both author and publisher.

Published by Manchester University Press
Oxford Road, Manchester M13 9NR, UK
and Room 400, 175 Fifth Avenue, New York, NY 10010, USA
www.manchesteruniversitypress.co.uk

Distributed exclusively in the USA by
Palgrave, 175 Fifth Avenue, New York NY 10010, USA

Distributed exclusively in Canada by
UBC Press, University of British Columbia, 2029 West Mall,
Vancouver, BC, Canada V6T 1Z2

British Library Cataloguing-in-Publication Data
A catalogue record for this book is available from the British Library

Library of Congress Cataloging-in-Publication Data
A catalog record for this book is available from the Library of Congress

ISBN 13: 978 0 7190 8182 8

First published 1999 by Durham Modern Languages Series

This edition first published 2010 by Manchester University Press

Printed by Lightning Source

Contents

Acknowledgements	5
List of Illustrations	6
Federico García Lorca: list of works mentioned in this volume	7
Introduction, *Michael Thompson*	9
The Lorca Fiesta: celebrating the centenary in Newcastle, *Sebastian Doggart*	19

1. Reassessing the impact of Lorca's work

Lorca's Legacy: writing in the institution, *Paul Julian Smith*	31
Lorca 1919–1929, *Gwynne Edwards*	43
García Lorca: after New York, *David Johnston*	57
'Poetry that gets up off the page and becomes human': poetic coherence and eccentricity in Lorca's theatre, *Michael Thompson*	67
Lluís Pasqual's unknown Lorcas, *Maria Delgado*	81
Lorca, Don Cristóbal and the Carnivalesque, *Cariad Astles*	107
Learning from the Master: Lorca's homage to Picasso, *Jacqueline Cockburn*	123

2. Creative Responses

The Death of Lorca, *Merryn Williams*	145
The night journey, *John Clifford*	146
Ode to Federico García Lorca, by Pablo Neruda, translated by *Sebastian Doggart*	164
Notes on *Voyage to the Moon*, *Frederic Amat*	169
Irish ReLorcations, *Colin Teevan*	175
Looking for Lorca: a legacy in the Americas, *Caridad Svich*	191
Directors' panel discussion: Alison Andrews, Hayley Carmichael, John Clifford, Sebastian Doggart, Paul Hunter, David Johnston, Alan Lyddiard	207

3. Translating Lorca

'Combined tactics' in translating Lorca, *Nicholas Round*	225
Translators' panel discussion: John Clifford, John Edmunds, Gwynne Edwards, David Johnston, Nicholas Round, Colin Teevan, Merryn Williams	237
'Sixteen Wounds of Love': translations of 'Llagas de amor' by John Clifford, Candida Clark, Sebastian Doggart, John Edmunds, Gwynne Edwards, James Flint, Paula Guarderas, Brendan Kennelly, John Kerr, Alistair Robertson, Nicholas Round, Caridad Svich, Colin Teevan, Mark Westcott, Merryn Williams	261
The Maiden, the Sailor and the Student, translated by *Sebastian Doggart*.	279

To Gerda Voûte Breuers, for all her wisdom and kindness, and to Alan Lyddiard, for his inspired leadership at Northern Stage and his enthusiasm for Lorca and all things Andalusian.

Acknowledgements

The editors would like to thank Northern Stage, the Spanish Embassy in London and the Publications Board of the University of Durham for generous subventions towards the publication of this book. Many thanks are also due to all the contributors, who have given their time, talents and energy with enormous generosity. Special thanks to Oliver Gaiger for designing the front cover. In addition, we are grateful for the editorial suggestions of Caroline Voûte, Mark Hawkins-Dady and Frances Clarke; for Chloë Veltman's vital contribution as rapporteur to the conference; for the humour and personal support of Rosie Hunter and Tony Doggart; and for the efficiency and good judgement of Janet Starkey and Peter Whyte in the preparation of the volume for DMLS.

Northern Stage's *Lorca Fiesta* of May–June 1998 was supported by the European Regional Development Fund, the Spanish Embassy, London, La Tasca Restaurants, San Miguel, Northern Arts, the National Lottery Arts for Everyone Programme, and Newcastle upon Tyne City Council.

Copyright material on pp.261–82 is reproduced by kind permission of the Herederos de Federico García Lorca and on pp.164–7 by kind permission of the Fundación Pablo Neruda. Many thanks to William Kosmas and Carmen Balcells for their co-operation in this respect.

List of Illustrations

The Moon Comes Out, Federico 1	22
The Moon Comes Out, Federico 2	22
Théâtre Sans Frontières' *Cuentos de Amor*	23
Told By An Idiot's *I Weep at My Piano*	24
Gabrielle Jourdan as Lorca in *Poet in New York* by Gwynne Edwards	54
Magician with fan in Lluís Pasqual's production of *El público* (Madrid, 1987).	92
Silly Shepherd	93
Juliet and horses	94
Naturaleza muerta con botella de ron "Jamaica" (1925)	126
Guitarra (1927)	129
Composición con instrumentos musicales (1927)	130
Nocturno frutero con dos limones (1934)	132
Teorema de la copa y la mandolina (1927	132
Payaso del guante (1925)	134
Payaso con guitarra (1925)	134
Payaso de rostro desdoblado (1927)	136
Retrato de Dalí (1927	139
Dama en el balcón (1927)	139
Retrato de dama española sentada (1929)	141
Images from *Voyage to the Moon* by Federico Amat	168

Federico García Lorca:
works mentioned in this volume

Title	Date of Composition	Title in English
El maleficio de la mariposa	1920	*The Butterfly's Evil Spell*
Cristobical	1920–1922	*Cristobical*
Los títeres de cachiporra: Tragicomedia de don Cristóbal y la señá Rosita	1922	*The Billy-Club Puppets: Tragicomedy of Don Cristóbal and Mistress Rosita*
La niña que riega la albahaca y el príncipe preguntón	1923	*The Girl Who Waters the Basil and the Prying Prince*
La zapatera prodigiosa	1925	*The Shoemaker's Wondrous Wife*
Mariana Pineda	1925	*Mariana Pineda*
Amor de don Perlimplín con Belisa en su jardín	1925	*The Love of Don Perlimplín for Belisa in His Garden*
La doncella, el marinero y el estudiante	1926	*The Maiden, the Sailor and the Student*
Posada	1927–1928	*The Inn*
El paseo de Buster Keaton	1928	*Buster Keaton's Walk*
Quimera	1928	*Chimera*
El público	1930	*The Audience*
Así que pasen cinco anos	1931	*Five Years from Now*
El retablillo de don Cristóbal [second version of *Los títeres de cachiporra*]	1931	*Don Cristóbal's Puppet Show*
Bodas de sangre	1932–1933	*Blood Wedding*
Yerma	1934	*Yerma*
Doña Rosita la soltera o el lenguaje de las flores	1935	*Doña Rosita the Spinster, or The Language of Flowers*
La casa de Bernarda Alba	1936	*The House of Bernarda Alba*

Comedia sin título   1936   *Play without a Title*

Film Script
Viaje a la luna   1929   *Voyage to the Moon*

Verse

Poema del cante jondo	1921	*Poem of Deep Song*
Canciones	1921–1924	*Songs*
Romancero gitano	1924–1927	*Gypsy Ballads*
Poeta en Nueva York	1929–1930	*A Poet in New York*
Sonetos del amor oscuro	1935–1936	*Sonnets of Dark Love*

Introduction

Michael Thompson

The year 2007: the Conservative Prime Minister, William Hague (try to imagine it ...), taking part in events to celebrate the centenary of the birth of a gay left-wing poet and playwright, declares 'Today England is called Wystan', while copies of Auden's verses are showered over York. An unlikely prospect, perhaps. In Spain, though, they have Federico García Lorca, and their conservative Prime Minister, José María Aznar, showed boyish eagerness as he announced on 5 June 1998, the centenary of Lorca's birth, that 'España hoy se llama Federico' ('Today Spain is called Federico') and proved to the assembled media that he could recite from memory a few lines from the *Romancero gitano*. Meanwhile, the city of Granada was bombarded from a helicopter with 100,000 leaflets containing a selection of Lorca's poetry.

Aznar's enthusiasm at the Residencia de Estudiantes in Madrid on 5 June was only slightly dented by an awkward question suggesting that there was some irony in his appropriation of a figure long seen as an icon of the Left and despised or ignored by the political forefathers of Aznar's Partido Popular. Asked whether he felt that he could identify ideologically with Lorca, he replied evasively: 'Representa, junto con Cervantes, uno de los grandes símbolos de nuestras letras. Algunos se empecinan en que discutamos de cosas sin mucho sentido. No hay que obstinarse en viejas historias o en ideologías' ('He stands alongside Cervantes as one of the great symbols of our literary heritage. Some people insist on trying to get us to talk about things that have little meaning. There's no point in going on about the past and about old ideologies').[1] In a way, such a tribute represents a significant posthumous triumph for Lorca: the enduring fascination of his

---

[1] *ABC* (6 June 1998), 13.

personality and his work have in the end overcome the hostility and unease provoked by the moral and political implications of his texts, by the perplexing difficulty of some of them, and by the author's own sexuality. Not only is his place in the literary pantheon assured, but he is deemed to be public property, unproblematically accessible to all. None of the other centenaries of events of 1898—the most significant were the end of Spain's empire and the birth of the poet Vicente Aleixandre—generated as much interest or excitement in Spain. One of the Franco regime's favourite poet-playwrights and propagandists, José María Pemán, was also born in Andalucía in 1898, but little effort was made to celebrate his life and work. Even if he had not shared the same Christian names, Aznar—anxious to distance his party from the authoritarian past of the Spanish Right—would not have dreamt of announcing to the nation on Pemán's birthday that 'España hoy se llama José María'.

Institutionalised tributes of this kind tend, however, to be concerned with the construction of monuments. They set out to chisel off the spiky bits, smooth down the rough edges and conceal the contradictions, fixing in stone an image of the man and his art and ultimately limiting their potential impact. In contrast, Paul Julian Smith emphasises in the study that opens the first section of this volume the importance of recognising 'García Lorca' as a site of struggle: a personality and a body of work which are—and must continue to be—appropriated, reappropriated and contested by numerous interests and in various ways. The issues around which the struggle takes place are political, sexual, historical and literary; to do with gender, cultural identity, emotional response, and approaches to reading, translation and performance. This book is a record of a centenary celebration that set out not to build a monument but to open up a space in which some productive struggles could take place, a number of Lorcas could be let loose, and a range of creative and analytical interpretations could be played off against one another.

The path leading to the Newcastle Playhouse's Lorca Fiesta goes back to 1995, when Alan Lyddiard and a small group of actors developed *Looking for Lorca*, a 'work in progress' as part of an extended process of preparation for the Northern Stage production of *Blood Wedding* the following year. Lyddiard had been struck by the poetic power that emerged from Brendan Kennelly's translation,[2] and had immersed himself in an investigation of Lorca and the cultural traditions of Andalucía. The resulting production of *Blood Wedding* was an extraordinary fusion of cultural influences, boldly setting off the potential cliché of flamenco against music from Northumberland and Scotland, combining folk traditions with modern dance (choreographed by Salud López from Sevilla), and putting Spanish dancers alongside actors from England, Scotland and Ireland. The high point of Kennelly's text, a pulsating adaptation of the Moon's speech, was thrillingly performed by Richard Clews in a spectacular white flamenco-style dress, the bare stage transformed by a series of mirrors into a hallucinatory labyrinth of sharp edges, reflections and shadows.[3] Various elements of that production re-emerged in pieces performed in the 1998 Fiesta: members of the *Blood Wedding* cast performed in Told By An Idiot's *I Weep At My Piano*, in *Cuentos de Amor* by Théâtre Sans Frontières, and in Lyddiard's own show based on Lorca's poem 'Llanto por Ignacio Sánchez Mejías', *The Moon Comes Out, Federico*, once again with choreography by Salud López.[4]

The conference at which the papers in this volume were delivered was an integral part of the Fiesta, running alongside the theatrical and musical performances and films, being informed by them and responding to them, involving some of the performers in discussions, and generally sharing the party atmosphere that comes naturally to the Playhouse. The event brought together theatre practitioners—writers, directors, actors and translators—and academics (and some who fit both descriptions) to celebrate and interrogate Lorca's legacy from a variety of perspectives. What emerges strongly from the talks, debates and poems published here, and from the Fiesta as a whole, is that this is very much a live, dynamic legacy. Above all, the contributors bring out

---

[2] Federico García Lorca, *Blood Wedding*, translated by Brendan Kennelly (Newcastle: Bloodaxe, 1996).
[3] Alan Lyddiard discusses his approach to the production in the directors' panel discussion reproduced in this volume (see pp.201–10).
[4] The performances in the Fiesta are described in more detail in Sebastian Doggart's introduction.

the continuing relevance of Lorca's work and the creative and interpretative challenges it poses.

The volume is in three parts. While the first part, 'Reassessing the impact of Lorca's work', has a primarily academic focus, all the contributions are designed to be accessible to a non-specialist readership. The pieces in the second part, 'Creative responses', are inspired above all by the contributors' own creative activity, although those by Caridad Svich and Colin Teevan also make an important contribution to the scholarly dimension of the collection. The third section, 'Translating Lorca', includes discussion of the principles and problems involved in the translation of Lorca's texts as well as examples of the practice.

Paul Julian Smith, Professor of Spanish at the University of Cambridge and author of numerous ground-breaking books on Spanish and Latin American literature, theatre and film, provides a sophisticated overview of the García Lorca phenomenon to open the first section. Since the paper he gave at the conference had already been committed for publication elsewhere, what is published here covers similar issues but is taken from the introduction and conclusion to his recent book, *The Theatre of García Lorca: text, performance, psychoanalysis* (reproduced with the permission of Cambridge University Press). As well as opening up some fundamental questions about perceptions and manipulations of Lorca's public image and about the reception of his texts by readers/spectators, directors and critics, the inclusion of this piece here serves a useful function in drawing our readers' attention to a book that is essential reading for all students of Lorca's theatre. **Gwynne Edwards**, Professor of Spanish at the University of Wales (Aberystwyth), author of *Lorca: The Theatre Beneath the Sand* and *Dramatists in Perspective: Spanish theatre in the twentieth century*, and prolific translator of plays by Lorca and other Spanish playwrights, surveys the key developments in Lorca's life and work between 1919 and 1929 and suggests intimate connections between the author's personality and his plays. **David Johnston**, Professor of Hispanic Studies at Queen's University Belfast, has written extensively on Spanish theatre and on the principles and practice of translating for the stage. He is also well known as a translator of Spanish plays (most recently Valle-Inclán's *Divine Words* and Lorca's *The Public*, both for

BBC Radio 3) and a writer (most recently, *¡El Quijote!*, for London's Gate Theatre, *Hambone's Day* for BBC2 and *The Shadow of the Wedding*, BBC Radio 3). His paper focuses on the next phase in the evolution of Lorca's theatre: the sharpening of social awareness in his work after 1929, and the centrality of the issue of 'otherness'. **Michael Thompson**, Lecturer in Spanish at the University of Durham, has published articles on and editions of the work of various contemporary Spanish dramatists; my contribution to this volume is an analysis of Lorca's concept of poetic theatre, emphasising linguistic playfulness, the integration of verbal and non-verbal languages and the frequently eccentric quality of the poetic logic of his plays. **Maria Delgado**, Lecturer in the School of English and Drama at Queen Mary and Westfield College, University of London, has translated plays by Valle-Inclán and edited a recent issue of *Contemporary Theatre Review* entitled 'Spanish Theatre 1920-95: Strategies in Protest and Imagination', *In contact with the gods?: Directors talk theatre* (Manchester UP, 1996) and *Conducting a Life: Reflections on the theatre of María Irene Fornes* (Smith & Kraus, 1999). She discusses innovative productions by the Catalan director Lluís Pasqual, showing how his iconoclastic approach responds to and illuminates the elusiveness and self-conscious theatricality of Lorca's experimental texts. **Cariad Astles**, who teaches puppet theatre, Latin American theatre and community theatre at the University of Plymouth, is engaged in PhD research into popular puppet theatre and the carnivalesque, and runs a puppet theatre company, Theatre Carnivalesque, brings out the importance of Lorca's puppet plays, discussing what are often regarded as minor texts in the light of theories of carnival and Lorca's ongoing project of theatrical experimentation. (This talk was nicely complemented in the Fiesta by the production of *The Billy-Club Puppets*. The puppet-show style proscenium arch constructed for the production served as a frame for most of the conference talks.) **Jacqueline Cockburn**, Head of History of Art at Westminster School, is working on a doctoral thesis on García Lorca's drawings at the University of London. Her publications include *The Spanish Song Companion* written in collaboration with Richard Stokes (Victor Gollancz, 1992). Her paper (colourfully illustrated at the time with slides, of which, unfortunately, only the Lorca drawings can be reproduced here), shifts the focus from the theatre to Lorca's drawings, discussing his debt to Picasso and the fusion in both artists of avant-garde experimentalism with deep roots in Spanish cultural traditions.

The second part of the book opens with three poetic tributes to Lorca. **Merryn Williams**, poet, Thomas Hardy scholar and editor of the journal *The Interpreter's House*, has published a volume of translations of Lorca's poetry. The text that appears here, 'Death of Lorca', is from her latest book of poetry, *Sun's Yellow Eye* (National Poetry Foundation, 1997). **John Clifford** is the author of about fifty scripts in every medium (theatre, radio, TV, film, opera and puppet theatre), and lectures at a Drama School (Queen Margaret University College, Edinburgh). His best known theatre works include *Losing Venice, Great Expectations, Ines de Castro* and *Light in the Village*. His translation of Calderón's *Life is a Dream* opened at the 1998 Edinburgh Festival and has recently played at the Barbican and in New York. He is currently working on a new libretto for *The Magic Flute*, and the translation and adaptation of a Galdós novel for BBC Radio 4. His reading at the conference of the poem published here, 'The night journey', was a moving, mesmerising tour de force. **Sebastian Doggart**, organiser of the Fiesta and conference, and director of a performance at the Fiesta based on *Poeta en Nueva York*, contributes a new translation of the startlingly surrealist 'Oda a Federico García Lorca' by the Chilean poet Pablo Neruda, who became a close friend of Lorca while living in Spain (1934-38). Next, the celebrated artist, stage designer and film-maker **Frederic Amat** gives an account of the tribulations suffered by Lorca's screenplay *Viaje a la luna* and by his attempts to film it, characterising the text as a secretive 'dialogue between dream and wakefulness'. The intention had been that he would be at the Fiesta to introduce the world premiere of his film, which in the event was not complete. He nevertheless presented a vivid description of the project, accompanied by slides of stills and artwork from the film. **Caridad Svich** is currently resident playwright at the Mark Taper Forum Theatre in Los Angeles. She is co-editor of *Out of the Fringe: Contemporary theatre and performance* (TCG/Nick Hern), and of *Conducting a Life: Reflections on the theatre of María Irene Fornes*. Her English-language translations of García Lorca's plays and poems are collected in the forthcoming volume *Federico García Lorca:*

Impossible theatre (Smith & Kraus), and her play *Alchemy of Desire* was performed at the Hackney Empire Studio Theatre in August-September 1999. Her account of the inspirational effect of Lorca's work on her writing for the stage and on that of other dramatists in the USA and Latin America combines personal experience and illuminating analysis in a highly distinctive way. **Colin Teevan** was appointed Writer-in-Residence at Queen's University, Belfast in 1997, where he is now Head of Drama. His original stage plays include *The Big Sea, Here Come Cowboys, Tear Up the Black Sail, Buffalo Bill Has Gone to Alaska, Vinegar and Brown Paper, The Crack and the Whip, Iph. . .* and, most recently, *Svejk*. He has translated for the stage from several European languages, most recently *Marathon* and *Cuckoos* from Italian, which have been produced at the Gate Theatre, London. His work is published by Oberon Books and Nick Hern Books. He has written on a range of theatre issues for international journals and anthologies, and is a co-founder and former Artistic Director of Galloglass Theatre Company, Ireland. His piece sets out an entertaining and revealing survey of connections—both real and fanciful—between Lorca and Ireland, arriving in the process at some new ways of defining elements of Spanishness in Lorca's 'rural trilogy'. The final component of this section is an edited transcription of a round table discussion on the problems and joys of directing and performing Lorca's theatre. Sebastian Doggart emphasises the openness of the texts; Alan Lyddiard and Alison Andrews describe their approaches to *Blood Wedding* and *The Billy-Club Puppets*; John Clifford celebrates the beauty, precision and explosive power of the words of Lorca's plays; Paul Hunter and Hayley Carmichael (of Told By An Idiot) talk about their response to Lorca's texts in the light of their brilliantly devised piece based on his relationship with Dalí and Buñuel.

In one way or another, all the contributions to this volume are concerned with the continuing challenge of making Lorca's work available and intelligible to English-speaking audiences, and the third section addresses the issue of translation directly. **Nicholas Round**, Professor of Hispanic Studies at the University of Sheffield, author of numerous studies on medieval, Golden Age and modern literature and translator of Spanish and Portuguese plays, describes his pragmatic approach to working in collaboration with John Edmunds on a translation of *El amor de don Perlimplín*, an experience that generated valuable insights into the nature of translation for the stage as a process of dialogue and negotiation. Professor Round also sets the ball rolling in the translator's panel discussion, emphasising the need for an adroit 'management of knowledges'. Merryn Williams and Gwynne Edwards discuss the problems of translating verse, while John Edmunds focuses on the specifics of translating for actors—the importance of identifying the key rhythms and breathing patterns implicit in the original text and attempting to create comparable rhythms in the translation. Colin Teevan argues that the two crucial factors in successful translation of drama are a sound knowledge of stagecraft and a meaningful emotional link with the text, and John Clifford advocates 'trusting the characters'—allowing the dynamics of the dialogue to generate the right language in the translation. Participants in the panel discussion and other translators took part in a demanding creative challenge: to produce new versions in English of Lorca's sonnet 'Llagas de amor' from the *Sonetos del amor oscuro*. The results of the challenge are published here as 'Sixteen Wounds of Love': some of them expertly crafted sonnets staying close to the form and imagery of the original, others daring adaptations that reinterpret Lorca's lines in astonishing ways. A new translation by Sebastian Doggart of Lorca's short play *La doncella, el marinero y el estudiante* concludes the volume on an intriguing note of whimsicality.

Many Lorcas are evoked here: a personality that was playful but troubled, childlike but aesthetically sophisticated, sentimental but socially committed, and a body of work rooted in literary, pictorial and folk traditions yet also startlingly modern, inventive and relevant. Some of that work (notably *Viaje a la luna*, *El público* and the *Sonetos del amor oscuro*) has become available only relatively recently; both the recent discoveries and the more familiar work continue to inspire new readings, translations and performances around the world. The *duende* that came out to play on Tyneside for a couple of weeks in 1998 provided eloquent evidence of the undimmed power of that inspirational influence, and all the participants were grateful to Sebastian Doggart for bringing us together to celebrate it. I leave it to Sebastian himself to give a fuller account of the performance side of the Fiesta.

The Lorca Fiesta:
celebrating the centenary in Newcastle
Sebastian Doggart

'How tragic!' lamented Queen Sofía of Spain in 1998, in front of the bed where Federico García Lorca was born, when reminded of his execution in 1936 by Franco's henchmen. Far away from the Queen, in Tokyo, a performance in Japanese was taking place of *Bodas de sangre*, Lorca's classic tragedy of a woman loved by two men. In Egypt, another of Lorca's love tragedies, *Yerma*, was being rehearsed in Arabic. At Cambridge University, a multimedia lecture was being given on The Lorca Cult. Neneh Cherry, Michael Nyman and Compay Segundo were recording a CD of tribute songs. Shooting had just finished on a Hollywood movie starring Andy Garcia as Lorca. In 1998, the centenary of his birth, his work and memory had never been more alive.

This book is directed at readers both familiar with, and new to, Lorca. It is a tribute to an extraordinary polymath whose influence continues to be felt across the world. As well as one of the twentieth century's most important dramatists and poets, Lorca was influential as a lecturer, screenwriter, painter, guitarist, pianist, puppeteer, producer, director and actor. The contributors to this book reflect the many facets of Lorca's creative work: academics, poets, translators, novelists, film-makers, painters, theatre directors, and performers. Indeed, there may soon be as many Lorcas as there are Shakespeares. His identities proliferate, as light through a prism, and his legacy becomes richer with every new reading or viewing. Lorca has touched millions with his visions of the natural world, his insight into human passions, and his seductive mastery of language. These are the fire, blood, and the alphabet of this book's title.

This book grew out of the 1998 Lorca Fiesta in Newcastle-upon-Tyne, the largest event outside Spain to commemorate the centenary of his birth. It was Alan Lyddiard, artistic director of Northern Stage, who conceived the idea of the Fiesta, and I worked with him, Mandy Stewart and their team to produce a two-week festival of drama, music, contemporary dance, flamenco, puppetry and film that culminated in Lorca's birthday celebration on 5 June. The festival attracted large audiences from all over Britain. Newcastle turned out to be an appropriate location for capturing the living spirit of Lorca. If he could have got over nostalgia for the orange blossom and sensual heat of southern Spain, he would have felt at home in the north-east of England, where economic neglect and a proud sense of identity compare with Lorca's own native Andalucía. Indeed, if Lorca were to go to a football match today at St James' Park, he would find a blood-driven energy similar to a bullfight in Sevilla. On pub-crawls in Gateshead he would feel echoes of the bacchanalian pilgrimage of an Andalusian *romería*. And he would be drawn to the pagan and Christian forces of Antony Gormley's sexually ambiguous Angel of the North, which was assembled during preparations for the festival.

The programming of the festival sought to avoid hackneyed folkloric representations of Lorca. There was no more place for gypsy *Bodas de sangre* than for patronising or prurient vindications of his sexuality. The intention was to show Lorca as our global contemporary, to affirm him as an avant-garde artist, and to challenge other artists to respond to him personally and innovatively. The result was ten new productions premiered at the festival. One of the most audacious projects was *The Moon Comes out, Federico*, a collaboration between Northern Stage and the Sevilla-based company Octubre Danza. It fused story-telling, contemporary dance, and live *cante jondo* (deep song) to enact Lorca's long poem 'Lament to Ignacio Sánchez Mejías', his toreador friend who was fatally gored in a bullring in 1934. Lorca viewed Sánchez Mejías' death as 'an apprenticeship for my own death. There are moments when I see the dead Ignacio so vividly that I can imagine his body, destroyed, torn apart by worms and brambles, and I find only a silence which is not nothingness, but mystery.' The production played poetically with this association. It began with the poem's final stanza: 'Not for a long time, if ever, will be born an Andalusian so noble, so rich in adventure. I sing of his elegance with words that moan and remember a sad breeze in the olive trees.' As the guitar struck up plaintively, the 'Moon' appeared, her red hair spilling over a long white dress. She cast a deathly shadow as Ignacio's 'Present Body' danced with his 'Absent Soul'. The show concluded with a moving scene in which an eight-year-old boy played Ignacio/Federico, set to a haunting Kyrie from the African mass, Misa Luba.

Many of the Fiesta's productions had a strong biographical element. The physical theatre group Told by an Idiot devised a witty dream piece, *I Weep at My Piano*, about the passionate and naughty relationship between Lorca and two other leading artists of the 1920s European avant-garde, Salvador Dalí and Luis Buñuel. Hayley Carmichael played Lorca as a Chaplinesque clown, pining over unreciprocated love for Dalí and teased brutally by Buñuel. An interesting pattern emerged of women portraying Lorca, and Carmichael was one of three actresses playing him, with Esperanza Martínez in *The Moon Comes out, Federico*, and Gabrielle Jourdan in *Poet in New York*. The latter was a monologue that combined Lorca's letters, poems and drawings to evoke his seminal journey to the United States and Cuba in 1929-30. Another strongly biographical piece was Foolsyard Theatre Company's staging of Peter Straughan's *The Ghost of Garcia Lorca which can also be used as a table*, a kaleidoscope of memories of Lorca, presented by 'Salvador Dalí': 'He could limp and play the piano,' Dalí says of his close friend, 'I forget the rest.'

As for Lorca's own work, the festival focused on material rarely seen on British stages. BBC newscaster-turned-translator John Edmunds directed a rehearsed reading of what Lorca's surviving sister Isabel considers to be his finest play, his 'erotic comic-strip', *Amor de Don Perlimplín con Belisa en su jardín*, newly translated as *How Dom Perlimplin Adored Belisa, and in His Garden Tried to Please Her*. Perlimplin was hilariously played by Murray Melvin, better known for his part in *A Touch of Frost* and as Reverend Run in Stanley Kubrick's *Barry Lyndon*. Another unusual text was *The Billy-Club Puppets*, produced by students from the University of Northumbria. They presented themselves as a contemporary version of Lorca's Barraca theatre troupe, and made imaginative use of video projection, life-size marionettes, and Geordie jokes. Meanwhile, the theatre's bar and foyer were painted with Moorish fountains, lizards, mares and other Lorcan images and became the stage for Théâtre Sans Frontières' *Cuentos de Amor*. The performers sang, danced on tables, and manipulated puppets

Northern Stage's The Moon Comes Out, Federico *at the Newcastle Lorca Fiesta (June 1998)*

Théâtre Sans Frontières' Cuentos de Amor *at the Newcastle Lorca Fiesta*
(May 1998)

Told By An Idiot's I Weep at My Piano *at the Newcastle Lorca Fiesta (May 1998)*

to enact some of Lorca's poems and to tell the story of *The Little Girl who Waters the Basil Plant and the Prying Prince*, first performed in 1923 by Lorca and Manuel de Falla for the children of Fuente Vaqueros.

'Fundamentally, I am a musician,' Lorca once said. He had a deep love of flamenco, especially the 'dark sounds' of *cante jondo*, in which he sought to find 'the black torso of the Pharaoh'. He played the classical guitar and helped to popularise *cante jondo* by writing new lyrics. His trip to New York brought him into contact with jazz, blues and gospel, and in the smoky bars of the port of Havana, he danced to *son*, *danzón*, *boleros* and *contradanzas*. Lorca's love of music lay at the heart of the Fiesta's programme. Carlos Bonell performed some of Lorca's own settings for guitar in the recital *All Shall Know I Have Not Died*. Israel Galván, one of Spain's most acclaimed young flamenco dancers, packed out the Newcastle Playhouse with his tribute to Lorca, his feet flying to the lament of the *soleá* and the *seguirilla*.

The climax of the festival was Lorca's birthday on 5 June, for which the organisers recreated the music and atmosphere of Havana, one of the places that most touched his heart. 'This island is a paradise,' he wrote to his mother, 'if ever I get lost, look for me either in Andalusia or in Cuba.' Marietta Veulens, a Cuban musician, led a specially formed quintet, playing the dance music which accompanied Lorca's own heady Havana nights, and two professional dancers taught the steps to over 800 revellers in the banqueting hall of the Civic Centre in Newcastle.

Lorca was also fascinated by film: 'The cinema has for me an indescribable magic, a freedom beyond compare. When we enter the darkness of the cinema, it is as if we close our eyes and begin a journey mapped by the imagination [...] Of course I love the theatre, and the theatre does amazing things, but the cinema is more versatile, more free, and so more poetic.' The festival screened numerous films, directly and indirectly inspired by Lorca. There was a season of works by Luis Buñuel, both his friend and one of his fiercest critics, who later wrote of Lorca: 'Of all the human beings I have ever known, Federico was the finest. He was his own living masterpiece.' This season included a screening of *Un chien andalou*, which Lorca was convinced was written contemptuously about him. There was also the British premiere of *The Disappearance of García Lorca*, a thriller about a young writer who returns after eighteen years to investigate who murdered Lorca, and why. As proof that Lorca has now been appropriated by mainstream European-American culture, he was played by Hollywood heart-throb Andy Garcia, who said of his relationship to the character:

> As a Cuban living in America, I am an exile, cut off from, and missing, my country and my cultural roots, so I can identify deeply with Lorca, but with a difference. He was a homosexual, a social exile in a sexually intolerant society. He lived among friends who loved him, and yet even his closest male and female friends never suspected his true sexual identity. The fear of non-acceptance was a terrible cross for him to bear. Yet I see him as a humorous guy, a man who liked to clown with his friends. I wanted to bring this aspect of him through, within the context of the movie.

Lorca himself wrote one screenplay, *Voyage to the Moon*, over two days in 1929. The script consists of seventy-two scenes, an enigmatic montage of mutating images, suggesting a search for an impossible love. After an abortive attempt in the 1930s to film it, the manuscript went missing until 1989 when it was found in a bedside table in Oklahoma. Subsequently, various people tried to produce it but always failed, making the project seem jinxed. In 1997, the Lorca Foundation, run by his heirs, commissioned the producer Javier Martín-Domínguez to make the film. The director was originally the Catalan painter and film-maker Frederic Amat, who had worked with Lluís Pasqual—arguably Lorca's finest contemporary stage director—on the first production in 1986 of *The Audience* at Milan's Piccolo Teatro. The film started shooting in late 1997 with Spanish performance artist La Ribot among the cast. It was due to have its premiere at the Newcastle festival, but, during shooting, Amat and Martín-Domínguez fell out. Amat walked off the set, and Martín-Domínguez took over the direction. Amat complained to the Lorca Foundation about Martín-Domínguez's interpretation. The Foundation took Amat's side and banned the screening of the completed film. Meanwhile, Amat began shooting a new version of the screenplay, alas too late to be completed in time for the festival. However, Amat flew over from Spain to give an illustrated talk on his multimedia approach to filming, the text of which is included here. Whether the film will ever be screened is a new Lorca mystery.

As well as celebrating Lorca's artistic legacy, the Fiesta sought to stimulate academic debate through a three-day international conference, which brought together scholars, directors, translators and writers to challenge the way Lorca is taught, performed and understood in Britain. The conference was billed as 'One Hundred Years of Lorca: Poetry, Politics and Perversion'. The intention behind the word 'perversion' was a play on Lorca's taste for pagan shock, but the Lorca Foundation objected to it on the grounds that it presented an inappropriate image of the poet, and the subtitle was eventually dropped. Professor David Johnston chaired the conference with great diplomacy, bridging the fierce divisions amongst Lorca academics. Most of the papers and discussions are included here.

One of the most interesting debates centred on the translation of Lorca's work. Ted Hughes said once that 'Lorca cannot be Englished'. However, this was a view fundamentally challenged by the underlying principle of the festival: the belief that Lorca's work touches people beyond cultural and linguistic boundaries. As a practical way of refuting Hughes's remark, we asked a number of writers, poets and novelists to translate into English one of Lorca's most complex poems, the sonnet 'Llagas de amor'. Their brief was to be true to the spirit, not necessarily the letter, of the original. Look at the results, published in Part Three, and decide for yourself whether it translates effectively into English. These sixteen versions reveal a rich and honest diversity of personal responses. Such diversity in responses to Lorca ensures that he will continue to seduce, intrigue and challenge in the twenty-first century.

1

Reassessing the impact of Lorca's work

Lorca's Legacy: writing in the institution[1]
Paul Julian Smith

Text, Performance, Psychoanalysis

In 1994 the Fundación Federico García Lorca moved to new quarters in Madrid, hard by the Residencia de Estudiantes, of which García Lorca himself had been the most celebrated student. In 1995 the Huerta de San Vicente outside Granada was opened as a 'Museum-House' ('Casa-Museo') dedicated to García Lorca. Purchased eleven years before by the Town Council, it was filled with 'furniture, pictures, and original objects from the house as it was when García Lorca lived in it', at a time when he composed some of his best known plays and poems.[2] At the opening ceremony García Lorca's niece Isabel García Lorca played the poet's arrangement of a popular song on his own piano. *El País* reported that the Museum 'seal[ed] the reconciliation between García Lorca and Granada'; and that together with the birthplace in Fuentevaqueros (also a museum to the poet)[3] and the Fuente de Lágrimas ('Spring of Tears') of Alfacar, where the poet's remains are believed to lie, the Huerta de San Vicente 'complete[d] a Lorcan route' or tourist trail.[4]

The Fundación, with its catalogues and manuscripts, the Huerta and birthplace with their relics and collectables, each would seem to signify in its different way the definitive institutionalisation of García Lorca in Spain, the poet's consolidation as an academic and popular icon on the

[1] The text of this paper is adapted from the introduction and conclusion of my book *The Theatre of García Lorca: text, performance, psychoanalysis* (Cambridge University Press, 1998), with the kind permission of Cambridge University Press.
[2] From an anonymous text on the back of the Huerta's publicity leaflet, dated 1995 and published under the auspices of the Ayuntamiento de Granada.
[3] The Casa-Museo Federico García Lorca in Fuentevaqueros is administered by the Diputación Provincial de Granada.
[4] Alejandro V. García, 'Lorca y Granada sellan la reconciliación con la apertura del Museo de la Huerta de San Vicente', *El País* (11 May 1995).

verge of the centenary of his birth. Moreover *El País*'s stress on 'reconciliation' suggests the termination of an extended period of mourning, one marked by the full incorporation of García Lorca into the Madrid academy and the Granadan establishment towards which in his lifetime he felt such ambivalence: Isabel García Lorca is reported to have wept on hearing the address by Laura García Lorca de los Ríos, the director of the Huerta, in which she presented the house as 'an extension of the body [of the poet], an extension of his imagination'.

Outside Spain also it appeared that García Lorca had achieved an untouchable status: for example, it was reported that in the United Kingdom he had surpassed Brecht as the most performed foreign playwright.[5] Yet it is a commonplace of cultural studies that any public figure (writer, politician, movie star) is a site of struggle, and one aim of my book is to examine the constitution of what I have called elsewhere the 'author function' in relation to García Lorca,[6] to tease out those contradictions which trouble the smooth surface of institutional prestige and historical reconciliation. More specifically, the increasing acknowledgement of García Lorca's homosexuality must problematise the very notion of a 'legacy' of García Lorca which is to be preserved and consecrated by family, region, and nation state. Lesbian or gay artists whose relationships remain invisible or unrecognised by law, may not be best served by those who legally inherit what remains of their name and property. As Luis Fernández Cifuentes has persuasively argued, it was the nature of García Lorca to seduce.[7] And this seduction (etymologically 'leading astray') means that García Lorca's life and work are irreducible to bare facts, 'original objects', or plot synopses. But this need not mean that the glamour of his figure or the rapture produced by and celebrated in his work can simply be assigned to an ineffable 'magic' or 'duende'. Rather I will suggest that this shuttling

---

[5] David Johnston, 'Las terribles aduanas: the fortunes of Spanish theatre in English', *Donaire*, 1 (September 1993), 21.

[6] 'Lorca and Foucault', *The Body Hispanic: gender and sexuality in Spanish and Spanish-American literature* (Oxford University Press, 1989), 106–109. It is to distance myself from the cult of 'Lorca' and to call attention to the author function that I use the full name 'García Lorca' throughout the book.

[7] 'La verdad de la vida: Gibson versus Lorca', *Boletín de la Fundación Federico García Lorca*, 4 (1988), 92.

between concept and affect (between thought and feeling) so characteristic of García Lorca's theatre should itself be submitted to analysis, and most specifically to psychoanalysis as the vocabulary of passion, in all senses of the word. As we shall see, passion, like seduction, leads to the greatest of threats and of pleasures: the loss of a sense of self (of García Lorca's and of our own).

Cultural studies as a discipline is only now emerging in Peninsular Hispanism.[8] But if, as has been recently argued, 'the modernizing project' of Spain in the 1920s and 1930s involving the 'incorporation of popular and mass cultural forms particularly marked [...] the Spanish avant garde';[9] and if García Lorca's work is itself characterised by both 'avant garde experimentalism and traditional elements',[10] then García Lorca must remain a key figure in any new approach to Spanish culture, as he was in more traditional literary studies. In my stress, then, on the historical, commercial, and ideological conditions of García Lorca's 'production' (of his self and of his theatre) I thus seek to make a contribution to this emerging field. However, unlike many practitioners of performance studies and some theatre professionals who engage in 'director's theatre', I do not contest the importance of the text. And if the 1990s have seen an institutionalisation of García Lorca in Spain at least, they have also seen a number of publications which have changed the corpus of García Lorca's writing and will perhaps transform our present understanding of its canonicity. Thus we have seen the appearance, much delayed, of three substantial collections of juvenilia: prose, poetry, and drama; of the first free-standing edition of the *Sonetos del amor oscuro*, previously included only in the last edition of the complete works; and the first Spanish edition of the unproduced film script *Viaje a la luna* based on access to the original manuscript.[11] There

---

[8] See Helen Graham and Jo Labanyi (eds), *Spanish Cultural Studies: an introduction* (Oxford University Press, 1995), 1.
[9] Helen Graham and Jo Labanyi, 'Culture and Modernity: the case of Spain', ibid., 7.
[10] Graham and Labanyi, 70 (picture caption).
[11] *Prosa inédita de juventud*, ed. Christopher Maurer; *Teatro inédito de juventud*, ed. Andrés Soria Olmedo; *Poesía inédita de juventud*, ed. Christian de Paepe (Madrid: Cátedra, 1994). *Sonetos del amor oscuro; Poemas de amor y erotismo; Inéditos de madurez*, ed. Javier Ruiz Portella (Barcelona: Altera,

is little doubt that further unpublished works held by the Fundación will continue to emerge.

The misadventures of García Lorca's manuscripts have by now a long history: if *Viaje a la luna* had appeared in both complete and incomplete form in English translation before it did so in the Spanish original, then, notoriously, *El público* had been the object of a full-length critical monograph in both Spanish and English before permission was finally given for the text itself to appear.[12] The precedence of commentary over original in this case is a deconstructive irony noted by critics such as Luis Fernández Cifuentes.[13] But this postponed publication is the clearest case of a divergence between the playwright and the family who inherited his copyright: for García Lorca had published in his lifetime the most explicitly homoerotic fragment of the play, the dialogue of the Figure of Bells and the Figure of Vine Leaves; and he had repeatedly insisted that *El público* and the other 'unplayable' plays constituted his real, true theatre.

There has thus been increasing critical interest in García Lorca's experimental plays, and there seems little doubt that an earlier publication of the unplayable plays would have counteracted the pernicious and pervasive folkloric stereotypes which still determine foreign responses to García Lorca: the recently revised *Oxford Companion to the Theatre* simply fails to mention the experimental plays, focusing, as ever, on the so-called rural trilogy.[14] If the 'impossible' theatre was, as García Lorca declared, destined for the future, we are now that audience, and we have an ethical responsibility to respond to its challenge, a responsibility denied to earlier generations of scholars and theatre-goers. Such a burden cannot leave us indifferent, intellectually or aesthetically.

1995). *Viaje a la luna*, ed. Antonio Monegal (Valencia: Pre-textos, 1994).

[12] Rafael Martínez Nadal, *Lorca's 'The Public': a study of his unfinished play ('El público') and of love and death in the work of Federico García Lorca* (London: Calder & Boyars, 1974).

[13] *García Lorca en el teatro: la norma y la diferencia* (Zaragoza: Universidad de Zaragoza, 1986), 278.

[14] Phyllis Hartnoll (ed.), *Oxford Companion to the Theatre*, 4th ed. (Oxford University Press, 1995), 314.

In tandem with this revision of the corpus of García Lorca's theatre comes the proliferation of critical approaches. While the history of what has been called 'the politics of theory in post-Franco Spain'[15] has meant that Spanish criticism remains predominantly within its linguistic and philological tradition, US scholars in particular have produced a wide range of readings, in addition to the exemplary historical and textual work of, say, Christopher Maurer and Andrew A. Anderson: a contemporary scholar or student can pick and choose amongst feminist, gay, and deconstructive García Lorcas, to cite only the most familiar.[16]

In the book I formulate some controversial interpretations of four major plays, which I take in reverse order of composition and increasing order of conceptual complexity and anti-naturalism. Thus of *Yerma* I argue that the central, sterile protagonist can be read as an 'intersexual type'; and that when she strangles her husband at the climax of the play she is, following Gregorio Marañón's recommendation to Spaniards of García Lorca's time, suffocating the seeds of the opposite sex which lie deep within her. *Bodas de sangre*, I argue, dramatises a lost object or relation: the young, male body and its confrontation with that of the other, a mutual penetration of 'two men in love', as Langston Hughes's translation puts it. This confrontation cannot be staged by García Lorca, but is, much later, by Carlos Saura in his flamenco film version. In *Así que pasen cinco años* the hesitations of the protagonist, his postponed engagement and deferred desires, are read as characteristic of the Gidian youth, more desired than desiring, unable or unwilling to integrate romantic love and genital pleasure. Finally, on *El público* I argue, in the context of Lluis Pasqual's

---

[15] See the introduction to Silvia L. López, Jenaro Talens and Darío Villanueva (eds), *Critical Practices in Post-Franco Spain* (Minneapolis: University of Minnesota, 1994).

[16] One early feminist reading is Julianne Burton's '"The Greatest Punishment": Female and Male in Lorca's tragedies' in Beth Miller (ed.), *Women in Hispanic Literature: icons and fallen idols* (Berkeley: University of California, 1983), 259-79. An early gay reading is Paul Binding's *Lorca: the gay imagination* (London: GMP, 1985). Luis Fernández Cifuentes's work combines sophisticated deconstructive argument with historical scholarship in an exemplary way. Antonio Monegal's 'Unmasking the Maskuline: Transvestism and Tragedy in García Lorca's *El público*', *MLN*, 109 (1994), 204-16 rehearses the deconstructive *topoi* of the mask and performance.

production, for a connection between the play's twin arguments on theatre and on homosexuality, a connection which focuses on the perilous and provisional status of both, caught as they are between the subjective and the social, the personal and the public.

'Doing Lorca'

This paper began with the transfer of the Fundación García Lorca to the same site as the Residencia de Estudiantes in Madrid; and with the opening of the Casa-Museo in the Huerta de San Vicente, presented in *El País* as an act of postponed 'reconciliation' between the poet and his home town. The true story as told in the regional press was, however, more complex. For García Lorca's archive had originally been offered to Granada council, which had rejected it. When it and the regional government of Andalucía later requested the archive be transferred from Madrid, generously offering the recently opened Huerta de San Vicente as its site and pledging an annual subsidy of five million pesetas, the director of the Fundación, Manuel Fernández Montesinos, was said to have refused their offer. The Andalusian *Ideal* reported that the Casa-Museo, in its current, more modest incarnation, had recently been closed because of the town council's delay in paying its employees' wages.[17]

This continuing struggle between centre and periphery staged around the figure of García Lorca was also seen at an auction of unpublished manuscripts by the poet. On this occasion the national State exercised its right of first refusal by spending almost five million pesetas and thus leaving both the Fundación and the Casa-Museo empty handed. *ABC* reported that the final destination of the documents would be decided by the then Socialist Minister of Culture, Carmen Alborch.[18] This acquisition was part of Madrid's cultural policy at the time: a

---

[17] J.L. Tapia, 'La Fundación García Lorca rechaza su traslado a Granada', *Ideal* (5 April 1996).
[18] Natividad Pulido, 'El Estado adquiere los textos inéditos de Lorca por casi cinco millones de pesetas: Alborch decidirá si van a la Biblioteca Nacional o a la Fundación del poeta', *ABC* (21 February 1995).

substantial portion of Buñuel's papers was also to be bought later for a much larger sum.

Hence García Lorca remained a site of struggle in Spain, as he was abroad. If in the 1990s he was the foreign playwright most frequently staged in Britain, still references to Brecht far outnumbered those to García Lorca in the British quality press.[19] Even as García Lorca's universal genius is proclaimed, still his influence on theatre in general is restricted: the fact that there is no standard adjective in English derived from his name, equivalent to the familiar 'Brechtian', would confirm that this is the case. Moreover, it is difficult to trace any conceptual or intellectual influence abroad, analogous to that of Brecht once more, which might be attributed to his 'impossible', experimental works. Presented as ever as a seductive icon rather than a playwright of substance, García Lorca was the subject of yet another biopic: in winter 1995 Marcos Zurinaga began shooting the stereotypically titled *Blood of a Poet*, starring Esai Morales and Andy García. Based on Ian Gibson's books, the film was intended in familiar fashion to focus not on the life or the work of García Lorca, but rather on his death.[20]

In Spain critics continued to complain about García Lorca scholars' supposed 'obsession with sex and politics', with one venerable figure from Granada claiming that this tendency had 'rendered uncongenial ["antipática"] the figure of Lorca, who was congeniality ["simpatía"] itself, the most vibrant joy and youthfulness of a whole glorious period of our literature.'[21] In a hermetic 'Spanish literary system'[22] which jealously preserved its immunity from the critical fashions of English-speaking countries, it remained difficult to acknowledge that 'congeniality' might be culturally conditioned or dependent on the

[19] In *The Guardian* references to García Lorca rose from 9 in 1990 to 25 in 1994, before falling to 8 in 1995; the figures for Brecht are 66, 98, and 50, respectively. I have consulted *The Guardian on CD ROM*.
[20] Private communication with Benedict Carver, contributor to *Screen International* (7 December 1995).
[21] Antonio Gallego Morell, *Sobre García Lorca* (Granada: University of Granada, 1993), Introduction, unpaginated.
[22] Darío Villanueva, 'The Evolution of the Spanish Literary System', in José Colmeiro, Christina Dupláa, Patricia Greene, and Juana Sabadell (eds), *Spain Today: essays on literature, culture, society* (Hanover NH: Dartmouth College, 1995), 139–47.

suppression of those very factors (such as homosexuality) which a national literary tradition would have most difficulty in assimilating. It is perhaps not in scholarly studies but in Frederic Amat's artistic works, endlessly repeated graphic traces intended for a travelling theatre that was never to be built, that we find one of the most touching and challenging responses in the Spanish state to García Lorca's restlessly experimental legacy.[23]

Like French productions of García Lorca in the 1950s and 1960s, Spanish productions in the 1990s oscillated between folklore and abstraction. The most transparent example of the first tendency was Luis Olmos's production of *La zapatera prodigiosa* for the Teatro de la Danza de Madrid, which, after completing a national tour, played the capital's Teatro La Latina from September to November 1995. The venue was significant: this was the first time that a García Lorca play had been staged in this 'popular theatre'. The director reported in an interview that his company specialised in 'strong doses of music, dance, colour, and, of course, theatre';[24] while publicity material also stressed 'light, colour, and fun ["alegría"] with the unmistakable magic of the great Andalusian poet!'. While this popularising approach may well serve as an antidote to the sometimes anaesthetic 'quality' versions of García Lorca (and most certainly achieved a more resounding commercial success), in Olmos's case a short and fragile text was swamped by lavish and garish staging, in which the actors were poorly integrated with professional dancers, on sabbatical from the Compañía Nacional de Danza and the Ballet Nacional de España.

At the opposite end of the spectrum came Lluis Pasqual's *Haciendo Lorca* for the Centro Dramático Nacional and the Théâtre de l'Europe, which played Madrid's subsidised Teatro María Guerrero in April and May 1996. Originally announced as a radically pruned production of the text of *Bodas de sangre*, *Haciendo Lorca* reduced theatricality to a bare minimum: two actors (Nuria Espert and Alfredo Alcón); a bare black

---

[23] Amat has also made artworks on the theme of the body and AIDS such as 'Anatomía'. See my 'Fatal Strategies: the representation of AIDS in the Spanish state', *Vision Machines: cinema, literature, and sexuality in Spain and Cuba, 1983–93* (London: Verso, 1996), 108.

[24] Ritama Muñoz-Rojas, 'Lorca entra por primera vez en el teatro de La Latina', *El País* (17 September 1995).

set against which the actors were slowly transported on cranes; a text composed of fragments of *Bodas, Yerma, Así que pasen cinco años*, and *El público*. Coldly received in Andalucía,[25] the somewhat reworked piece received an ecstatic welcome in Madrid. As *El País* reported, the sense of a unique occasion derived in part from the fact that this was 'the last premiere of the Socialist era' and the last cultural event at which socialite Minister of Culture Alborch would be present.[26]

While audience and press feted Pasqual as Spain's most international director, recently awarded the French Légion d'Honneur, his innovatory *Haciendo Lorca* is to be read in the context of a newly nationalist programming policy for the Centro Dramático Nacional: it had earlier been announced that the Madrid Centro would focus for that season on twentieth-century Spanish plays.[27] Just as the rapturous reception at the María Guerrero had been underwritten by the news (just announced) that the victorious but minority Partido Popular was to form a government with the Catalan regionalists, so the shift from experimental to classical programming was acknowledged by Pasqual himself to be a response to 'this time of disappointment and anguish' in which arts professionals awaited with the rest of the nation an as yet untried right-wing government. Pasqual thus feels a need to return to unfinished business with the 'all too familiar' García Lorca ('el Lorca de toda la vida'). But he also stresses the contribution of his actors: Espert, who had starred as *Yerma* in Víctor García's famous production, and Alcón, who had played the Director in Pasqual's own. Pasqual claims they are 'the last great masters with a direct line [to the poet], a specific way of doing Lorca. It was now or never.' Here we find once more that sense of the fragility and pathos inherent in the theatrical event and in the contribution of actors, who in the course of their careers exhibit to the audience the trace of time in their bodies: few of those present at the premiere of *Haciendo Lorca* could have failed to be aware of the role played by the playwright, by the actors,

---

[25] Margot Molina, 'Fría acogida en Sevilla al estreno de "Haciendo Lorca" de Lluis Pasqual', *El País* (20 April 1996).
[26] Rosana Torres, 'El equipo de lujo de "Haciendo Lorca" ofreció en Madrid el último estreno de la etapa socialista', *El País* (28 April 1996).
[27] Itziar Pascual, 'La escritura española de este siglo, apuesta del Centro Dramático Nacional', *El Mundo* (5 September 1995).

and by their director in the theatre of the transition to democracy and of the subsequent 'disillusion' with the Socialist government.

But the intense affects experienced by many in the audience of *Haciendo Lorca* (*El País* speaks of 'rejoicing and tears') are not merely generalised emotion; rather they are also part of what Freud called an 'economics of pain': a work of mourning or progressive 'detachment from an object [whose] significance is reinforced by a thousand links'.[28] The experience of the theatre, continuously repeated in time and diffused in space, constructed through the accumulation of countless memory traces and affective charges, would seem to be exemplary of just such an economic process. It is a process in which a figure such as García Lorca is gradually endowed with an affective charge and significance whose limits cannot simply be defined.

Freud writes in his case study of female homosexuality that one way of breaking off a love relation is through identification of the lover with the object.[29] I have argued that, merging with their fantasies of García Lorca, many critics and spectators regress to a nostalgic narcissism in which their very own poet (whether sacrificial blood victim or congenial genius of 'our literature') reflects back to them what they already know. There are recent signs in Spain, however, that mourning may be coming to an end; and that with the consequent liberation of affect García Lorca is being incorporated into new and exciting contexts which could not previously have been anticipated. One of these signs is Pasqual's *Haciendo Lorca* itself, with its radical disrespect for the integrity of García Lorca's text. Another is Joaquín Cortés's dance version of 'El diálogo del amargo' ('The Dialogue of the Bitter One'), which formed part of his highly successful flamenco fusion dance show *Pasión gitana* (*Gypsy Passion*), first performed in March 1995. Staged as an amorous *pas-de-deux* between two male dancers, and with García Lorca's poetry recited over the dance, this is one of the first examples of a Spanish 'queering' of García Lorca. The Cortés who revels in his Cordovan heritage but acts for Almodóvar and models for Armani; the Cortés who displays a muscular male torso while dancing in and with

---

[28] 'Mourning and Melancholia', *On Metapsychology*, Penguin Freud Library 11 (Harmondsworth: Penguin, 1991), 251, 252.

[29] 'The Psychogenesis of a Case of Homosexuality in a Woman', *Case Histories II*, Penguin Freud Library 9 (Harmondsworth: Penguin, 1991), 384.

the flounces of a flamenco skirt, is a fine example of a cultural phenomenon who refuses to be confined to any one side of the paradigm: tradition and modernity, centre and periphery, gay and straight.

Giving a new twist or shade to García Lorca's most famous line of poetry, the lesbian and gay students' group of Madrid's Complutense University have named themselves 'Rosa que te quiero rosa' ('Pink how I love you, pink').[30] Beyond the continuing critical focus on such motifs as ritual sacrifice and the wounded heart in García Lorca,[31] I would suggest more attention be paid to such manifestations of love and of survival as those to be found in the varied cases of Pasqual, Cortés, and 'Rosa...'. While cultural figures and activities of this kind which draw on García Lorca's legacy will clearly have more cogency in Andalucía and the Spanish state, a greater awareness of the challenge posed by García Lorca's experimental drama may help to extend the reach of a putative 'García Lorca century' beyond Spain's borders, as Pasqual has already attempted in such an exemplary fashion at the Théâtre de l'Europe. The sometimes oblique but always fruitful engagement I trace in my book between García Lorca and Marañón, Hughes, Gide, and, finally, Freud, is offered as a further step in this direction.

Conservative commentators, frightened by the rise of regionalism, have raised the question of 'what remains of Spain'.[32] García Lorca must be a primary example of a cultural remainder which will survive to be interpreted in new ways appropriate to the new and unfamiliar circumstances of a rightist government. But García Lorca's legacy can be read not as a testimony to the persistence of the nation state and a national literature, but rather as a pointer to their ruins. The García Lorca who staged the dance of the two Figures in *El público* in a Roman Ruin is also the García Lorca who shares with later gay Spanish writers a sense of 'the disruptive and erotically transgressive potential in

---

[30] 'Rosa que te quiero rosa', Aula 500, Facultad de Ciencias Políticas, Campus Somosaguas, Madrid.
[31] David Johnston (ed. and trans.), *Yerma and the Love of Don Perlimplín for Belisa in the Garden* (London: Hodder and Stoughton, 1990), 3.
[32] Federico Jiménez Losantos, *Lo que queda de España* (Madrid: Temas de Hoy, 1995).

the landscape of ruins and classicism'.[33] He may also have more than a little in common with the young Freud who experienced 'A Disturbance of Memory on the Acropolis'.[34] Succumbing to déjà vu before García Lorca's all too familiar literary monument, but also anxious (like Freud in Athens) not to outstrip our father if we go too far beyond him in our work of interpretation, surely we shall never abandon our first love. However, we should attempt to rearticulate that nostalgic passion and maudlin cult of the past characteristic of the García Lorca author function as an ethics directed towards the future: as the affirmation of life in the face of inevitable mortality and the gift of the self to others as testimony to the passage from the subjective to the social.[35] Such are the ultimate implications (at once textual, performative and psychoanalytic) of doing the theatre of García Lorca.

---

[33] One later writer is Luis Antonio de Villena; see Chris Perriam, *Desire and Dissent: an introduction to Luis Antonio de Villena* (Oxford: Berg, 1995), 45. See also Villena's own 'La sensibilidad homoerótica en el *Romancero gitano*', *Campusi*, 11 (December 1986), 27-30. In spite of its title, this piece is illustrated, as is so often the case in Spain, with etchings which focus on female nudes.

[34] 'A Disturbance of Memory on the Acropolis', *On Metapsychology*, 443-56. In this late piece Freud remembers how he once felt a sense of déjà vu amongst the ruins which he attributes to an unconscious fear that he had outstripped his father, a man of commerce who would never visit Athens and would not have appreciated it if he had.

[35] I take these themes from Fernando Savater's *Ética como amor propio* (Barcelona: Grijalbo Mondadori, 1995), *passim*.

Lorca 1919-1929

Gwynne Edwards

Lorca's great plays were written in the seven years which preceded his death in the Summer of 1936: *El público* in 1929-1930; *Así que pasen cinco años* in 1931; *Bodas de sangre* in 1933; *Yerma* in 1934; *Doña Rosita la soltera* in 1935; and in 1936 *Comedia sin título* and *La casa de Bernarda Alba*. These years were, then, the full flowering of Lorca's genius—and we should not forget the poetry, in particular *Poeta en Nueva York*—but the seeds of that flowering were already manifesting signs of strong growth in the previous decade. The years 1919 to 1929 saw Lorca based in Madrid yet at the same time umbilically tied to his native Granada. In cultural terms, he was exposed to major developments in the arts in Europe, yet equally drawn to particular Spanish traditions. It was a time of influential friendships, which in turn fed into his work. And his personal life was marked by emotional crises which became a significant factor in his creative output. The aim of this essay is to show how these separate threads became closely and strikingly woven into the fabric of Lorca's work. 1919 proved a significant year in Lorca's life, for it began his association with the Residencia de Estudiantes in Madrid, which became so crucial to his personal and artistic development. The Residencia, based on the Oxbridge college model, sought to offer students a high-quality liberal education, and by the time Lorca arrived it had a total of 150 students. As part of their policy, the authorities at the Residencia invited distinguished individuals to lecture to the students. They included H.G. Wells, G.K. Chesterton, Albert Einstein, Marie Curie, François Mauriac, Hilaire Belloc, John Maynard Keynes and Paul Valéry. Many famous musicians and composers also appeared there: Manuel de Falla, Andrés Segovia, Igor Stravinsky, Francis Poulenc and Maurice Ravel. When Lorca arrived at the Residencia in November 1919, he encountered an atmosphere which was artistically and intellectually stimulating.[1]

Cultural life in Madrid was also an inspiration. Friends of Lorca from Granada introduced him to a wider intellectual circle and to developments in the arts which were taking place both in and outside Spain. At the Madrid Arts Club, the Ateneo, Lorca encountered young Spanish poets such as Gerardo Diego, Pedro Salinas and Guillermo de Torre. The latter was a prime mover in the movement called 'ultraísmo', which advocated that art should express the modern world of machines, radios, aeroplanes, ships, photography, and so on. Torre and others, such as Ramón Gómez de la Serna, were admirers of Cocteau, Picasso, Juan Gris, Diaghilev, Marinetti, and others. The general attitude was one which rejected the values of the past and favoured all those modern movements—Dadaism, Cubism, Futurism—which sought to overturn traditional values. In many respects Lorca was to remain faithful in his work to many Spanish traditions, but there are also other aspects of his writing which embrace the world of the *avant-garde* and which owe much to the years spent at the Residencia.

Lorca's friendships at the Residencia also proved highly influential, especially those with Luis Buñuel and Salvador Dalí. Buñuel had arrived in 1917 and had already made a reputation as a tough, uncompromising character. He was not yet the film-maker that he would later become, but in temperament he was already the subversive individual who would make so many hard-hitting films. A lover of sport, Buñuel was in many ways the personification of Spanish *machismo*. In his autobiography of 1982, *Mi último suspiro*, he speaks of his insatiable desire for women and, when he was young, of his dislike of homosexuals. In Madrid, he and his friends used to wait for gay men to emerge from public conveniences in order to attack them. In this context Buñuel's relationship with Lorca is very interesting, in particular his refusal to believe that Lorca was truly gay. Other friends of Lorca at that time also claim that they were unaware of his true inclinations, though perhaps they preferred to remain silent about a delicate subject. Otherwise, Buñuel's memory of Lorca in the early

---

[1] The most detailed account of Lorca's life is that by Ian Gibson, *Federico García Lorca: a life* (London: Faber and Faber, 1989).

twenties was of his immense charisma. He was the centre of attention in any group through his lively manner and conversation, his infectious laugh and his general enthusiasm. In terms of cultural and artistic influence, Buñuel's impact on Lorca was less at this time than Lorca's on him. To some extent the reverse would occur later, after Buñuel's departure for Paris in 1925 and his success as an *avant-garde* filmmaker.

Salvador Dalí arrived at the Residencia in September 1922. From the outset he cut an arresting bohemian figure, though soon his appearance became that of a young man-about-town, the hair cut short and slicked back in the style of Rudolph Valentino. But despite his appearance and behaviour, Dalí was at bottom pathologically timid and much in awe of the much more socially brilliant Lorca, admitting that 'the personality of Federico García Lorca produced an immense impression on me.'

Five months after his arrival in Madrid, Lorca had his first play staged: *El maleficio de la mariposa*. The Teatro Eslava was run by Gregorio Martínez Sierra, who admired European *avant-garde* theatre, favoured innovation, and hated the dull naturalistic Spanish theatre of the time. Having heard Lorca recite the story of an injured butterfly which was cared for by a colony of cockroaches, one of whom fell in love with the butterfly but died of a broken heart when it finally flew away, Martínez Sierra suggested that he turn the piece into a play. It opened at the Eslava on 22 March 1920, provoked a hostile reaction, and was taken off after a handful of performances. Despite its failure *El maleficio de la mariposa* contains all the essential ingredients of Lorca's later work, in particular the themes of love and frustration. The prologue to the play contains a plea that love be recognised at all levels, and, even if it suggests here that love exists between the insect characters of the play just as strongly as it does between human beings, there is also the implication that the love of one man for another should be accepted:

> I ask you to inform all men, poet, that love is born with the same intensity at all levels of existence. [...] In Nature all things are equal.[2]

---

[2] Translation by Gwynne Edwards in Federico García Lorca, *Plays: Two* (London: Methuen Drama, 1990), 84.

El maleficio de la mariposa also attempted to strike a blow at the dull, unimaginative naturalism of much of the theatre of Lorca's time. The characters have a marked symbolic quality: the young male cockroach embodies the passion of youth; the butterfly the beauty he seeks; the scorpion and the glow-worms the inevitable destruction of his dream. In addition, the play's settings are highly stylised—stage-pictures which underline the emotional experiences of the characters, and in which lighting, music and movement are essential ingredients. Lorca's dramatic technique thus reveals from the outset that concern for the integration of different elements—language, stage-design, movement (including dance), and lighting—which was favoured by theatre innovators outside Spain, by Maurice Maeterlinck, W.B. Yeats and Edward Gordon Craig.[3] In 1920 he was already developing the theatrical style which would distinguish a play like *Bodas de sangre* with its stark stage-pictures and its universal characters—Mother, Bride, Bridegroom, Moon, Death.

But if Lorca was embracing the *avant-garde*, he was also turning to Spanish tradition, a second essential characteristic of his work. Influenced from childhood by Spanish folk music, lullabies and the like, Lorca became acquainted in the autumn of 1919 with the famous Spanish composer, Manuel de Falla, twenty-two years older than himself. Falla had already enjoyed great success with such works as *El amor brujo* and *Noches en los jardines de España*. Moreover, Falla also settled in Granada permanently and Lorca's friendship with him reinforced his own interest in Spanish folk music, in particular the gypsy music known as *cante jondo*, deep song, more generally known as flamenco song. In the summer of 1921, Lorca was having flamenco guitar lessons with two gypsies from Fuente Vaqueros, and was friendly with several flamenco singers and guitarists. He and Falla also visited the caves of the Sacromonte, on the edge of Granada, where the gypsy community lived. In this context it is important to emphasise the two men's part in the organisation of the 'Festival of Deep Song' which took place on the 13 and 14 June 1922 in the Alhambra's Plaza de los

---

[3] For the influence of these theatre innovators on Lorca, see Gwynne Edwards, *Dramatists in Perspective: Spanish Theatre in the Twentieth Century* (Cardiff: University of Wales Press, 1985), chapter 3.

Aljibes; and Lorca's volume of poetry, *Poema del cante jondo*, on which he worked prior to the festival. In addition, some months before the Festival, Lorca lectured on '*Cante jondo*. Primitive Andalusian Song', at the Arts Club in Granada. He sought to explain the origin of 'deep song' in the East, in India, its arrival—with the gypsies—in Andalusia, and the way in which he believed it to be the true expression of the Andalusian soul. The songs of 'deep song' are characterised by the anguish of hopeless love; of finding oneself in a situation in which fate is hostile and death inevitable; of knowing that one is condemned to inevitable suffering. Lorca's attraction to 'deep song' suggests connections with his own sexual frustration and his growing conviction that, like the gypsy, he was an outsider, marginalised in his case by his homosexuality. In embracing *cante jondo*, Lorca both found himself and a voice, a style, which in one way or another would characterise much of his mature work, in particular the three rural tragedies: *Bodas de sangre*, *Yerma*, and *La casa de Bernarda Alba*. But even in the more obviously *avant-garde* works, *El público* and *Así que pasen cinco años*, the passionate expression and vivid images of *cante jondo* are very much in evidence. Lorca's work is thus distinguished by the close integration and interweaving of both traditional and *avant-garde* elements.

This point can be illustrated in a different way in relation to *Mariana Pineda*, on which Lorca began to work in the latter part of 1923. The subject matter is highly traditional, for the story of Mariana Pineda was an important part of the history of Granada in the nineteenth century, and as a child Lorca had heard the stories and ballads about her. Moreover, he was attracted by the theme of Mariana not only as the victim of politics, but also as the victim of love. The themes of love, frustration and death, previously rehearsed in *El maleficio de la mariposa*, as well as in *Poema del cante jondo*, are again to the fore, the insects of the earlier play transformed now into their human equivalents who are, in turn, Lorca himself. When, in Act 2, Mariana speaks of 'the taste of love that burns my mouth',[4] she is as much a projection of her creator's yearning as was the youthful and handsome

---

[4] Translation by Gwynne Edwards in Federico García Lorca, *Plays: Three* (London: Methuen Drama, 1994), 25.

cockroach. And when she is abandoned by her lover, she expresses that deep frustration which Lorca too felt in his mid-twenties and which would later become an increasing preoccupation.

While the subject of *Mariana Pineda* is traditional, its dramatic technique is decidedly *avant-garde*. The prologue, for example, takes place before the curtain rises, the curtain has designed on it 'the now vanished Moorish gateway of the Cucharas and a view of the Bibarrambla Square in Granada', and this picture 'is framed in a yellowish border, like an old print' (*Plays: Three*, 3). From the outset, there is, therefore, an emphasis on stylisation, and this is continued in the settings for the play's three acts, which Lorca significantly called *estampas* (engravings), which suggests that what we are to see on stage is not merely a historical picture, but one in which there is the bold, stark, uncluttered effect of an engraving. The simplicity and boldness of settings and costumes are, of course, strongly symbolic, the white walls suggestive of Mariana's innocence and purity; the mauve and red of Mariana's dresses a pointer to her spilled blood; the black of the chief of police's clothes, an image of the evil which will destroy her. Although the story and the characters are historical and in that sense realistic, Lorca's stylised treatment of his material transforms it into something much more universal, an experience of love, hope, despair, and death, with which we can all identify; a traditional subject presented in that modern, stylised manner championed by such painters as Dalí and Picasso.

Mariana Pineda also illustrates another side of Lorca: his political sympathies. The play, set during the oppressive reign of Ferdinand VII, is much concerned with the oppression of liberal ideals. When Lorca wrote it, the government of the day had just been overthrown by the military dictatorship of Miguel Primo de Rivera who at once introduced a series of repressive measures. Although Lorca intended writing the play before the military coup in September of 1923, it would be unrealistic to think that such a major political event does not find an echo in the play. It is worth remembering that, even if Lorca's father was a wealthy landowner, he also had strong left-wing sympathies and would support the Second Republic of 1931–1936. When Primo de Rivera was finally forced to step down, Lorca became part of the Republic's educational programme with the touring theatre company *La Barraca*. Later he would support various foreign left-wing organisations, read his poems at a mass meeting in the Madrid Workers' Club, and appear on May Day waving a red tie from a window in the Ministry of Communications. But the seeds of all this were sown much earlier, as *Mariana Pineda* suggests.

Another aspect of Lorca's work concerns his fascination with puppets. While he was preoccupied with *cante jondo*, he was also writing the puppet farce the *Tragicomedia de don Cristóbal y la señá Rosita*, the first draft of which he completed in 1922. Lorca's interest in puppet plays can be explained in various ways. Clearly, he was eager to resurrect the tradition of the Andalusian puppet play, which by the 1920s was fast disappearing. For the most part he recognised, of course, its potential for broad comedy, though his own puppet plays and farces also contain important social comment. But, in addition, the puppet play allowed Lorca to escape from the strictures of the commercial and naturalistic theatre.

On many occasions Lorca complained about the economic and artistic control exercised by the theatre impresarios of his day: 'That a man, by the mere fact of availing himself of a few millions, should set himself up as a censor of plays and arbiter of the theatre is intolerable and shameful.'[5] The puppet theatre, in which the dramatist controlled the performance, effectively freed him from such commercial concerns and from the vanity of star actors and directors. In addition, the puppet figure could express action and emotion in a bold, simple manner far removed from the stale realism of the commercial theatre. Lorca declared:

> Bad words acquire frankness and freshness when they are spoken by puppets [...] Let us fill the theatre with fresh wheat and from it let there spring the bold words that will confront the tediousness and vulgarity to which we have condemned the theatre.[6]

Although it is not a puppet play, *La zapatera prodigiosa* illustrates perfectly the points made above. A draft of it was completed by the end

---

[5] In an interview of 1934 published in *El Sol*. Federico García Lorca, *Obras completas* (Madrid: Aguilar, 1986), III, 1630. The translation is my own.

[6] From the ending of *El retablillo de don Cristóbal*. The translation is my own.

of 1926, though it did not receive its first performance until 24 December 1930, when it opened at the Teatro Español in Madrid to considerable acclaim, the Shoemaker's Wife played brilliantly by Margarita Xirgu who, three years earlier, had taken the lead part in *Mariana Pineda*. *La zapatera prodigiosa* has as its subject the traditional story of an old man, the village shoemaker, married to a lively, vibrant young woman. Lorca called the play a 'violent farce', and it certainly lives up to that description in the vigour of its action, the liveliness of its characters, and the boldness of its language. But Lorca, as he often did, also used comic situations for the exploration of serious themes, particularly the patriarchal structures of village life and the stifling effect of the traditional honour code. The Shoemaker and the Wife are ridiculed by the villagers, their lives circumscribed by public opinion—a theme which would reach fruition in the three great rural tragedies.

At the same time, the exploration of social issues does not prevent Lorca from investing his 'violent farce' with more poetic and universal qualities. He himself drew attention to this aspect of the play: '*La zapatera* is a farce, but more than that it is a poem about the human spirit and the latter is the only really important character in the play.'[7] The young woman personifies the universal clash between illusion and reality, dream and disillusionment. This pursuit of impossible dreams is given its most visual and dramatic form at the moment in the play when she pursues the butterfly and it escapes her. But she dreams of love too, as does the Shoemaker of kindness and companionship. This universal theme of longing and aspiration invariably ending in frustration runs through all Lorca's work

As for its style and technique, *La zapatera prodigiosa* again struck a powerful blow against the stale realism of Spanish theatre in the 1920s and early 1930s, for Lorca's play uses stage-settings, lighting, costume, and music in the integrated *avant-garde* manner mentioned previously. When, for instance, the butterfly enters the Wife's room and she and the child pursue it, darkness is descending, they speak in whispers, and the child quietly sings a song which begs the butterfly to stay. The interplay of lighting and movement, combined with the sound of the

---

[7] In an interview of 1933 published in *El Sol* (*Obras completas*, III, 1620).

voices, creates a beautiful, magical, poetic effect which is not only at the opposite pole from realism but which is also quite unusual in a play of this kind. At the same time, though, the attack on the realism of Spanish theatre is achieved through Lorca's use of what are essentially puppet-play techniques. Movement, gesture and language are often bold and exaggerated. The characters frequently express themselves in vigorous action and language, the Wife beating her head with her hands, stamping her feet, raging at her neighbours, while the slanging matches between her and her husband have the knockabout character of a Punch and Judy show. *La zapatera prodigiosa* is, then, a play in which Lorca again brilliantly combines aspects of modern theatre with traditional elements.

Another play which should be included under this heading, though again it is not a puppet-play, but a farce, is *Amor de don Perlimplín*. Lorca started work on it in the summer of 1925 and had virtually finished it by the beginning of 1926. The plot again concerns the marriage of an older man to a young woman, but the traditional story is handled in a totally original and personal manner. There are, of course, grotesque and farcical elements: the ridiculous contrast between the fifty-year old Perlimplín, hesitant and inexperienced in love, and the young and beautiful Belisa, half-naked on her balcony; and Perlimplín on his wedding-night, fast asleep while Belisa entertains five lovers. Beneath these farcical elements there are, however, serious themes. In Perlimplín, Lorca explores the theme of sexual impotence, and its relevance to himself is very clear. Perlimplín's impotence stems from a fear of castration and from his earlier domination by his mother. In this context it should not be forgotten that Lorca's mother, Vicenta Lorca Romero, was a powerful influence on him and that his own work (see his drawings) contains many castration motifs in the form of severed hands. At all events, Perlimplín, in the play's final scene, disguises himself as a handsome young man in a red cloak and, before killing himself, succeeds in that guise in convincing Belisa of his love for her. The point appears to be that only through fantasy, by pretending to be someone else, can he become sexually potent, and it is the realisation of this fact which destroys him. To that extent the play is a dramatisation and an exploration of Lorca's own sexual problems, a much more personal statement than *La zapatera prodigiosa*. The stage-technique, of course, is typical Lorca: bold sets, colourful costumes, a particular mood—as in the final scene in the garden—created by the interplay of lighting, costume and music. The stylised character of Lorca's approach to his plays is, therefore, much in evidence once again. Salvador Dalí, it seems, was initially extremely enthusiastic about the play, possibly because, complex character that he was, he saw in it the psychological and sexual meaning described above. The relationship between Lorca and Dalí was, indeed, a close one in the mid-twenties, and needs to be understood in relation to Lorca's work.

In the Spring of 1925 Lorca spent Holy Week with the Dalí family at Cadaqués on the Costa Brava before returning with them to the family home at Figueras and then going off with Salvador to Barcelona. Prior to 1925 Dalí's sister, Ana María, had figured prominently in her brother's paintings, but after Lorca's visit to Cadaqués he effectively displaced her, the head of the poet/dramatist appearing more and more in Dalí's work. As for Lorca, his feelings towards Dalí became more intense as a result of the visit to Cadaqués and, during the months which followed, he appears to have suffered a deep depression, doubtless caused by the separation from Dalí. It was at this time that he wrote *Oda a Salvador Dalí*. It was almost a year before Lorca and Dalí met again. The painter returned to the Residencia in May 1926 and left there a month later, having been dismissed by the Academy of Fine Arts for refusing to be examined by its board. It was, perhaps, during these weeks that Lorca made sexual advances to Dalí, at least according to the latter. Forty years later he said this: 'He was homosexual, as is well known, and desperately in love with me. He tried to sodomize me twice.'[8] It is, of course, unwise to have too much faith in anything that Dalí said, such was his tendency to self-publicity and self-aggrandizement, and his denial of his homosexuality can certainly be questioned. Lorca's next encounter with Dalí occurred in connection with the première of *Mariana Pineda* in Barcelona in 1927, for which Dalí designed the sets. The drawings of both men at this time point to their close relationship. Lorca's drawing 'El beso' ('The Kiss') portrays his own head on which he has superimposed that of Dalí, their lips meeting, and Dalí's paintings clearly reveal the emotional conflict

---

[8] In an interview with Alain Bosquet published in 1966. See *Entretiens avec Salvador Dalí* (Paris: Pierre Belfond, 1966). The translation is my own.

which Lorca's presence caused in him: 'Honey is Sweeter than Blood' and 'Little Ashes', with their severed heads, are pointers to Dalí's sexual impotence, and to an involvement with Lorca to which he did not care to admit.

By 1928 Lorca's involvement with Dalí was further complicated by his attraction to a sculptor, Emilio Aladrén Perojo, eight years younger than himself. Such was Lorca's passion for the young sculptor that he made every effort to promote his artistic talent, minor as it was. But over the next year things began to go very wrong for Lorca. Although his volume of poetry, *Romancero gitano*, was an enormous success when it was published in July 1928, Dalí regarded the poems as old-fashioned and stereotyped, and Buñuel described them as 'flamenco dramatism', far removed from the work of those he regarded as the great poets of the day.[9] Both men were, of course, turning their back on anything traditional in favour of the irrational and the iconoclastic, but their criticisms must have hurt Lorca a good deal. Buñuel's relationship with Dalí—artistic rather than sexual—was becoming closer and his resolve to undermine Dalí's feelings for Lorca much stronger. In early 1929 Buñuel and Dalí were working on their film, *Un Chien andalou*, in which the effeminate protagonist may well have been modelled on Lorca. Certainly Lorca thought so, not least because Andalusians at the Residencia were known as 'Andalusian dogs'.[10] For him the film was an act of betrayal by two of his closest friends, while Dalí and Emilio Aladrén were both beginning to move away from Lorca in terms of their personal lives. For a variety of reasons, then, Lorca had good cause to fall into the depression which, in June 1929, led to his leaving Spain for New York, where he would spend nine months.

The experience of New York would prove crucial in many ways, not least in relation to his writing. To attempt to analyse it in any detail here would, of course, involve going beyond the limits of this essay, but it is important to mention one aspect of Lorca's work which was at least in part stimulated by his visit to New York: his fascination with the cinema. It should not be forgotten in this respect that the group

---

[9] Dalí in a letter to Lorca, written in September 1928, and Buñuel in a letter to José Bello, written in the same month.

[10] J.F. Aranda, *Luis Buñuel. Biografía crítica* (Barcelona: Editorial Lumen, 1975), 65, n.1.

Gabrielle Jourdan as Lorca in Poet in New York *by Gwynne Edwards*

which lived at or were connected with the Residencia de Estudiantes in Madrid (including Lorca, Buñuel, Dalí and Rafael Alberti) were all in love with the cinema. Amongst other things, they admired the comics of the silent films (including Charlie Chaplin, Harold Lloyd and Buster Keaton) whose crazy antics they regarded as almost surrealist. It is no accident, then, that in 1925 Lorca should have written a short prose dialogue entitled *El paseo de Buster Keaton,* in a way his own tribute to the silent cinema. This short piece describes Buster Keaton riding his bicycle in the outskirts of Philadelphia, where, having murdered his four children, he pursues butterflies which escape him and encounters a prostitute who propositions him. Although *El paseo de Buster Keaton* has a striking visual quality reminiscent of film, it is really more literary than cinematic, a piece to be read rather than seen. In terms of its meaning it has, like all Lorca's work, clear autobiographical elements. Buster Keaton, an innocent in a hostile, harsh, materialistic world, searches for a happiness he cannot find, and in accepting the prostitute's proposition acknowledges the loss of his innocence. Undoubtedly Lorca saw something of himself in the characteristically melancholy face of Buster Keaton, but in its portrayal of an urban landscape in which man is effectively dehumanised, this short piece also anticipates Lorca's actual experience of New York four years later.

In the autumn of 1928 there was set up in Madrid the Cine Club, which hired different cinemas in the city for the screening of *avant-garde* films. Lorca attended regularly. Moreover, Buñuel, now in Paris, provided the Cine Club with the latest films and also with information about the latest trends in cinema. It was, no doubt, the experience of what he saw at the Cine Club, as well as the appearance of Buñuel and Dalí's film, *Un Chien andalou*, in 1929, which inspired Lorca to write his own screenplay, *Viaje a la luna*, in New York. Although he had not seen the Buñuel-Dalí film, he was familiar with its content and style and attempted to produce a script along the same lines. Divided into seventy-one short sequences, *Viaje a la luna* does not suggest a journey through space, rather a spiritual and emotional journey in search of impossible love and ending in death. There is no narrative here, only a series of images which move into each other and convey the chaotic processes of the unconscious mind, many of them pointing to sexual anxiety. Such is sequence 44: 'On the screen a moon appears, outlined on a white background, which fades into a male sex organ and then into a screaming mouth.'[11] In short, *Viaje a la luna* is a kind of graph of the emotional torment which overwhelmed Lorca in early 1929 and which took him to New York later in the year; and it closely parallels *Poeta en Nueva York* and the two Surrealist plays, *El público* and *Así que pasen cinco años*, both written during the next few years.

In conclusion, the ten-year period examined here reveals very clearly the close connection between Lorca's personal life and his work, and, above all, the great variety of the work itself: an insect play, a historical play, farces, puppet-play, film-script, poetry, all embracing traditional and *avant-garde* elements. Lorca is, in truth, one of the great innovators of the twentieth century, someone constantly searching for new ways of expressing himself. It is ironic, therefore, that Buñuel and Dalí should have ridiculed him for his traditionalism. Dalí in particular was to become a kind of self-parody in his life and his painting, endlessly repeating himself and with less and less effect. Buñuel, though a great film-maker throughout his career, continued to plough more or less the same furrow. In contrast, Lorca's work surprises by its sheer variety and constant experimentation. One suspects that, had he lived longer, he would have written even more startling plays and perhaps tried his hand at cinema.

---

[11] For the text, see Federico García Lorca, *Obras completas*, ed. Arturo del Hoyo, 22nd ed., (Madrid: Aguilar, 1986), II, 1139–48.

García Lorca: after New York
David Johnston

In 1929 a deep artistic and personal crisis led Federico García Lorca to New York. Whatever the informing details of the crisis were, and, as is the case in much of Lorca's life and work, many of them are shrouded both in critical coyness and his own care not to leave much written testimony of his intimate world, the effect of New York on his subsequent work is clear. This article is not centrally concerned, however, to give a blow-by-blow account of the events of the last six years of Lorca's tragically foreshortened life, in the wake of his return from what was in poetic terms the richly formative experience of New York—the reader interested in investigating this chronology is referred to Ian Gibson's fascinating account of Lorca's life.[1] Rather it seeks to assess, albeit in broad terms, the impact of this formative experience on Lorca's subsequent work, to trace the process of artistic and personal assimilation—particularly through the rural trilogy—through which crisis becomes the stuff of growing commitment.

A generally held nutshell view of Lorca's work is that it revolves relentlessly around a single conceptual issue, that is of instinctual life thwarted by socialisation and control. It is a clash which Lorca dramatises powerfully both in his poetry and his theatre. Clearly rooted in his own experience of sexual difference in a rigidly codified society, it is a central concern which lends itself to a variety of readings, from a cultural *topos* originating in Greek tragedy and achieving its maximum expression in the drama of the Spanish Golden Age, to stock views inherited from the Romantics and Freud.

Perhaps another way of considering Lorca's work, however, is as a disturbed, frequently obsessive, probing of hostile Otherness. The writer is unable to divert his gaze from the bleak laws of our condition and the oppressive codes of our society just as, in his lament for the death of his friend, the bullfighter Ignacio Sánchez Mejías, he is unable to divert his gaze from the dreadful trail of blood, underscored by the

---

[1] *Federico García Lorca: a life* (London: Faber & Faber, 1990).

impotence of the refrain 'Que no quiero verla' ('I don't want to see it'). In that sense, Lorca's work centres not so much on a clash which, no matter how deep and intimate its origins, remains conceptual, but rather flowers from the dark root of confrontation: the artist's exploration and exorcism of the darkness that is both embedded within us (socialisation, the internalisation of the law) and operates relentlessly around us (history, the functioning of the law).

If we look at Lorca's work in this way, we can perhaps arrive at a clearer notion of the importance of New York for his subsequent work. New York is perhaps inevitably experienced in terms of a striking otherness by any European, even today. But in terms of Lorca's obsessed investigation of an otherness that is simultaneously social, sexual and political, the city becomes an objective correlative for hostile otherness, Lorca's personal wasteland. In that sense, the real title of the resulting book of poetry *Poeta en Nueva York* is more accurately, as Lorca himself suggested, 'Nueva York en un poeta'. Lorca draws the city into himself, with its febrile but ultimately mechanistic rhythm of life, its relentless pursuit of Mammon, its rejection and marginalisation of the blacks, and in doing so he advances his understanding of the human heart of darkness. In the words he was to put into the mouth of Bernarda Alba in 1936, 'the more you know your own illness, the better'.

One of the New York poems which marks a key stage in this artistic advancement is 'New York: Oficina y denuncia' ('New York: Office and Denunciation'). On one level the poem clearly heralds a new social commitment, a moving away from literary forms which linger in the realms of the subjective or the philosophical. More particularly, it announces a determination to sharpen the focus of Lorca's poetic investigation of hostile otherness, drawing it from the realm of myth, of timeless Civil Guards and gypsies, denizens more of the tradition of *cante jondo,* or deep song, than of any specific time or place, moving away from the self-consciously *commedia dell'arte* shrouding of characters like Don Perlimplín or the shoemaker's wondrous wife, and re-constructing instead through his art a hostile otherness which is historically, socially and, indeed, politically intelligible.

The final image of the poem is worth further comment. It is a crucial expression of the poet as sacrificial victim, an image of immolation which occurs elsewhere in the New York sequence. It is foregrounded in the poem which Lorca chose to open the collection: 'Vuelta de paseo' ('Back from a Walk'). But the agents of sacrifice in the later poem are now quite different, as is the poet's view of the relationship between art and a socially constructed reality. The poet is no longer 'the heaven-murdered one', but now bows before the artistically inevitable responsibility of protest; protest, both psychological and ecological, at the violence we commit on nature, and protest at the uncaring subjectivity of an art devoted to the solitary self. This protest carries with it not just the suggestion of the immolation of the self within the project of a committed art (this is a piece of pseudo-Marxism which Lorca would not have seriously entertained) but more graphically the sense of the pain arising from his own active identification with the haunted victims of a very real world in which acquisition ('oil') has substituted the natural flow of things ('the Hudson'):

> What shall I do? Set landscapes to order?
> Order loves that become photographs
> and then splinters of wood and mouthfuls of blood?
> No... no... I shall denounce.
> I denounce the conspiracy of these deserted offices
> from which no agony shines forth,
> which obliterate the projects of the forest,
> and I offer myself to be eaten by emaciated cattle
> when their bellowing fills the valley
> where the Hudson flows, drunk on oil.

All of this is not to say that upon his return from New York Lorca was to throw himself whole-heartedly into the creation of a body of work whose primary line of engagement was social or political. But the poet clearly saw in drama the opportunity to speak to an audience in numbers. He inserted theatre in general, and tragedy in particular, into a potentially progressive dynamic. This sense of theatre as an instrument of potential reform is, of course, fraught with difficulties. But let us proceed with it unchallenged for the moment in order to discuss what Lorca may have considered the role of theatre to be at a time of heated political debate as Spanish republicanism sought to construct a new national project from the jaws of a fundamentalist construct of Spanishness.

In early 1935 a special performance of Lorca's new play—*Yerma*—was arranged for an audience of theatre people. He addressed them with a manifesto which gives eloquent testimony to his awareness of the social responsibilities of the theatre:

> The theatre is a school for laughter and tears, an open forum where we can put old or misguided moralities to the test and embody in living examples the eternal truths of the human heart.

There are three related issues here: the idea that theatre can and should re-orientate the spectator towards what Lorca considered to be the most precious fulfilment of one's being: the emotions; that theatre had a role in the debate between modernisation and traditionalism raging at that time in Spain; and that performance is the key to an impact which derives from emotional response but whose goal is fundamentally an advancement of knowledge.

It is as if, having emerged from the artistic cauldron of New York, the poet has mustered the emotional strength to begin to diagnose his own illness, to interrogate the otherness which has both confronted him externally as a system of hostile social codes and which has become part of him, the product, above all perhaps, of parental attitudes. And to recognise that this illness, this otherness, has a public dimension: the trilogy of *Bodas de sangre*, *Yerma* and *La casa de Bernarda Alba*, written in 1933, 1934 and 1936 respectively, is rooted in the poet's realisation that what he is telling is not solely a private issue (although this is the level at which it is inevitably experienced with greatest pain), nor is it a *topos* of cultural marginalisation, but that it is an historical trauma whose roots and whose potential development are all wholly identifiable both within a Spain asserting its future in the face of entrenched traditionalism and a Europe sliding through growing authoritarianism towards conflict.

The tone of Lorca's description of the theatre as a school, of course, reflects the general cultural project of Republican Spain. The more utilitarian aspect of this is seen in Lorca's acceptance of the commission to direct La Barraca, a student group whose remit was to bring the classics of Spain's Golden Age to the towns and villages of the country.

As a talented director and lucid *dramaturg*, Lorca clearly identified the central issue of Golden Age theatre as the clash between the codified self and non-codified self. He was no less aware that this was a theatre which was national in the sense that it dramatised the clash between desire and the law as a primary issue of public concern, and this further sharpened his sense of theatre as a place where the invisible should be made visible, where the explicit politics and moralities of the law should be put to trial and the invisible politics and moralities of private desire given a public airing and explored in terms of both social control and intimate crisis.

As a result of the advancement of diagnosis and the strengthening of resolve which was New York, Lorca's rural trilogy establishes hostile otherness both in terms of recognisable socio-political patterns of traditional Spain and of the authoritarian consciousness. For example, it is clearly important to *Bodas de sangre*'s status as ritualistic drama that the inevitable failure of the young lovers is seen as being not solely a result of star-crossed destinies, but that it has also been brought about in some way by the archetypal father and mother figures (descendancy as power and as memory/tradition). But the mother and father are also identifiable in terms specific to their time and place, the father as a caricature of greed for land, the 'pacto de la sangre con la tierra', the blood-bond with the land which has been a defining axis of Spanish traditionalism, and the mother as the chilling voice of a society without peace, of tribes without reconciliation. It is the Father's lust for land which occasions the break-up of Leonardo's relationship with the Bride before the action proper of the play even begins, and it is precisely the Mother's obsession with the knife which leads her to virtually placing it into her son's hand as she drives him out from the wedding in pursuit of the wayward lovers. The *navaja* ('knife') is a recurring sign in Lorca's poetry, plays and drawings, taken, as are so many of his motifs and icons, from an observed reality. If one were translating the force of the word into an Irish situation, then its direct equivalent would be 'the gun', and it was precisely this sense of a real place inhabited by real violence which Brendan Kennelly develops in the last few lines which he appends to his version of the play.[2] Both knife and gun are readily intelligible correlatives for a certain type of social and historical violence, both potent agents and harbingers of a destruction whose causes are known to all. In other words, the first mention of the 'navaja', highlighted as it is at the beginning of the play, creates a shiver of expectation as the audience confronts the tragedy of a relentless chain of cause and effect which it recognises as being its own trauma.

Lorca's interrogation of hostile otherness, his plunging into a heart of darkness which is simultaneously culture-specific and universally human, eventually and inevitably discovers the nothingness which lies at the heart of the authoritarian consciousness, the vacuum of idea and value which masquerades as the discourse and structures of power. Absence and negation are powerful elements in Lorca's dramatic universe. Where they are most powerfully evoked is through his poetry, that living poetry which is of the stage, when characters speak from the very heart of their being. The difficulties of rendering this poetry convincingly into English have been discussed at length by a number of translators, as have the problems faced by English-speaking actors, whose training is largely still inspired in the methods of Stanislavsky, when it comes to actually having to speak it. But we also must bear in mind that although there is more of a tradition of verse drama in Spain, and that Lorca was consciously modelling his theatre along these lines, the poetry of Lorca's own original Spanish text has in performance something of the effect of an estrangement—and specifically in the way in which Brecht described his *Verfremdungseffekt* as 'the things of everyday life lifted out of the realm of the self-evident'.

[2] The additional words are spoken by the Mother:
>In the very roots of pain
>Where death is born
>And love dies
>And I am left
>With the torn, dirty remnants of a dream,
>A dream that I must change,
>In this blood-haunted place,
>Into a dream of peace.

Federico García Lorca, *Blood Wedding*, a new version by Brendan Kennelly (Newcastle: Bloodaxe, 1996), 79.

It seems curious to mention Lorca and Brecht in the same breath, but Lorca's experience of New York had led him to a deeper than ever conviction that what makes life most precious is also most absent from the codes of our living. Unlike Brecht, however, Lorca does not superimpose an estrangement effect on his theatre in order to prompt the spectator towards a rigidly rational analysis. It is rather his own answer to the threat of total behaviourism, the destructive intrusion of the public into the private. Paul Valéry, a poet much admired by Lorca, insists on the inescapable commitment of poetic language to the negation of our most ingrained codes. According to Valéry the images of this language 'ne parlent jamais que de choses absentes' ('only ever speak of absent things'). This is exactly what Lorca's richly imagistic drama achieves. It disrupts the established discourse of behaviourism with forceful expressions of the intimate self, of the right to be, beyond all morality and all theology. Lorca's characters, in the deepest expression of their intimate being, inhabit an amoral and godless universe, and his poetry gives voice to that part of the self that extends beyond the social imperatives of both God and morality.

Lorca would have had no difficulty in seeing his own expressed view that happiness is the goal of life as a statement of politics. To give voice to the silenced self, the yearning for an absent happiness, is to challenge the established order of things, to imply a different way of being. It was Gabriel Marcel who wrote that 'through the emotions I discover that "this concerns me after all"', and through the *duende* of performance the spectator is ineluctably drawn into a shared community of emotion. The real artistic achievement of the rural tragedies is the speaking of what Marcuse thirty years later was to call a 'non-reified language', a way of communicating the 'intimate denied' as an absence not only deeply felt in the individual life but also as the defining reality of a public space delimited by the spirit of negation.

Lorca himself referred to the poetic nature of his theatre as 'la poesía que se levanta del libro y se hace humana. Y al hacerse, habla y grita, llora y se desespera' ('a poetry which stands up from the page and becomes human. And as it does so, it cries out, it weeps and it despairs'). It is this poetry, together with its marked contrast to the flintier, hard-edged speeches redolent of self-control and traditionalism, which creates the characteristic complicity of Lorca's rural trilogy. It is perhaps worth emphasising at this point that I am not describing poetry in terms of its formal characteristics, but rather, in the case of Lorca, as the dramatic tension between language rigidly organised and language strikingly violated. As Lorca meditated, as all significant playwrights must do, upon the nature of audience complicity, he developed through his work a performance theory (which I have referred to above in typical Lorcan shorthand as *duende*). At the heart of this theory lies the performance of emotion (as Lorca's definition of stage poetry quoted above makes clear), the communication by the actor of the surface of emotion to an audience which will not only feel the sting of absence (the 'dark wound' of art) but which will also be led by the depth of emotional response (empathy plus recognition) into a confrontation with the absences and negations operative within the intimate life of each spectator. There can be no doubt that Lorca's rise to prominence in Britain in the 1980s is in great part due to the response at that time to this dramatic project, the redefining of community via the formal equivalent of an audience united through the democracy of the emotions rather than the elitism of intellect. As a Thatcherite society increasingly defined the individual in terms of the freedom to acquire, many turned to Lorca's vision of the individual more radically defined in terms of the dissident extension of selfhood. The playwright's experience of naked materialism in New York, the pursuit of money at the expense of life (the image of a stockbroker hurling himself from an office window haunted Lorca), and the throng of heaving crowds in which individuals seemed willingly to sink their identity ('Landscape of the Vomiting Multitudes' and 'Landscape of the Urinating Multitudes') were, in their way, a prefigurement of radical monetarism. The lesson was not to be lost.

Lorca's later theatre is, in every sense, primarily about making what is invisible or repressed in society visible on stage. In terms of the shock waves it directs at its audience, it is a body of work structured on formations of desire in tension with the spirit of acquisition or control, on pleasure as a political issue. The boldness of much of Lorca's theatre, particularly after New York, is that it imagines woman with pleasure as her object, and that the object is sexual. Why Lorca should be concerned with the sexual as a site for oppression is obvious. What is rather less obvious is that when what is being made visible on stage is desire, felt and expressed as an imperative of nature, that desire then transforms itself into a force wholly intelligible within the particular codes and repressions of the individual spectator. In other words, Lorca's plays speak simultaneously of female and gay sexuality because they are above all else a vehicle which gives voice to the force of desire. Pleasure and desire move from the realm of concept into the domain of passion; they are not simply named but recreated through the force of poetry, and that is how they are experienced by the audience.

In a similar way, both O'Casey and Joyce were also concerned to use a richly figurative and emotionally-laden language to reflect the same tensions at play in an Ireland where the dead hand of traditionalism sat equally heavily upon the new national project. The received wisdom is, of course, to compare Lorca with Synge. Both reacted against the ethos of a place anchored to stagnation. And when Synge put sex on the stage of Dublin's Abbey theatre for the first time, he was very nearly lynched. Lorca, of course, nearly thirty years later, was not so lucky. He didn't get away with it.

The problem with some of the English translations of Lorca's plays is that they allow Lorca's perceived status as a 'poetic dramatist' to blind them to what Nicholas Round terms the 'rough-edged, risk-taking quality' present in all of his plays. Whether we see this quality as informing Lorca's stage language or as the subversive spirit upon which his sense of complicity is founded, or indeed both, the radical impact of this theatre should be clear. Lorca's post-New York plays are disruptive of the dominant cultural and linguistic codes of their original Spanish context, ineluctably leading the audience into the embracing of an otherness which has otherwise been largely banished from their lives.

In that sense, while Lorca was clearly delighted to return to a Spanish way of life after his experience in New York, it is idle in the extreme to speculate on how authentically 'Andalusian' the context and expression of his later theatre may or may not be. At the heart of this theatre is the radical exposition of difference, of deviance from the law (in the way that Lope de Vega, for example, would have understood, if not wholly applauded, this latter proposition). Lorca is more concerned to deconstruct the essentials of this culture than he is to celebrate them, dramatising its social and political pillars and moral imperatives as a single force of hugely hostile otherness—from the institution of marriage, the absorbent sense of community, the relentless capitalist ethic of work and acquisition, to the driving aspiration to reputation (the honour code). Lorca never seeks to minimise the cohesive strength of these forces—dramatised linguistically in terms of inanimate strands of imagery, scenically as walls that divide and exclude, and cosmically, most forcefully perhaps in *Bodas de sangre*, in terms of the conspiracy of the Beggar Woman and the Moon.

Quite simply, he has been all too aware, from the first burgeoning of his sexuality, that society has a relentless capacity to manipulate and control the subversive world of the instincts. But his stay in New York, his confrontation with urban modernity, has also taught him that society can find ways of sublimating this world through alternative schemes of production and acquisition. And as it does so, it atrophies the individual's capacity to grasp the real alternatives. This is the real lesson that Leonardo wants to teach the Bride in the forest scene of *Bodas de sangre*. His simple disavowal of the community imperative— 'if I thought as others do'—unmasks the assumption that it is community which is the real, the rational. This is the rebirth of the individual consciousness outside the productive apparatus, outside the social codes, outside tribal memory, outside language as the agent of moral thought to which personal feelings and capacity for independent action must be surrendered. In the anonymity of New York, Lorca has seen how easily consciousness is obliterated by reification, by the inherited consensus of the general necessity of things. Of course, the Bride eventually returns to the community, but the ultimate meaning of *Bodas de sangre*, like all of Lorca's plays, is located not in its narrative line, but in the form of its telling, in its poetry.

Lorca's theatre is a coherent interrogation and cogent deconstruction of authoritarianism and of the reified consciousness that political analysts and social philosophers like Wright Mills, Marcuse or Reade decades later were to identify as lying at the heart of contemporary disaffection. But through the poetry of his plays he plotted for his audience to feel and to grasp alternatives. This is what makes Lorca's later theatre genuinely subversive: its emotional charge is the foreshadowing of a different way of being. To grasp the alternatives is, of course, both to understand the contradictions and lament the apparent impossibilities. This is what theatre has been doing since Aeschylus, and Lorca was always fully aware of the great truths of the tradition of tragedy from which he saw himself as deriving and to which he sought to contribute. But after New York, his tragic sense was a distinctly modern one.

'Poetry that gets up off the page and becomes human': poetic coherence and eccentricity in Lorca's theatre

Michael Thompson

In an interview of April 1936, Lorca made this memorable pronouncement:

> El teatro es la poesía que se levanta del libro y se hace humana. Y al hacerse, habla y grita, llora y se desespera. El teatro necesita que los personajes que aparezcan en la escena lleven un traje de poesía y al mismo tiempo que se les vean los huesos, la sangre.[1]
> (Theatre is poetry that gets up off the page and becomes human. And as it does so, it talks and shouts, weeps and despairs. Theatre requires the characters who appear on stage to be clothed in poetry but at the same time to let us see their bones, their blood.)[2]

This paper discusses the implications for interpretation and performance of Lorca's definition of theatre as poetry, drawing examples from four plays: *Así que pasen cinco años*, *Bodas de sangre*, *Yerma* and *La casa de Bernarda Alba*.

In the last five years of his life Lorca spoke frequently and passionately about the theatre: as art, as entertainment, as a platform for political ideas and the moral conscience of the nation, as a profession and a business in a state of crisis.[3] In these interviews and talks he insists on using the word *poeta* to refer to himself as playwright, and always links theatre with poetry. The key terms he uses to define his vision of poetry, and by extension theatre, are: *imaginación, invención*

---

[1] Federico García Lorca, *Obras completas* (Madrid: Aguilar, 1986), III, 673 (hereafter *OC*).
[2] Translations of all quotations are mine, unless otherwise stated.
[3] Volume III of the Aguilar *OC* contains an extensive collection of Lorca's lectures, programme notes, articles, interviews, speeches and letters.

(inventiveness, creativity or creative skill), *inspiración, fantasía, evasión* (that is, avoidance of the obvious or escape from conventional logic), *libertad, descubrimiento* (startling discoveries but also revelation), *realidad, misterio, contradicción*. He pursues a Romantic ideal of sublime inspiration, while at the same time insisting upon roots in popular culture, observation of reality and formal experimentation. He stresses immediacy, a very everyday kind of poetic inspiration, but also magic and mystery:

> La poesía es algo que anda por las calles. Que se mueve, que pasa a nuestro lado. Todas las cosas tienen su misterio, y la poesía es el misterio que tienen todas las cosas. (*OC*, III, 671)
> (Poetry is something that walks down the street. Something that moves around, that we can feel as it goes by. All things have their mystery, and poetry is the mystery that all things have.)

He makes it absolutely clear that the mere use of verse in a play is not the point: 'El verso no quiere decir poesía en el teatro. [...] No puede haber teatro sin ambiente poético, sin invención' (*OC*, III, 628) ('Verse is not the same as poetry in the theatre. [...] There can be no theatre without a poetic atmosphere, without invention'). The point is the complete integration of *teatro* and *poesía*.

Lorca was not the only playwright in Europe in the 1920s and 1930s experimenting in this way.[4] However, for the moment I prefer to make brief comparisons with two more recent Spanish dramatists. José Ruibal makes a very eloquent case for an *avant-garde* 'teatro poético total':

---

[4] For a study of Lorca's work in the context of European poetic drama, see A. Hinchliffe, *Poetic Drama* (London: Methuen, 1977). A brief but useful discussion is included in John Lyon, 'General Introduction' to Federico García Lorca, *Yerma*, trans. Ian Macpherson and Jacqueline Minett (Warminster: Aris & Phillips, 1987), 18–26. The closest parallels are with Jean Giraudoux and Jean Cocteau in France and T.S. Eliot and Christopher Fry in England. Some of the best discussion in English of the functioning of Lorca's dramatic imagery is in two Critical Guides: C.B. Morris, *García Lorca: Bodas de sangre* (London: Grant & Cutler, 1980) and *García Lorca: La casa de Bernarda Alba* (London: Grant & Cutler, 1990).

Un teatro donde lo poético no está cifrado en las metáforas brillantes ni en la decoración de la trama. Un teatro donde lo poético es la misma médula del drama: un teatro concebido como totalidad poética. Este teatro parte de que la idea de la obra, su núcleo promotor, es una concepción poética. Partiendo de ahí tanto el lenguaje como los demás elementos que concurren en la expresión dramática, por estar sometidos a una estructura poética, funcionarán poéticamente: lo poético no aparece como un medio, sino como un resultado integrador.[5]

(A form of theatre in which the poetic dimension is not merely a matter of brilliant metaphors or ornamentation of the action. Theatre in which poetry is the very core of the drama: theatre conceived as a poetic totality. The basis of this kind of theatre is that the central idea of the play, its motive force, is a poetic concept. It follows from this that both the language and the other elements that make up dramatic expression will function in a poetic way, since they are subject to a poetic structure: the poetic dimension is not a means but an integrating result.)

Ruibal's plays are less lyrical than Lorca's and address specifically political issues much more directly, yet the emphasis on creative freedom and on the integration of the multiple languages of theatre is similar. The other parallel I would like to draw is at first sight a less encouraging view of poetic theatre. In José Sanchis Sinisterra's play *Los figurantes* (1993), the extras in a historical drama lock the leading actors in their dressing-rooms and take over the theatre. While hanging around on the stage wondering what to do next, they come across an actor from another production sleeping in a piece of scenery who seems to have been there for some time. He recounts how in one production he used to sleep through the whole show, propped up on his pike:

> PRISIONERO 3°—¿En escena?
> METALÚRGICO 8°—Sí: es que era en verso...
> PRISIONERO 3°—Ah, claro...[6]
> (3RD PRISONER—What, on stage?

---

[5] José Ruibal, *El hombre y la mosca* (Madrid: Fundamentos, 1977), 107-8.
[6] José Sanchis Sinisterra, *Los figurantes* (Madrid: SGAE, 1993), 40.

> 8TH METALWORKER—Yeah: it was all in verse, you know the kind of thing.
> 3RD PRISONER—Oh, I see...)

However, the key moment of the play is when all these specialists in walk-on parts begin to discover their own alternative form of theatrical expression, elemental and wordless:

> Paulatinamente, se eleva una sencilla melodía coral, repetitiva, monocorde, casi inarmónica al principio y apenas audible. Acompañará la serie de extrañas, insignificantes acciones con que cada uno de los diecinueve personajes va a intentar descubrir cuál puede ser su papel en la obra que querrían representar... si se les diera la oportunidad. (85)
> (Gradually, we begin to notice a simple choral melody, repetitive, monotonous, almost discordant at first and barely audible. It will form an accompaniment to the series of strange, insignificant actions by means of which each of the nineteen characters attempts to work out what role he or she might play in the work that they would like to perform... if they got the chance.)

The movements are individual at first, but begin to combine into coordinated 'group sequences' until they are interrupted by the restoration of the old regime. Although Lorca's statements, like Ruibal's, emphasise the centrality of verbal language, they also suggest the possibility that the essence of theatricality lies in a strange kind of physical poetry such as that proposed by Sanchis Sinisterra.

Defining theatre as essentially poetic implies that the foundation on which a play is constructed is not necessarily a story, a situation or a set of characters, but can instead be conceived as a single image or concept. Around this poetic core complex layers of associations are built up by means of words, staging and movement. Rather than a line going from the beginning to the end of a story, the structural image we should be thinking of here is circular: a poetic nucleus surrounded by a series of concentric circles (like dropping a stone in a pond). The physical presence of the actors, processes of characterisation and interaction, the stage space and the impression it creates of a social, physical or imaginary environment, story and dramatic situations, all constitute ways of 'making the poetry human', but everything is part of the 'poetic totality'. An actor, a movement, a prop or a lighting effect can be regarded as a component of the signifying structure—in Ruibal's words, 'un elemento básico'. Lorca's image of the 'traje de poesía' (suit of poetry) in which dramatic characters should be clothed may seem misleading, apparently suggesting that the poetry is merely ornamental. However, I believe that the point of the remark is that this 'traje' represents the essence of the character, revealing the bones and the blood through the skin, as it were.

The most obvious way in which poetry makes its presence felt in Lorca's plays is in the form of verse: formalised language in traditional metres, in most cases either sung or recited as a monologue. Sometimes the verse has a ceremonial function, acting as a vehicle for community rituals (the lullaby, the wedding songs, the girls' winding song and the final lament in *Bodas de sangre*; the washerwomen's song and the songs at the pilgrimage in *Yerma*; the religious ritual and the harvesters' song in *La casa de Bernarda Alba*). In these cases, the use of verse does not violate the diegetic logic of the drama, but it does set up symbolic elements that will be developed in other parts of the play and introduces a degree of stylisation which necessarily conditions the whole performance, demanding to be complemented by music and dance. In other cases, the verse acts as a vehicle of individual reverie or fantasy, or else as a universalised language spoken by figures that are themselves entirely symbolic (the songs of the 2nd Friend, the mannequin, Harlequin and the girl in *Así que pasen cinco años*; the moon's monologue in *Bodas de sangre*; the opening lullaby and Yerma's soliloquies in *Yerma*; María Josefa's songs in *La casa de Bernarda Alba*). For Yerma and María Josefa, verse is a secret language of anguish and desire, in which they take refuge from the prosaic logic of the figures of authority around them (Juan and Bernarda).

Verse is employed sparingly as a vehicle for spoken dialogue between characters in *Así que pasen cinco años* and *Bodas de sangre*, and not at all in *Yerma* and *La casa de Bernarda Alba*. In a sense, this is a more intrusive use of verse, more disruptive of the illusion of reality on stage. It is in most cases the language of ritualistic exchanges between symbolic or supernatural characters. The passionate dialogue between Leonardo and the bride in the forest in *Bodas de sangre* is the only example in these plays of two human characters talking to one another in verse. The scene is charged with tremendous emotional and sexual intensity, yet the verse also lends it a certain formality and strangeness. The two lovers are no longer speaking with their own individual voices: they are possessed by a shared language which taps into the symbolic undercurrents of the play.

Although the sections in verse have an important function in consolidating the main elements of symbolism in each play, much of the poetic language takes the form of dialogue in prose intensified by metaphor (and words not obviously metaphorical but acquiring symbolic significance through repetition and association). At this level, poetic elements appear throughout all four plays, tending to burst through initially bland dialogue in ways that can be surprising. While the opening conversation of *Así que pasen cinco años* between the young man and the old man is undeniably puzzling, it consists initially of phrases that could feature in ordinary speech. Then the old man suddenly says: 'Me gusta tanto la palabra recuerdo. Es una palabra verde, jugosa. Mana sin cesar hilitos de agua fría' (*OC*, II, 500) ('I love that word: remember. It's a green, juicy word. Cold water trickles out of it endlessly'). The preceding image of a child saving sweets to eat them later then comes to stand for a wider idea of deferring the fulfilment of desire. Similarly, the beginning of *Bodas de sangre* moves from short everyday phrases to a poetic outburst, as the mother speaks of 'un hombre hermoso, con su flor en la boca' ('a handsome man, with a flower in his mouth'),[7] referring to the knife as 'the serpent' and to a man as 'a bull' (702-3). The process of turning the first mundane reference to a knife into the key symbol of the play has been set in motion. Although *Yerma* begins with a song, the opening dialogue is once again staccato and prosaic. Juan makes the first poetic move, but his simile is conventional—'se ponen fuertes como el acero' ('they get as hard as steel'). Yerma's is more striking: 'tú cada vez más triste, más enjuto, como si crecieras al revés' (804-5) ('you're getting sadder and sadder, more and more dried up, as if you were growing backwards'). She picks up his word 'enjuto' and introduces the first

---

[7] This is a deliberately literal translation. David Johnston's version captures the sense of the phrase very well: 'An angel of a man, in the flower of his life' (*Blood Wedding* (London: Hodder & Stoughton, 1989), 30).

element of a pattern of water symbolism that will form the core of the play.

There is no sudden flash of metaphor at the beginning of *La casa de Bernarda Alba* as in the other plays; instead, imagery is integrated less conspicuously into popular speech from the first exchanges between Poncia and the Criada. Bernarda uses figurative turns of phrase in a hard, clinical, conventional way, as if she means them literally: 'En ocho años que dure el luto no ha de entrar en esta casa el viento de la calle. Hacemos cuenta que hemos tapiado con ladrillos puertas y ventanas' (985) ('In these eight years of mourning not even a breeze will get into the house from the street. As if we had bricked up the doors and windows').[8] In contrast, however, Adela produces distinctive, startling, creative imagery that in itself is a significant part of her rebellion against Bernarda's stifling, anti-poetic rigidity: 'Mirando sus ojos me parece que bebo su sangre lentamente' (1016) ('When I look into his eyes it's as if I'm slowly drinking his blood').

Once the symbolic patterns have been established verbally, other sounds become significant by association: the noise of the storm, the car horn and the chiming of the clock in *Así que pasen cinco años*; hoofbeats and the two violins in *Bodas de sangre*; sheep and bells in *Yerma*; the church bells, the noise of the stallion kicking and sounds made by people outside the house in *La casa de Bernarda Alba*. The absence of sound becomes one of the most significant features of the intricate and finely calculated acoustic texture of *La casa de Bernarda Alba*. The sound of musical instruments as part of the action is at times indicated in stage directions, usually as accompaniment to songs. The notion of poetic totality would, however, justify extensive use of extra-diegetic music in productions of all four plays—not merely as atmospheric background, but as one more integrated component of the sign system.

Visual elements of staging add further richness to the poetic structure: the blue lighting, some of the costumes, the miniature theatre and the forest, the cards and the illuminated ace of hearts in *Así que pasen cinco años*; the colours of the rooms in the first act, the knife, the

---

[8] Ramsden's edition (Manchester: Manchester University Press, 1983) corrects this line to 'Haceros cuenta que hemos tapiado ...' (14).

orange blossom, the movement of actors around the Novia in Act 2, the red wool and more blue light in *Bodas de sangre*. Although *Yerma* is more restrained in this respect, focusing almost exclusively on the figure of the protagonist herself, the fertility dance of the third act introduces some powerful elements of visual symbolism. *La casa de Bernarda Alba* presents a stark background against which Bernarda's stick, María Josefa's lamb and white dress, and Adela's fan and green dress stand out vividly.

Finally, the actors not only speak poetry, they embody poetry. Returning to Ruibal's terminology, we could say about Lorca's characters that 'más que salir las palabras de sus bocas, son ellos quienes salen de la boca de sus palabras' ('rather than the words coming out of their mouths, it is they who come out of the mouths of their words').[9] Certain roles are exclusively symbolic constructions, without names, histories or motives (but with surprisingly strong desires in some cases), representing ideas, psychological processes or superhuman forces: the dead child and the cat, the rugby player, the mannequin, and Harlequin and the clown in *Así que pasen cinco años*; the woodcutters, the moon and the beggar woman in *Bodas de sangre*; the male and female dancers in *Yerma*. The unseen Pepe el Romano could be said to fulfil the same function in *La casa de Bernarda Alba*. Even the parts designed to convey a complex, emotionally convincing sense of character are associated with verbal and visual symbolic elements that define their function within the overall poetic structure while simultaneously encapsulating powerful evocations of human experience. The development of the characterisation of Adela in *La casa de Bernarda Alba*, for example, is an impressively subtle exercise in suggestion and interaction, yet she ends up constituting a very simple, elemental representation of desire and rebellion. An actor performing the role of Leonardo in *Bodas de sangre* has opportunities to explore guilt, resentment, pride, lust, rebellion and so on, but must find a way of simply being the man on his horse, the dark torrent, the force of the sea. The stylisation inherent in the poetic approach makes the use of some element of dance in performances of all these plays particularly

---

[9] José Ruibal, *Teatro sobre teatro* (Madrid: Cátedra, 1984), 38.

appropriate.[10] The translation of the elemental physicality of Lorca's imagery into bodily movement to music puts into practice in a very direct way the theory of 'poetry that gets up off the page and becomes human'.

The written word is of central importance as the source of the poetry: 'el teatro [...] no es más ni menos que literatura' (Lorca, *OC,* III, 615) ('theatre [...] is no more nor less than literature'). But it reaches the audience as part of a multimedia stage language in which spoken words are integrated with all the other signifying elements we have discussed.

The impact of poetry in *Así que pasen cinco años*, *Bodas de sangre*, *Yerma* and *La casa de Bernarda Alba* is multiple and contradictory. At times the effect is one of abstraction or universalisation of particular experience. In *Bodas de sangre*, the fight of two men over a woman is elevated to the status of a ritual sacrifice, the grief of the mother expressed in terms of eternal human destiny and the cycle of the seasons. At the same time, though, the poetry is to do with the intensification of sensations, with concrete, earthy, corporeal realities. Poetry is the language of the imagination but also of the body. Merely hearing the sound of Leonardo's voice is likened by the bride to getting drunk and sinking into a bed of rose petals. Yerma's tender conversations with her imagined child are shot through with pain: 'tronchada y rota soy para ti' (808) ('I'm being ripped and torn apart for you'). Adela's language is a threat to Bernarda because it speaks vividly of individual desire and specific bodily sensations: 'por encima de mi madre saltaría para apagarme este fuego que tengo levantado por piernas y boca' (1015–16) ('I'd jump right over my mother to quench this fire that's burning up my legs and in my mouth'). The moon in *Bodas de sangre* may be a representation of an abstraction, but it expresses its longing for blood in alarmingly physical and emotional terms (776–77). Even the dreamy young protagonist of *Así que pasen*

---

[10] Alan Lyddiard's 1996 production of *Blood Wedding* at the Newcastle Playhouse, inspired in part by Saura's film of Gades's dance version, built a great deal of dance (choreographed by Salud López) into the action. A particularly striking effect was the doubling of the characters of Leonardo and the bride in Act 3, scene 1: dancers interpreted in movement the lines spoken by the actors.

cinco años discovers a language of sensuality—of blood, flesh, pain and urgency.

The symbolic structures produce a very effective condensation of meaning while at the same time creating a sometimes extravagant excess of meaning. The poetry serves to unify and elucidate, but also generates fragmentation, uncertainty and mystery; it is satisfying and reassuring yet frequently disconcerting. There are big, elemental symbols that bind a play together: the horse, the moon and blood in *Bodas de sangre*, the fertile countryside and flowing water in *Yerma*; the house itself in *La casa de Bernarda Alba*. However, images are often repeated, elaborated and made contradictory, and the poetic logic can be decidedly odd. There is surprising, disconcerting imagery in them all, and a crucial moment of strangeness near the end of each one.

Así que pasen cinco años is cryptic from start to finish, an unsettling mixture of metaphysical anguish and whimsical imagination. What is often underestimated about this work is its playfulness. Life, love and death are repeatedly presented in terms of games played by children and adults (the dead child and the cat, the friends, the rugby player, the sinister clown and card players), while the text itself is an exuberant exercise in playing with words. Interwoven with mysterious and troubling images are crazy poetic inversions of logic. At one moment in the first act, the old man interrupts the playful fight between the young man and the first friend in order to recover his hat:

>VIEJO—(*Entrando gravemente.*) Con permiso... (*Los jóvenes se quedan en pie.*) Perdonen... (*Enérgicamente, y mirando al* JOVEN.) Se me olvidará el sombrero.
>
>AMIGO—¿Cómo?
>
>VIEJO—(*Furioso.*) Sí, señor. Se me olvidará el sombrero... (*Entre dientes.*), es decir, se me ha olvidado el sombrero.
>
>AMIGO—¡Ahhhhh!... (512-13)
>
>(OLD MAN—(*Entering solemnly.*) Excuse me, gentlemen... (*The young men stand up.*) Forgive me... (*Forcefully, staring at the* YOUNG MAN.) I'll forget my hat.
>
>FRIEND—What?
>
>OLD MAN—(*Furiously.*) Yes, I said I will forget my hat... (*Through clenched teeth.*) That's to say, I have forgotten my hat.

FRIEND—Ahhhhh!...)

The stage directions are crucial to the comic effect. The mixing of the sinister with the playful culminates in the final scene, in which the death of the protagonist is staged in a manner that is charmingly silly. As soon as the card players have forced him to play his ace of hearts, an image of the ace lights up on a bookcase; one of the players takes out a pistol and fires a dart at the heart, which disappears; as the young man clutches his chest, the same player produces a pair of scissors and snips the air (594).

The imagery of the rural plays is more accessible, yet each has a strange poetic logic of its own. At the beginning of *Bodas de sangre*, the mother's metaphor of men as bulls is obvious, but she also refers, more surprisingly, to her virile dead as geraniums (703). The central symbol of blood becomes quite unstable, acquiring multiple associations with life and death, then just before the climax the woodcutters have a peculiar conversation that plays on these contradictory meanings:

> LEÑADOR 3º—¡La sangre!
> LEÑADOR 1º—Hay que seguir el camino de la sangre.
> LEÑADOR 2º—Pero la sangre que ve la luz se la bebe la tierra.
> LEÑADOR 1º—¿Y qué? Vale más ser muerto desangrado que vivo con ella podrida.
> [...]
> LEÑADOR 1º—Ahora la estará queriendo.
> LEÑADOR 2º—El cuerpo de ella era para él y el cuerpo de él para ella.
> LEÑADOR 3º—Los buscan y los matarán.
> LEÑADOR 1º—Pero ya habrán mezclado sus sangres y serán dos cántaros vacíos, como dos arroyos secos. (773-4)
> (3RD WOODCUTTER—Blood!
> 1ST WOODCUTTER—Blood chooses the path that must be followed.
> 2ND WOODCUTTER—But blood that sees the light of day is drunk by the earth.
> 1ST WOODCUTTER—What does that matter? It's better to be bled dry than to go on living with your blood stagnant in your veins.
> [...]

1ST WOODCUTTER—He'll be making love to her now.
2ND WOODCUTTER—Her body was for him and his body for her.
3RD WOODCUTTER—They'll find them and kill them.
1ST WOODCUTTER—But by then his blood will be mixed with hers and they'll be like two empty jugs, two streams run dry.)

An alarming equation seems to be being made between sex and violence, between the greatest intensity of life and the proximity of sudden death. The moon's thirst for blood a moment later is not just macabre but can be dangerously erotic, and the play's final image of the knife penetrating startled flesh is disturbingly phallic. The *grito* ('cry' or 'scream') can be taken as one of pain or ecstasy (or possibly even childbirth).

Yerma and other characters around her have some bizarre ideas about fertility and conception. She uses the hopeful image of weeds growing out of stones softened by the rain, and is enchanted by María's impression that she has been impregnated by her husband whispering to her: 'me parece que mi niño es un palomo de lumbre que él me deslizó por la oreja' (812) ('I feel like my baby is a dove of light that he slipped into my ear'). Yerma imagines her child as already existing but trapped inside her, or else inside her husband, needing to be freed by the power of poetic speech, which Juan does not possess. The culminating element of oddness is the climax of the play, in which Yerma overpowers and strangles Juan, then says 'he matado a mi hijo' (880) ('I have killed my child'). Her strength comes not just from the force of her will or her desire: it is a poetic strength. She has shown herself all along to be more powerful than Juan in poetic terms, for her speech is rich and imaginative, while his is dull and prosaic. The poetic logic of the notion that a potential baby already exists inside Juan is that by killing him she has literally killed her child.

The opening stage direction of *La casa de Bernarda Alba* indicates that 'un gran silencio umbroso se extiende por la escena' (973) ('a great shady silence spreads across the stage'), suggesting that the silence of the empty stage should somehow be made visible, tangible. As the atmosphere of heat and confinement builds up, the impression that the silence imposed by Bernarda is physically oppressive becomes stronger and stronger, reinforced by small things the characters say. Bernarda refers to 'el silencio del peso del calor' (1025) ('the silence made heavy by the heat'), and Poncia remarks to the maid: '¿Tú ves este silencio? Pues hay una tormenta en cada cuarto' (1054) ('Do you see this silence? Well there's a storm brewing in every room'). Much of the point of the figure of María Josefa is that she cuts through this silence and challenges Bernarda's control of language. She speaks nonsense, plays with words and rhymes, and leaps from one strange metaphor to another: '¿Por qué una oveja no va a ser un niño? [...] Pero él os va a devorar porque sois granos de trigo. No granos de trigo. ¡Ranas sin lengua!' (1058) ('Why can't a lamb be a baby? [...] But he'll devour you all because you're just grains of wheat. No, not grains of wheat. Frogs with no tongues!'). Adela also eventually challenges the silence and the hegemony of the single voice of authority. When she makes the defiantly illogical declaration 'aquí se acabaron las voces de presidio' (1063) ('this is the end of prison voices') as she breaks her mother's stick, she makes explicit the link between Bernarda's physical instrument of repression and her attempt to control speech.

The overall effect of Lorca's strategy of poetic theatre is to blend tradition with innovation and to fuse the verbal and visual languages of theatre. The texts (as printed scripts but also as performances) make their aesthetic opacity evident, focusing the audience's attention on form, sound, texture and movement (that is, they do not purport to be merely transparent containers of meaning). Ideas and feelings are presented in startling, unsettling ways that challenge audiences' perceptions, producing an effect of defamiliarisation. Lorca's theatre is self-consciously poetic and self-consciously theatrical, productively playful in various senses—child's play, word play, role play. All this adds up to an ambitious project: to blow apart what Mosquito at the beginning of the *Tragicomedia de don Cristóbal* calls 'the theatre of the bourgeoisie'[11] and fill the stage with passion and magic. Poetry that gets up off the page and becomes human on the stage demands imaginative productions that capture the symbolic unity of each piece but are also sensitive to the mystery and the bizarre dissonances of Lorca's distinctive poetic logic.

---

[11] *OC*, II, 105.

Lluís Pasqual's Unknown Lorcas[1]
Maria M. Delgado

Examining the year 1998, centenary of both Brecht and Lorca, the contrasting ways in which both writers were commemorated throws up a range of interesting questions around where their significance lies. Both were vigorously celebrated in their own countries of birth. The Brecht centenary was, not surprisingly, centred on the Berliner Ensemble, the company founded by the playwright-director in 1949. Discussions, however, also surfaced around where definitions of political theatre now lie and whether Brecht's models still hold relevance for contemporary audiences. In addition, the publication of John Fuegi's revised biography claiming that three of the playwright's lovers composed a significant amount of plays such as *Threepenny Opera,* and the protracted suing of his publishers by heirs of Brecht's lover and secretary Elisabeth Hauptmann for backdated royalties, cast a sordid but not unlucrative cloud over the Berlin celebrations.[2]

The Lorca centenary proved an altogether less scandalous affair.[3] It began as soon as the new year was celebrated with *Una Mirada a Lorca*, an event in Granada attended by the king and queen, clearly

---

[1] I would like to thank Pascal Sénatore of the Odéon-Théâtre de l'Europe for providing me with access to a video version of *Haciendo Lorca*. Ros Ribas has been both kind and generous in allowing me access to his photographs of Pasqual's work. Thanks are also due to Frederic Amat and Marco Carniti for discussing with me their work with Pasqual, and to Lluís Pasqual for his generosity and support of my research. This article is dedicated to Maribel San Ginés for all the assistance she has provided in its preparation and in all my previous writings on Pasqual.

[2] For one of the more recent features on the scandals surrounding the centenary celebrations see Amelia Gentleman, 'Brecht reputation at stake', *The Guardian* (25 May 1998), 9.

[3] There has, though, been a marked amount of attention in the press to the controversy over the filming of Lorca's screenplay, *Viaje a la luna*, which Frederic Amat realised without the collaboration of producer Javier Martín-Domínguez after Martín-Domínguez tried to assume directorial responsibility for the venture.

offering their endorsement both of the poet-playwright marginalised by the Franco regime, and of the Año Lorca celebrations which the event officially inaugurated. Held at the appropriately named Auditorio Manuel de Falla in Granada, it featured excerpts of pieces by the poet's friend, de Falla, as well as other composers admired by Lorca, including Stravinsky, Debussy and Albéniz. Two piano pieces, 'Pensamiento poético' and 'Granada' , composed by Lorca in his youth, were played by Daniel Ligorio, and the young actor Juan Diego Botto recited a series of poems written by Lorca between the ages of eighteen and twenty-two. Francisco Merino provided a rendition from *Don Cristóbal*, the puppets of Fernando Gómez and Pilar Gálvez offered the 'Nana del Galapaguito' performed to a recording by La Argentinita accompanied on the piano by Lorca, while singers Enrique and Estrella Morente offered a kaleidoscopic collage where the emphasis was not on a singular writing subject but rather on a mythical entity, both celebrated and interrogated through his writings, compositions, acknowledged musical influences and collaborations.[4] There was no attempt to define Lorca, rather the eclectic programme sought to self-consciously construct a Lorca where disparity was staged and where the elusive shifting persona of the playwright became part of the spectacle: a being constructed from the works, a series of masks where the point of origin is never located, a brilliant game of mirrors where reflections of truth and lies merge to present a series of events which never deliver a unified reality.

I have chosen to begin my paper by focusing on this event, because although conceived by Jorge de Persia, the programme was directed by Lluís Pasqual to designs by Frederic Amat, with the Granada City Orchestra and the Chorus of Barcelona's Palau de la Música conducted by Josep Pons. Pasqual, Pons and Amat are all Catalans, who have collaborated on numerous previous occasions. All are associated with Barcelona's Teatre Lliure of which Pasqual was a founding director in 1976. Pons was, until recently, music director of the Lliure's Chamber Orchestra, which he founded in 1985, and Amat, one of Spain's foremost painters and a former design pupil of Lliure co-founder Fabià

---

[4] For further details of the event see Carlos Tarín, 'La música abre en Granada el Año Lorca', *El Correo de Andalucia* (16 January 1998), 6.

Puigserver, has designed a number of Pasqual's most recent productions.⁵ All three began their careers in Catalonia, all received recognition abroad for their work with Spanish texts and scores, all have worked with foreign companies, and all recognise a diversity of international influences on their work. In addition, with the exception of Amat's collaboration with Cesc Gelabert on *ZUMZUM-KA* which was seen at the Edinburgh Festival in 1998, and Pasqual's visit to London's Institute of Contemporary Arts in 1992, their work has rarely been seen in this country and has therefore received little coverage from an insular, domestic, news-centred English press.

Although I do not plan to speculate at length on the reasons for this, it does, I believe, relate to the fact that their work cannot be easily read via the stereotypes through which much of the Spanish culture exported to Britain is marketed. It is unfortunate that the more stolid stagings of the Teatro Clásico which visited the Edinburgh Festival in 1989 and the Spanish Arts Festival in 1994, drawing unfortunate comparisons with the Royal Shakespeare Company, have provided one of the only opportunities for British audiences to see text-based productions. Whilst the conspicuous attention generated by La Cubana, La Fura dels Baus, Comediants and Carles Santos has accorded visibility to their synthetic interdisciplinary approach to performance, Joaquín Cortés and Paco Peña have continued to provide an example of the lure of stereotypes in the fascination with Spain's cultural wares.

Lorca, too, has appeared to offer an easy point of contact with the country's more exotic customs and traits. It is especially the association of Lorca's rural trilogy with the Andalusian landscape and culture that has provided a recognisable point of contact for a foreign readership. The fact that Spain's cultural construction has been irrevocably linked with the culture of flamenco for about two hundred years has allowed Lorca's Andalusian-located work to be read and marketed through accessible clichés which may not be applied with the same ease to the work of his contemporaries or successors. As one of the first martyrs of the Civil War, he creates a romantic subject for exploitation, and his writings have been read as a mirror of his much publicised life, as

---

⁵ Amat has also provided illustrations for the Compact Disc covers of the majority of Josep Pons' recordings for Harmonia Mundi.

reflections of Andalusian life during the 1920s and 1930s, as elegies where his own death is anticipated, and as metaphors for his homosexuality, supposedly demonstrating how sexual and social deviancy leads to destruction.

Whilst I am not suggesting that the works can be reduced to the readings which we allocate and which may be dominant at any one time, oblique works, like *El público* and *Comedia sin título*, and the shorter plays, like *La doncella, el marinero y el estudiante* and *Posada*, have come to question the accepted image of Lorca as 'a colourful, castanet-clicking gypsy with a tragic social conscience'.[6] Where Pasqual differs from his contemporaries, José Luis Gómez, José Carlos Plaza and Núria Espert, is that he has granted a central position to works hitherto regarded as peripheral. While artistic director of the Centro Dramático Nacional at the Teatro María Guerrero (1983-1989), he presented a major Lorca season (1986-1987) where his own production of *El público* was framed within *Sonetos del amor oscuro,* a programme of recitals by Amancio Prada staged by Pasqual and first seen in the previous season, and *5 Lorcas 5*, a grouping of five short pieces directed by five different directors, including José Luis Alonso, Joan Baixas and Lindsey Kemp. The choice clearly indicated a wish to allow one of Spain's major directors, Alonso, to tackle Lorca for the first time, providing Kemp (who in *Cruel Garden* had created a grand elegiac reading of the poet's life and work) with an opportunity to refashion *El paseo de Buster Keaton*, and giving Baixas, founder member of La Claca, whose legendary show *Mori el merma (Death to the Monster)*, with puppets and masks designed by Joan Miró, had been one of the theatrical highlights of the transition years, the staging of *La doncella, el marinero y el estudiante*. Pasqual himself directed Antonio Banderas, then still predominantly recognised as a stage actor, in *Diálogo del amargo*.[7]

---

[6] John London, 'Introduction', *The Unknown Federico García Lorca* (London: Atlas, 1996), 7. Both *Posada* and *La doncella, el marinero y el estudiante* are published in new English translations therein.
[7] They had previously worked together on the Brecht version of Marlowe's *La vida del Rey Eduardo II de Inglaterra* (1983), where Banderas was Gaveston to Alfredo Alcón's Eduardo.

This season, presented on the fiftieth anniversary of his death, re-envisaged Lorca. Both a process of re-appropriation and scholarship, *5 Lorcas 5* was made up of short, predominantly unfamiliar works which reject narrative logic in favour of a dramaturgical structure which defiantly challenges the reassuring tendencies of the realist play. Although *Diálogo del amargo* and *La escena del Teniente Coronel de la Guardia Civil* inhabit more familiar gypsy territory, their inclusion within a programme which included more dissident fragmented pieces like *El paseo de Buster Keaton* and *La doncella, el marinero y el estudiante*, occupying an uneasy space between film and performance script, served to juxtapose these different Lorcas, thus destabilising any possibility of reading the dramatist through accredited values.

The Lorca dissection continued in 1987-1988 with a production of *Los caminos de Federico*,[8] a spectacle conceived with the Argentine actor, Alfredo Alcón. Seen in Madrid in June 1988, just after the revival of Pasqual's production of *El público*, it featured Alcón, who had trained with Margarita Xirgu in Buenos Aires, constructing a playful Lorca confiding in and flirting with his audience. In contrast to the grand theatrics of Kemp's *Cruel Garden,* the emphasis was on storytelling. Consisting of a collage of poems layered and folded over one another, the spectacle emphasised an inscribed body written, rather than a coherently structured whole. Here Lorca was examined as a commodity, transformed into the many identities societies have accorded him: prophet, seer, artist, musician, son, lover, social rights crusader, surrealist, director—a displacing gaze where the performing body replays historically defined identities which recognise that culture enjoys an ideological role.

The fact that Pasqual presented the premiere of the play *El público* while artistic director of the Centro Dramático Nacional (the Spanish National Theatre), an organisation receiving generous subsidy from the Ministry of Culture, suggests a recognition of the cultural value of the text. Dispensing with a reverential reading which might have presented this excavated script to a curious audience with a rigidly sacred precision, much like Ultz's 1988 production at Stratford East, Pasqual

---

[8] This was a co-production with the Teatro Municipal General San Martín in Buenos Aires. The production was first seen in Buenos Aires in July 1987.

and his designer Fabià Puigserver chose a more playful approach which recognised and celebrated not only the complex interaction of differing linguistic and dramatic discourses in the play, but also the specific function of the eccentric stage directions. Rather than simply providing a mimetic reproduction of the directions presented in the text, Pasqual and Puigserver chose to radically reinterpret them. Rejecting the proscenium stage, although commenting on its trappings in a series of complex and striking ways, Pasqual and Puigserver created a performance space which was both fluid and idiomatic. Moving away from reverential fidelity, they used the opening stage directions' stipulations of 'Decorado azul'[9] (blue decor), to create a playing area which recognised the colliding temporal systems at work when an avant-garde play from 1930 is staged for the first time in 1986.

It had been Pasqual and Puigserver's intention to premiere the play in Granada in a purpose-built mobile theatre designed by Puigserver and Amat. Although the scheme received initial backing from the Ministry of Culture, problems emerged over running and maintenance costs and the building was never realised. The intricate designs produced for the interior of the theatre by Puigserver and the exterior by Amat, published in 1988 as *El Teatro Federico García Lorca*,[10] demonstrate the need to reenvisage the performance space for plays like *El público* which gravitate around a fundamental questioning of established conventions of dramatic construction.

An understanding of the space consequently created in the Teatro María Guerrero for the play's Madrid run necessitates some prior knowledge of the work undertaken by Puigserver and Pasqual in the years before this production. For although it was their first Lorca venture, their working relationship had commenced in 1975 with *La setmana tràgica*, a Mnouchkine-inspired dramatisation of the failed revolt of 1909 devised from improvisational work with students from the Escola de Teatre de l'Orfeo de Sants in Barcelona. Customary

---

[9] Federico García Lorca, *El público*, ed. María Clementa Millán (Madrid: Cátedra, 1988), 119.

[10] Frederic Amat, *El Teatro Federico García Lorca* (Granada: Diputación Provisional de Granada, 1988). I would like to thank Eric Southworth for sending me a copy of his unpublished paper, 'Lorca and Theatre Architecture', which dedicates a section to this project.

actor-audience relationships were here challenged through an orchestration of space whereby the actors encircled the audience, subverting habitual framing boundaries.

Pasqual and Puigserver were to collaborate regularly until the latter's death in 1991, with Pasqual acknowledging the 'constant and living exchange'[11] that was a feature of all their projects. By the time they began working together the Polish-trained Puigserver was already an internationally recognised designer, having produced the much lauded canvas design for Víctor García's production of *Yerma* (1971).[12] Puigserver's membrane skin could be stretched, raised, lowered or folded as necessary to provide a plethora of different playing areas. 'Peter Brook says that set design for the theatre is divided into "before the canvas set and after the canvas set",' Pasqual has asserted, '*Yerma* was a tremendous contribution to contemporary theatre.'[13]

In Puigserver Pasqual found an imaginative designer who was willing to work beyond the parameters of baroque design and who, importantly, as John London has also indicated, considered stage design 'his vocation, rather than an activity into which he gradually passed alongside other jobs. It is difficult to overemphasise the professionalism of Puigserver's background in comparison to the general situation in post-War Spain.'[14] Puigserver was a craftsman with a meticulous eye for detail, insistent on working on every aspect of his design's construction. He was also a minimalist, stripping the stage of superficial decor, and capable of providing a visual analogy for the dramatic tension in the text. In 1976 Pasqual and Puigserver joined forces with

[11] Lluís Pasqual in Maria M. Delgado, 'Redefining Spanish Theatre: Lluís Pasqual on Directing, Fabià Puigserver, and the Lliure', *Spanish Theatre 1920-1995: Strategies in Protest and Imagination (3), Contemporary Theatre Review*, 7:4 (1998), 100.
[12] For a more detailed discussion of Puigserver's work see Guillem-Jordi Graells and Juan Antonio Hormigón, eds, *Fabià Puigserver: Hombre de teatro* (Madrid: Asociación de Directores de España, 1993) and Guillem-Jordi Graells and Giorgio Ursini Uršič, eds, *Fabià Puigserver: Scénographe* (Paris: Union des Théâtres de l'Europe, 1995).
[13] Lluís Pasqual in Maria M. Delgado, 'Redefining Spanish Theatre: Lluís Pasqual on Directing, Fabià Puigserver, and the Lliure', 101.
[14] John London, 'Twentieth-Century Spanish Stage Design', *Spanish Theatre 1920-1995*, 50.

Pere Planella to co-found the Teatre Lliure Collective, which they housed in a building in the Gràcia area of Barcelona renovated for nine million pesetas. Puigserver's design of the theatre provided the first multi-purpose auditorium in Spain; a performance space which could adapt to the requirements of each new project. That which is now seen as common practice was pioneered by Puigserver and Pasqual at the Lliure.

During the years following Pasqual's residencies at the National Theatre of Warsaw, where he assisted Adam Hanuszkiewicz on his 1976 production of Chekhov's *Platonov*, and at the Piccolo Teatro di Milano (1978) where he worked as Strehler's assistant, his collaborations with Puigserver demonstrated a fascination with working in the round, where the actors are especially vulnerable and unable to escape the presence of the audience, and an extraordinary capacity to conjure magical stage moments from elemental ingredients.[15] Since 1978 the productions staged at the Lliure have revealed a more subtle and stylish director, one who favoured an intense rehearsal period and who, following the opening of the production limited his fine tuning to listening to performances, allowing them to be 'adjusted to the audience', breathing with the audience,[16] recognising that productions shift and change with every performance and every audience. Theatre for Pasqual has always been what he himself terms 'a learning process' (215) a way of spending time with favourite plays, getting to know them and battling with their intricacies and demons. He has always been attracted to more oblique dramatic works and never felt the need to pursue a realist aesthetic. 'Realism in the theatre bores me', he has insisted: 'In the theatre, I demand of myself and of others the capacity for metaphor, for [...] poetry [...] : the capacity for a door to be many things, a door being the least of them' (215).

Any glance at the Lliure's programming over the past twenty-three years, or his choice of repertoire while artistic director of the Centro

---

[15] Pasqual discusses what he learned from his time in Poland in Maria M. Delgado, 'Redefining Spanish Theatre: Lluís Pasqual on Directing, Fabià Puigserver, and the Lliure', 91–92. For comments on his period at the Piccolo see Maria Delgado and Paul Heritage, eds, *In Contact with the Gods?: Directors Talk Theatre* (Manchester University Press, 1996), 214–15.

[16] 'Lluís Pasqual', *In Contact with the Gods?*, 215.

Dramático Nacional certainly indicates a marked responsibility and attraction on Pasqual's part to works which defy a linear logic and which concern themselves with duplicity, the split self, the relationship between differing registers of reality, conflicts between the rational and the impassioned, and the very art of theatre which depends for its existence on illusory practices.[17] Interestingly, he has often stated that if when he reads a play he knows how to do it then he will not stage it.[18] He continually postponed producing *El público*, announcing it for his second season as artistic director of Madrid's Centro Dramático Nacional but not daring to stage it at the time because it scared him.[19] When it was finally produced two years later, in 1987,[20] the production was regarded as part of an ongoing agenda of bringing to the stage dramatic works which had been branded 'impossible'.[21] As with his earlier production of *Luces de bohemia* in 1984, the staging provided an evanescent meditation on the text which recognised the existence of conflicting articulations and fragmentations and dispensed with psychological identity as the sole pivot on which interpretation of character turns.

Relocating the play text in a socio-cultural context which differs from that which engenders it, always involves a process of reinvention. The Pasqual/Puigserver reading of *El público* posited a recognition of the production process which questions the playwright's status as privileged

[17] For example, at the Teatre Lliure: Chekhov's *Les Tres Germanes* (1979), Marlowe/Brecht's *La vida del Rei Eduard II d'Anglaterra* (1978), Genet's *El balcó* (1982), Shakespeare's *Al vostre gust* (1983), and Goldoni's *Un dels últims vespres de carnaval* (1995). At the Centro Dramático Nacional: *Luces de bohemia* (1984), *Madre Coraje y sus hijos* (1986), and *Julio César* (1988).
[18] See 'Lluís Pasqual', *In Contact with the Gods?*, 208.
[19] See Maria M. Delgado, 'Redefining Spanish Theatre: Lluís Pasqual on Directing, Fabià Puigserver, and the Lliure', 95.
[20] Although the production opened at the Piccolo Teatro, Milan on 12 December 1986, its run at Madrid's Teatro María Guerrero began on 16 January 1987.
[21] Pasqual discusses this in ibid., 97. For a far fuller description of the production see Maria M. Delgado and Gwynne Edwards, 'From Madrid to Stratford East: *The Public* in Performance', *Estreno*, 16:2 (Autumn 1990), 11-18, 6. Paul Julian Smith also provides a reading of the production in *The Theatre of García Lorca: text, performance, psychoanalysis* (Cambridge University Press, 1998), 118-38.

point of origin, at the pinnacle of a hierarchical power structure which recognises the director as a supposedly secondary figure.[22] Rather than simply seeing their task as the extraction of meaning from Lorca's text, in interviews published to promote the production, Pasqual and Puigserver recognised their own engagement in a creative dialogue with the play.

Taking the direction of 'Las ventanas son radiografías'[23] ('The windows are X-ray negatives') as a starting point, director and designer moved to create an 'imaginary theatre',[24] perhaps even a theatre beneath the sand. Upstage the fossilised trappings of the proscenium arch stage and its reductive perspectivism created a glaring reminder of the theatre of the open air. Extracted from their habitual context the stiff plush red, gold, white and blue curtains stood starkly as a constant reminder of an architectural structure which no longer seemed relevant to the products framed within it. Recognising the traditions of theatrical interpretation in which they work and the expectations national and international audiences may bring to a Lorca or Pasqual/Puigserver production, the staging highlighted the interpretative and significant layers which form part of any theatrical product. Every production witnessed is intertextual, set against a background of prior performances, interpretations and meanings. The beauty of *El público*, as conceived by Pasqual and Puigserver, was the overt theatrical articulation of this process. Its subject became as much the dominant artistic referents of the time in which it was written as the contemporary situation in which it was being staged and performance history between these two temporal axes. As such, stage directions which Puigserver regarded as products of the surrealist context in which Lorca was immersed were radically reinterpreted.

Removing the stage and the orchestra stalls of the Teatro María Guerrero provided an expansive, almost circular playing area of

---

[22] A point made by Stratos E. Constantinidis in *Theatre Under Deconstruction?: A Question of Approach* (New York & London: Garland Press, 1993), 14.

[23] Federico García Lorca, *El público*, 119. The English translation which follows is taken from Henry Livings' translation of the play published in *Lorca Plays: Three* (London: Methuen Drama, 1994), 61.

[24] Lluís Pasqual, 'La verdad del amor y del teatro', *El público*, 40 (January 1987), 6.

sparkling blue sand, a transformative space which simultaneously served to evoke the circus ring, a lunar landscape, a beach, and a *corral* (seventeenth-century courtyard theatre). Only a single row of stall seats remained, primarily for the actors, a dislocated reminder of a theatrical model which was inverted as the audience observed actors watching other actors, hence denying the stability of a single field of vision. Both Pasqual and Puigserver have repeatedly commented on the ever-shifting nature of theatrical meaning.[25] Stage directions which may have seemed radical fifty years earlier are now read against a catalogue of artistic and technological innovations which has modified their impact. Refusing to efface the disparities between the theatrical and social codes of 1930 and 1987 provided a vibrant *mise en scène* where a collage of dramatic, rhetorical, literary, medical, cinematic, biblical, performative and sexual discourses all came into play. Narrative or thematic coherence was emphatically negated. Dramatist and director refused to endorse readings which would reduce the play to a single issue.[26]

Instead, the emphasis was on polyphony. In *El público*, the cumulative acts of realist dramaturgy are replaced by a 'Drama en cuadros'[27] (Play in frames). These 'frames' dispense with spatial or temporal coherence, offering an array of characters whose relations to each other are never concretely defined and using a variety of acting styles—from the *Tanztheater* of the white horses to the operatic register of Julieta's anguished soliloquies, to the seductive writhings of the Figura de Pámpanos (Figure of Vine Leaves) and Figura de Cascabeles (Figure of Bells), to the clinical, measured debate between the Prestidigitador (Magician and Director) in the final scene, to the awkward reciting of Juan Echanove's Pastor Bobo (Silly Shepherd). The choreographed movement resisted easy categorisation, recognising its own performative referents. Transitions of mood and tone are rapid

---

[25] See, for example, Lluís Pasqual, 'La verdad del amor y del teatro', 6–9, and Fabià Puigserver, 'Lo importante es el viaje', *El Público*, 40 (January 1987), 9–11.
[26] 'Sería reductor decir que esta obra trata solamente de la homosexualidad de Lorca' ('It would be reductive to say that this play is solely about Lorca's homosexuality'). Lluís Pasqual, 'La verdad del amor y del teatro', 7.
[27] Federico García Lorca, *El público*, 117.

in Lorca's language; here they were made visible thorough a dynamic physicalisation of action.

In the third scene of the play, when the Hombre 1 (First Man) claims he has no mask, the Director reveals that there is nothing but masks. In Pasqual's production, gender, sexuality, social and political interaction were all presented as imitative performance; a game in which the tension between visibility and invisibility found its most resonant manifestation through the character of the Prestidigitador, whose function lies in conjuring illusions. The theatrical trickery accompanying his entry for the final scene, fan in hand, silhouetted by a spot on a curtain some distance away, provided an alluring manifestation of the ephemeral intangibility of performance, becoming itself only through disappearance.[28]

Magician with fan in Lluís Pasqual's production of El público
(Madrid, 1987)

---

[28] A point made by Peggy Phelan in *Unmarked: the politics of performance* (London & New York: Routledge, 1993), 146.

Silly Shepherd

In *El público* as staged by Pasqual, theatricality was the definitive idiom. Costumes alluded to the play's various generic registers, and were not fixed to any definable period or tradition. In the case of the Pastor Bobo, part clown, part fool, multiple layers of costume mixed military insignia with signs of domesticity (an apron), profession (a sheepskin wipe), femininity (the earrings) and classical antecedents (a hose, a handkerchief tied around the head). Emphatic colour coding in a costume scheme dominated by red, white and black commented on the audience's expectations: Julieta (Juliet) dressed in sculpted white, Elena (Helen) positioned on platform pedestal heels, the Emperador (Emperor) in white toga and red cape. Signs of discontinuity soon appeared as Julieta was placed in an imagistic network dissonant from that in which the audience may have initially conceptualised her. Verbal and visual dislocation found their exquisite counterpoint as Julieta's encounters with the horses delineated a confrontation of performance styles, ideologies, icons and desires. The physically masked and visibly disembodied entities populating the stage provided a carnivalesque antagonism of conflicting roles.[29] Connections were teased and traced by an audience whose attempts to locate intentional meaning were continually frustrated.

Juliet and horses

---

[29] See David George, *The History of the Commedia dell' arte in Modern Hispanic Literature With Special Attention to the Work of García Lorca* (Lewiston/Queenston/Lampeter: The Edwin Mellen Press, 1995), 153-65.

It was the journey, the process of reading and interpretation, which was the crux of Pasqual's production. Positing the process as a journey with Puigserver in which the participants included Amat, musician and composer Josep Maria Arrizabalaga and actor Alfredo Alcón,[30] Pasqual acknowledged the ongoing capacity of texts to carry on meaning effectively forever. Interpretation can never be complete. The French philosopher Jacques Derrida writes of reading as 'transformational', denying 'a finished signified beneath a textual surface'.[31] Like the superimposed masks paraded before us at a dizzying speed in Pasqual's *El público*, when surfaces are displaced, they reveal other surfaces. When even gender and sexuality are presented as representation, the real is implicitly acknowledged as absent. Pleasure lies in the peeling away of the masks, the search for an elusive referent, a non-existent essence which can never be revealed. 'El amor, la felicidad sólo existen', Pasqual has affirmed, 'mientras los buscamos'[32] ('Love and happiness exist only while we search for them').

The interplay of light and darkness—flickers and shadows, expansive spots which sought out the characters and into which the characters slid—divided and controlled the performance space, creating multiple areas and contrasting perspectives. Intimate spaces, long corridors, and expansive arenas of decisive physical and ideological conflict all offered a malleability and fluidity of space which was physicalised through the encounters (physical, musical and visual) enacted across the space. The focus was on the performers interacting in a physical landscape where visibility was not necessarily desirable and where desire always exceeded the means by which it could be satisfied.

Superimposed performative masks seduced the audience into believing that beneath a role lies 'truth' but truth proved an elusive concept in Pasqual's staging. Absolutes were negated. Comparing the piece to a Mozart sonata, Pasqual consistently recognised the particularity of the reading of the play presented through the production: the many surfaces, reflections and prisms always denying a

---

[30] See Lluís Pasqual, 'La verdad del amor y del teatro', 6.
[31] Jacques Derrida, *Positions*, trans. Alan Bass (London: Athlone Press, 1981), 63.
[32] Lluís Pasqual, 'La verdad del amor y del teatro', 7.

definitive rendition.[33] The circular setting served to implicate the audience in a relationship which renegotiated private and public spheres. Pasqual has admitted in interviews that when he first read the play in 1978 'no entendí nada de nada' (6) ('I understood absolutely nothing'). On the eve of the production's opening he spoke of areas of the play 'que se han ido aclarando, otras que permanecen en la oscuridad total' (7) ('which have become clearer, others which remain in total darkness'). Pasqual's production may have begun with white lights permeating the darkness of the playing area, seeking to make visible the opaque, but visibility, as Pasqual recognises, has its limitations.

The critic Peggy Phelan writes of visibility as a 'trap'; it summons surveillance, and the law; it possesses 'voyeurism, fetishism, the colonialist/imperial appetite for possession'.[34] In Pasqual's production, the interplay of visibility and invisibility was brutally enacted on the body of El Desnudo Rojo (The Red Nude). Punishment becomes performative, mapped out on a naked body crucified on a metal bed frame, itself framed by a white sheet and then reframed again by a gold curtain. A public ceremony enacted on the most private of locations to an audience confronting the unexpected. The visibility of his genitalia, the invisibility of the four partially lit students debating *Romeo and Juliet* as their shadows climbed along the curtains behind the nude figure, the women dressed in black fumbling in the dark to make their way through the dimmed auditorium, all functioned as metaphors for a production which operated around the praxis of revelation: the revelation of Lorca's 'unknown' play, the revelation of an 'unknown' Lorca which refuses to reconfirm the populist associations of his best known works, the revelation of a different Teatro María Guerrero far removed from its habitual proscenium frame.

It is no coincidence that Pasqual's production was co-produced by Milan's Piccolo Teatro and the Théâtre de l'Europe, of which Giorgio Strehler was then also artistic director. Strehler's practice, based always on detailed research and a celebration of the transformative capacity of the stage, offered a model of theatre where the methodologies of

---

[33] Ibid., 6.
[34] Peggy Phelan, *Unmarked*, 6.

performance and the fluidity of the historical and contemporary function of a play text were of paramount importance. Playing in both Paris and Milan, *El público* offered Italian and French audiences a production which deviated sharply from cultural precedents and questioned popular conceptions of Lorca as a folkloric dramatist whose thematics were conveniently related to a Latin temperament. As with his later production of *Comedia sin título*, again seen in both Madrid and Paris, Pasqual promoted the Hispanic cultural heritage abroad without reducing it to a single hegemonic product. In the light of press reviews of the production's Paris and Milan performances, Paul Julian Smith comments on the continuing unease of critics about the play's homosexual theme and onstage nudity, teasing out the contradictory positions occupied by a staging which both celebrated the dramatist's universality and accommodation of multiple interpretations, and demonstrated the necessity to police 'the limits of decency, both at home and elsewhere'.[35]

While working on *El público*, Puigserver talked of his desire to work with plays which veered away from the obvious, where the language was poetic and where the emphasis was on showing rather than telling.[36] In 1989, *Comedia sin título*, Pasqual's final production as artistic director of the Centro Dramático Nacional, took another of the 'impossible' incomplete plays, described by Lorca as 'una obra en la que no puedo escribir nada, ni una línea, porque se han desatado y andan por los aires la verdad y la mentira, el hambre y la poesía'[37] ('a play in which I cannot write anything, not even a line, because truth and lies, hunger and poetry have been let loose and wander through the air') and reinhabited it to provide alternative spectator/performer configurations which disallowed complacent aestheticisation.

As with his production of *El público*, the play was reinvented as a reflection on the politics and function of theatre. Hinging on the slight plot of a revolution breaking out outside a theatre where rehearsals for *A Midsummer Night's Dream* are taking place, the play's narrative style

---

[35] Paul Julian Smith, 'The Lorca Cult: Theatre, Cinema, and Print Media in 1980s Spain', *Spanish Theatre 1920–1995*, 77.
[36] Fabià Puigserver, 'Lo importante es el viaje', *El Público*, 9–10.
[37] Quoted in José Monleón, 'El último Pasqual: *Comedia sin título*', *Primer Acto*, 230, (1989), 22.

provides a penetrating commentary on the construction of theatre and self. The ornate splendour of the Teatro María Guerrero was self-consciously placed on display, providing a frame for the rehearsals of Shakespeare's play which Pasqual included in his staging.

Critic Leonard Tennenhouse views *A Midsummer Night's Dream* as a study of 'authority grown archaic', where 'inversions—of gender, age, status, even of species—violate all the categories organising Elizabethan reality itself'.[38] Lorca's piece also constructs a space where chaos threatens the hermetic world enclosed within the proscenium frame. Imanol Arias, returning to the stage after a decade of working predominantly in film, presented an Autor (Author) who struggled to remain in control, directing proceedings from a lit auditorium where he was tormented by actors planted in the audience who verbally assaulted those struggling onstage.[39] Disorder enveloped the auditorium as an explosion from outside ruptured a section of the stage. As more of the stage collapsed and a cloud of dust fell over the audience, spectators dashed out in haste, ignorant of the illusion conjured by Pasqual and Puigserver. Pasqual views the play as 'muy alegre y terrible a la vez... una declaración de amor y de guerra al teatro'[40] ('very bright and terrible at the same time, a declaration of love and war on theatre'). Composed on the eve of the Civil War, it is for Pasqual both a denunciation of the evasive nature of the Spanish stage in the 1930s and, like *El público*, a manifesto for a theatrical practice which dispenses with the centrality of a single perception and reinvents the purposes and strategies of theatre in consistently disquieting ways.

---

[38] Leonard Tennenhouse, 'Strategies of State and political plays: *A Midsummer Night's Dream, Henry IV, Henry V, Henry VIII*' in *Political Shakespeare: Essays in Cultural Materialism*, eds Jonathan Dollimore and Alan Sinfield, 2nd edition (Manchester University Press, 1994), 111.

[39] His casting brought associations with the 'outsider' roles he had taken in films of the 1980s, perhaps most significantly the emotionally tortured terrorist in Uribe's *La muerte de Mikel* (1983) and the Robin Hood-like renegade of Vicente Aranda's *El Lute* and *El Lute II* (1987 and 1988). In all these films he provided forceful interpretations of elusive objects of desire on whom oppressed social groups could project their hopes and fantasies for the future.

[40] Ander Landaburu, 'Lluís Pasqual y Lorca son una fiesta en París', *Cambio 16* (November 1990).

As Lorca's 'impossible' plays oblige us to expand the dramaturgical vocabulary at our disposal and acquire new reading codes, so Pasqual, in providing alternative theatrical configurations, undermined the spectators' sense of themselves as a cohesive group, destabilising the recognised boundaries of audience and performer.[41] The street outside, a rumbling symbol of the Other feared by the closed-in audience, threatened to invade its complacent and illusionist existence. Panic set in and the boundaries between the private space of the auditorium and the undefined public space of the world beyond collapsed. Violence erupted in the interior body of the theatre; order could no longer be staged and the structures which upheld it fell apart.

In the opening moments of the play the Autor announces that 'ver la realidad es difícil. Y enseñarla mucho más'[42] ('to see reality is difficult. And to show it even more so'). Pasqual and Puigserver created a stage reality which they repeatedly foregrounded as representation, manipulating its vocabulary to reveal how 'the real is read through representation, and representation is read through the real'.[43] Reviewing the Madrid production José Monleón argued that it articulated not merely a possibility for a new methodology of theatre but a way of understanding its social function in times of political change.[44] In its provocative and unnerving spirit and its reframing of Shakespeare's disembodied play, the production stood against the boundaries of accepted or sanitised taste, the 'cultura de plástico' which Pasqual has repeatedly denounced for its corrupting and debilitating complacency.[45]

[41] Even those cast members, like Juan Echanove and Walter Vidarte, who had also featured in *El público*, were here allocated roles which stood in stark contrast to those they had played in *El público*, thus defying the expectations of sections of the audience who may have been expecting them to occupy more familiar territory.
[42] Federico García Lorca, *El público y Comedia sin título: Dos obras teatrales póstumas* (Barcelona, Caracas & Mexico: Seix Barral, 1978), 312.
[43] Peggy Phelan, *Unmarked*, 2.
[44] José Monleón, 'El último Pasqual: *Comedia sin título*', 27.
[45] Lluís Pasqual/Diego Muñoz, 'No me encuentro bien bajo la cultura catalana que representa Jordi Pujol', *La Vanguardia* (8 May 1995), 39. See also Ytak, *Lluís Pasqual: Camí de teatre* (Barcelona: Alter Pirene, 1993), 90-91. Paul Julian Smith has classified Pasqual's production of *El público* in similar terms 'as a challenge to the hegemony of a complacent Socialist government which

It is significant that Pasqual chose *Comedia sin título* both to close his tenure at the Centro Dramático Nacional and as his inaugural production as artistic director of the Odéon-Théâtre de l'Europe in 1990, a year after making his French language debut with a production of *Comme il vous plaira* at the Comédie Française. His arrival was decisively announced with a production that heralded the physical collapse of the existing Odéon. Previously shared between the Théâtre de l'Europe and the Comédie Française, Pasqual radically restructured the Odéon, creating a second performance space and encouraging international co-productions.

Staging *Comedia sin título* both in French as *Sans Titre* and in Spanish[46]—and assuming the role of the Autor in the Spanish-language production—he sought to emphasise cultural specificity through a focus on the problems inherent in translating Lorca into French and the different performance traditions of French and Spanish actors.[47] Rather than erase difference in search of some naive concept of cultural globalisation, Pasqual sought, both in the production and in his subsequent programming, to emphasise diversity and particularity. Referring to himself as more Spanish in Paris than he is in Spain, Pasqual contests the concept of international theatre.

As with Strehler before him, Pasqual's directorial choices can be classified as part of a vision of theatre as public service where traditions are revisited, revised and transformed. As Pasqual, Puigserver and Planella had conceived a social role for the Lliure within the landscape of Gràcia, so, with the Odéon-Théâtre de l'Europe, Pasqual looked to create the possibilities for a European theatre which went beyond political institutions or bland standardisation. *Comedia sin título* /*Sans Titre* was about the inauguration of a theatrical strategy which could offer a means of interrogating what the oscillating discourses of a new Europe might be and how theatre might participate in the debates raging

has restored the parameters of "normality" supported by politicians of other parties.' Paul Julian Smith, 'The Lorca Cult: Theatre, Cinema, and Print Media in 1980s Spain', 78.

[46] This was a strategy he was to repeat with the French and English productions of *Le Livre de Spencer* / *Spencer's Book* in 1994.

[47] Pasqual discusses this in 'Lluís Pasqual' in *In Contact with the Gods?*, 207–208, 215–16.

across the shifting boundaries of the continent.⁴⁸ In addition, it announced Pasqual's intersecting identities; a Catalan who collaborated with a regular designer, whose interests lay in metatheatrical dramaturgy, engaging with the myths of his own theatrical culture but working within a landscape whose otherness he acknowledged.⁴⁹

His subsequent *Haciendo Lorca* (*Making Lorca*) (1996) completed his five-year tenure at the Odéon. Originally conceived as a reworking of *Bodas de sangre*, for a cast of two, it mutated during rehearsal into a meditation on the play, centring on the characters of Death and the Moon. Adapted, dismantled and reorganised for Alfredo Alcón and Nuria Espert, the piece emerged like Peter Brook's recent performed essay on *Hamlet, Qui est là?,* as a process of weaving together research, reflections, relocated sections of the play, and juxtaposed sections from other texts. The emphasis was on narrative discontinuity where bodies of inherited meaning came together to comment on the conflicts played out in the writings.

The metaphor of a shifting ephemeral Lorca was brilliantly conjured by the design of the crane provided by Frederic Amat, the painter/designer who worked with Puigserver on *El público* and with whom Pasqual has, since the death of Puigserver in 1992, forged a new collaboration.⁵⁰ Pasqual locates in Amat 'the ability to sweep away all the incidental things and [...] reach beyond the single world that suggests a whole world'.⁵¹ The dark crane, operated by a team of four technicians, alluded to Puigserver's canvas membrane both in its

⁴⁸ Joan de Sagarra, 'Un Teatro de Estado no puede ser muy rentable', *El País* (6 October 1990).
⁴⁹ Franco-Argentine director Jorge Lavelli also opened his tenure as director of a French national theatre with one of Lorca's 'impossible' plays. His 1988 production of *Le Public* at Le Théâtre National de la Colline announced the theatre's agenda as the promotion of contemporary world writing rather than just that of France, and writing which was transgressive, violent, aggressive, which allowed the director a decisive role and which reflected Lavelli's artistic aspirations. For further details see Alain Satgé, *Jorge Lavelli, Des années soixante aux années Colline: un parcours en liberté* (Paris: Presses Universitaires de France, 1996), 1–7.
⁵⁰ Other ventures include *Tirano Banderas* (1992) and *Roberto Zucco* (1994).
⁵¹ Lluís Pasqual in Maria M. Delgado, 'Redefining Spanish Theatre: Lluís Pasqual on Directing, Fabià Puigserver, and the Lliure', 103.

audacity, its concrete physicalisation of the dramatics of the piece, and its creation of a visual environment which emphatically rejected mimetic realism. Propelling Alfredo Alcón across the stage whilst Nuria Espert hovered in pools of light below, first keeping them apart and then bringing them together, it offered a vertical organisation of space which stressed the capacity of technology and stage machinery to magnify, distort, and augment.[52] The presence of both Alcón and Espert, renowned Lorca performers whose readings of the writer's works as actors, and more recently directors, have been seen across Europe and Latin America, served to authenticate the production, but also significantly acknowledged the key role each performer had played in shaping Pasqual's conception of Lorca as dramatic material as well as the texture and shape of the piece itself.[53]

La oscura raíz, a two-hander performed intermittently since February 1998 by Pasqual and Nuria Espert, again foregrounds the journey of discovering and 'making' Lorca, rendering visible the very process of configuration. Although the genesis for the production came from a meeting between Lorca and Margarita Xirgu on the stage of the Teatro Goya in 1935, it moved beyond this encounter, with Espert reciting (and through that very act simultaneously recalling and implicitly acknowledging) sections of her most celebrated roles: Doña Rosita,

---

[52] This is a point made by Robert Lepage in Rémy Charest, *Robert Lepage: connecting flights* (London: Methuen Drama, 1997), 111.

[53] Pasqual has admitted seeing García's production of *Yerma* over forty times while it toured Spain in the early 1970s. See Maria M. Delgado, 'Redefining Spanish Theatre: Lluís Pasqual on Directing, Fabià Puigserver, and the Lliure', 92. Espert and Alcón belong to a group of actors with whom Pasqual has frequently worked. Having worked increasingly as a director in the last ten years, Espert first collaborated with Pasqual in 1978 when he directed Salvador Espriu's *Una altra Fedra, si us plau* (*Another Phaedra, If You Please*) for her company, going on to work with him again on *Medea* at the Teatre Grec in 1981. Alcón, who performed with María Casares in Margarita Xirgu's 1963 production of Lorca's *Yerma,* spent time in Madrid during the sixties working with José Luis Alonso. He returned in the mid-eighties where his roles at the Centro Dramático Nacional under Pasqual's direction included Eduardo in *La vida del Rey Eduardo II de Inglaterra* (1983), Lorca in *Los caminos de Federico* (*Federico's Steps*) (1988), and the agonised Director in *El público.*

undertaken with Jorge Lavelli in 1980, *Yerma*, and the poems she recalls narrating in her youth.[54] Pasqual's performance, juxtaposing poems, lectures, letters, and fragments of recalled dialogue, creates an ambiguous persona, at once director, performer, excavator and critic, recalling the Lorca he created in Edgardo Cozarinsky's film *La Barraca* (1994) but, in his contemporary attire and direct address to the audience, implicitly rebutting simplistic identification—he was clearly not Lorca incarnate—in favour of an interpretative position which recognised both the traces of past performances and the specificity of his own public and private identities.

Just as Pasqual has identified the significant role that Lorca's correspondence formed in his preparatory reading when planning to stage *El público*,[55] *La oscura raíz* also made concrete 'una línea de descubrir una y otra vez al poeta'[56] ('a process of discovering the poet again and again'). It is not, as the critic Juan Carlos Olivares acknowledges, about the construction of a character but rather a personal positioning before ideas and emotions which may be as much Pasqual's as Lorca's. It is a recognition of the impossibility of presenting a truthful or real Lorca, an understanding of the blurred and ever-shifting boundaries between truth and lies which is the territory of theatre and an articulation of the complex ways in which the self is mapped within cultural, social, economic and political parameters.

If *La oscura raíz* concerned itself with the resonance of Lorca's writings,[57] *Bengues*[58] (1998), a collaboration with Antonio Canales' dance company, is engendered from the destruction of *La casa de Bernarda Alba*, Lorca's least lyrical play, and its reinvention through

[54] See Barbotegi S.L., *La oscura raíz*, http://www.infoescena.es/Barbotegi/obras/1001.asp.
[55] See Maria M. Delgado, 'Redefining Spanish Theatre: Lluís Pasqual on Directing, Fabià Puigserver, and the Lliure', 96.
[56] Pasqual paraphrased in Juan Carlos Olivares, 'El pellizco de Lorca', *ABC* (12 February 1998).
[57] Resonance is here as not just what the texts say but the way they say it, reflecting what is being told and the mood of the characters, the musicality which demands it be spoken in a non-natural way, almost sung. See *Robert Lepage*, 127–28.
[58] The title comes from the gypsy word for devils.

the violent idiom of flamenco.[59] The dominant black-and-white colour scheme remains but the visual staticism is displaced by the frenzied temperament of the spectacle. Unlike Rafael Aguilar's version for Antonio Gades, where the lone male figure of Bernarda functioned as an abhorrent outsider distanced from the feminine society in which she exists, here all the cast, excepting María la Coneja's María Josefa, are male. As such all the characters are implicated within the system of restrictive surveillance which operates in the domestic space. Gender is posited as visibly imitative, with selected signs of femininity (the turn-of-the-century boots and earrings) worn by Canales' Bernarda serving to locate the feminine upon the male performing body. It holds with Pasqual's view that the feminine as created on the male is always more feminine precisely because it is performed through markings and defined through the masculine. As such it brutally articulates the manner in which the definition of woman is inscribed through its relation to the male.[60] Gender boundaries are constructed by a performance state that conspicuously juggles its own ambiguous insecurities. The subliminal artifice of theatre here de-fortifies the rigid codification that informs all the identities presented to us. Flamenco, which Pasqual had always consciously avoided working with, is here stripped of its showy folkloric adornments. The body as focal object of desire is contained, regimentalised and ultimately destroyed by the rules of a society whose political façade finds its counterpoint in *Guernica*, the dance tapestry based on Picasso's painting which was presented alongside *Bengues* and which serves to implicate Bernarda within a larger regime which endorses the fascism enacted in Picasso's 'Guernica'.[61] The body here functions as the text on which the intersecting discourses of political and cultural history are written. Each

---

[59] Lluís Pasqual in Pablo Peinado, 'Antonio Canales + Lluís Pasqual', *Zero Quincenal* (November 1997), 19.

[60] See Cristina Marinero, 'La Señora Canales', (*La Revista*) *El Mundo* (16 November 1997), 10. Peggy Phelan theorises this marking of the feminine by referring to Lacan's writings on the phallic function which posit that 'the frame of the phallic mark' permits visibility 'of that which she is not' ... 'The image of the woman is made to submit to the phallic function and is re-marked and revised as that which belongs to him'. See *Unmarked*, 17.

[61] A point made by Canales in Cristina Marinero, 'La Señora Canales', 12.

piece is a collage which, according to Canales, has no beginning or end, a reflection on the enduring significance of cultural products which have been situated within the turbulent socio-political context which engendered them.

A couple of years ago, while speaking at the Edinburgh Festival, the American director Peter Sellars drew attention to the malleability of the classics as 'something that is larger than anybody's particular point of view, and yet they have a moral dimension that won't go away'.[62] This moral dimension allows them to be appropriated, processed and reinvented for the demands of the social, political and cultural climate in which they are staged. Pasqual locates in such classical texts the capacity to ensure that an audience is shaken and confronted with alternative ways of seeing.[63] For director José Samano, discussing his Lorca tribute *Un rato, un minuto, un segundo*, performed by Lola Herrera and Carmen Linares at Barcelona's Tivoli Theatre in March 1998, the governing idea was to ensure the spectators left the theatre knowing exactly who Lorca was.[64] For Pasqual the proposition has always been more elusive; there is no essential Lorca, no infallible ideological position, no universal truth to be plucked from his diverse body of work.

'¡Quién sabe cómo era Lorca!'[65] ('Who knows what Lorca was like?') Pasqual stated while rehearsing *Cómo canta una ciudad de noviembre a noviembre,* a reconstruction of a lecture on the city of Granada, its music, smells, and taste, given in 1933 at Buenos Aires' Sociedad de Amigos del Arte and then later in 1935 at Barcelona's Casal del Metge. Presented at Barcelona's Teatre Lliure in May 1998, it featured Juan Echanove, collaborating with Pasqual on a Lorca text for the third time, and offering an evocation of the poet which consciously rejected imitative strategies in favour of a measured contemplation of

[62] Peter Sellars in conversation with Ruth Mackenzie at the Edinburgh Festival, 14 August 1995.
[63] See Nuria Cuadrado, 'El inflejo de una luz especial', *La Espera* (16 May 1998), 5.
[64] See Teresa Sesé, 'Lola Herrera y Carmen Linares evocan la figura de Lorca en el Tívoli', *La Vanguardia* (17 March 1998), 45.
[65] Jacinto Antón, 'Lluís Pasqual: ¡Quién sabe cómo era Lorca!', *El País* (12 May 1998), 36.

the musicality of a specific lecture, affirming the fascination of Granada's popular songs which Lorca knew and recreated on the piano. Arranged by Josep Maria Arrizabalaga, another collaborator on *El público* and *Comedia sin título*, the interplay of sounds, vocal and instrumental, offered a texture in which audience's attempts to visually identify with the poet were eluded by the silhouetted Echanove.

Echanove has admitted that his conceptions of Lorca are inextricably shaped by those of Pasqual.[66] Pasqual, too, has endeavoured to place the project within a configuration where the marks of their earlier ventures are recognised.[67] Cultural domination, as the critic Jonathan Dollimore remarks, 'is not a static unalterable thing; it is rather a process, one always being contested, always having to be renewed'.[68] Pasqual's productions indicate the multiple Lorcas that can be imagined, invented and dreamed when one is freed from a reductively intentionalist approach.[69] Each of his collaborations has demonstrated the capacity of these texts to offer modes of thinking about society which move beyond tame standardisation and cohesive consolidation towards a negotiation of those shifting parameters through which our lives are constantly redefined.

---

[66] Ibid.
[67] Lluís Pasqual, press release for *Cómo canta una ciudad de noviembre a noviembre* (May 1998).
[68] Jonathan Dollimore, 'Introduction: Shakespeare, cultural materialism and the new historicism', in *Political Shakespeare: essays in cultural materialism*, 14.
[69] Jacinto Antón, 'Lluís Pasqual: ¡Quién sabe cómo era Lorca!', 36.

Lorca, Don Cristóbal and the Carnivalesque

Cariad Astles

In Georges Bataille's essay 'The Big Toe', human life is described as 'seeing oneself as a back and forth movement from refuse to the ideal and from the ideal to refuse'.[1] Bataille thus locates the nature of human existence in the dialogue between spiritual and material aspirations, the one constantly attempting to shake the other off, but being irrevocably drawn back. He uses the metaphor of a foot wearing high heels to illustrate the point: the lofty heel vainly trying to distract from the essentially low and flat character of the foot (20–23).

This grotesque and carnivalesque image is useful when considering the work of Federico García Lorca for puppet theatre, although Lorca considered the refuse and the ideal not as opposing entities but as part and parcel of the same piece. Lorca is still little known as a writer for puppet theatre, except within the marginal world of puppet theatre itself. Amongst the vast body of Lorca scholarship there is little in-depth analysis or critique of his puppet plays, which are often considered to be experiments or minor works as a prelude to his greater plays. The studies that do exist are more commonly chronologies and accounts of his puppet activity or acknowledgements of his fascination with puppetry. I believe that the paucity of scholarly attention to Lorca's puppet plays lies—at least in part—in the consideration of puppet theatre as 'refuse': vulgar, simplistic, immature, full of crude sexual innuendo, and, despite this latter aspect, more suitable for children; whereas his great tragic plays aspire to the 'ideal'. I also believe that Lorca's puppet plays require consideration within a different framework from his plays for actors. The conventions and stylistic devices of puppet theatre, particularly those of popular origin, have their own frames of reference which are often counterpoised to those of conventional drama. We would be hard pushed to search for plot, dramatic tension or narrative thrust in *La niña que riega la*

---

[1] Georges Bataille, *Visions of Excess*, ed. and trans. Allan Stoehl, (Manchester University Press, 1985), 20–21.

albahaca y el príncipe preguntón or *El retablillo de don Cristóbal*. Our interest lies elsewhere: in ritual, in comic action and in carnivalesque festivity. The purpose of this study, therefore, is to demonstrate how Lorca's plays for puppet theatre and in particular his puppet anti-hero, Don Cristóbal, are carnivalesque rituals which challenge not only theatrical hegemonies but also life and death themselves.

I would like to include a brief outline of Lorca's journey through puppet theatre. This is partly to emphasise the point that puppetry for Lorca was an ongoing concern; indeed, *El retablillo de don Cristóbal* was not completed until 1931; Don Cristóbal accompanied Lorca to Buenos Aires in 1934 and *El retablillo* was performed in Madrid after his return. I will then point to aspects of the carnivalesque which I propose to discuss here; finally, I will examine Lorca's three puppet plays and the character of Don Cristóbal in the light of carnivalesque theory.

From letters, interviews and manuscripts we are able to trace Lorca's connection with puppet theatre to an early age. During the early 1900s, travelling puppeteers are known to have toured Andalucía and beyond with puppet shows (*cristobicas*) featuring the anarchic Don Cristóbal and the lover Currito del Puerto, both characters in Lorca's later shows. These puppet shows were probably improvised for the most part and passed from generation to generation through oral tradition; there are no records of texts. Lorca probably saw his first puppet show around 1905-1906, when he was seven or eight. This inspired him to begin a lifetime fascination: he turned a garden altar into a puppet stage and began to make puppet shows, enlisting the help of his family in the fabrication of the puppets; he is known to have entertained his family and friends on numerous occasions with his juvenile puppet farces.[2] When he was fifteen or sixteen, he bought himself a puppet stage; this coincides with his meeting the composer Manuel de Falla. These two became great friends and shared a passion for the possibilities of puppet theatre, which both were to explore jointly and separately. They shared a dream of creating a new puppet theatre with the 'idilio salvaje' Don Cristóbal and touring it not only through Andalucía but also to Europe

---

[2] Francisco Porras Soriano, *Los títeres de Falla y García Lorca* (Madrid: UNIMA, 1995), 23-24.

and America. Lorca frequently refers to this project of a *Cristobical* in letters to Falla and other friends. In a letter to Falla during the summer of 1922, Lorca writes: 'I am enthusiastic about the project to travel to the Alpujarras. You know how much I dream of doing some *cristobicas* full of Andalusian emotion and exquisite popular feeling.'[3] In the same letter he writes that he has seen 'unos cristobicas' in the village, performing 'de una manera aristofanesca'.

The same year, in Madrid, Lorca, Buñuel and Juan Chabás gave a talk on puppetry; they 'adopted' a puppeteer from the Parque del Retiro, Mayeu, and introduced him to the Residencia de Estudiantes. Lorca drafted a number of pieces for puppet theatre, including the first draft of *Tragicomedia de don Cristóbal y la señá Rosita*, or *Los títeres de cachiporra*, which he read to Falla and José Mora Guarnido in 1922. This piece was constantly rewritten and revised throughout Lorca's life and he was frustrated in his attempts to have it staged. On 6 January 1923 Lorca presented his famous evening of puppetry to around 120 people (a hundred of whom were children). This was his first public puppetry performance; he collaborated with Manuel de Falla and Hermenegildo Lanz on three pieces: *Los habladores* (*The Chatterboxes*) by Cervantes, *La niña que riega la albahaca y el príncipe preguntón*, adapted from a folk tale by Lorca himself, and a piece with flat figures, *Misterio de los Reyes Magos* (*Mystery Play of the Three Wise Men*). The puppet Don Cristóbal acted as master of ceremonies, engaging in improvised dialogue with the children. The puppet itself was made by Hermenegildo Lanz in Cubist style, a fact commented upon by Mora in *La Voz* of 12 January 1923: 'Cristobicas dressed in silk for the first time [...] he seemed as new as a cubist poem.'[4]

Throughout 1923 and 1924 Lorca refers to his 'títeres de cachiporra' and his hopes for performance; there were plans for a performance in Madrid alongside his play *Mariana Pineda* but the director, Martínez Sierra, pulled out, which upset Lorca considerably. Lorca's dream of a touring puppet theatre and his frustration when his puppet performances were not realised, are continual themes. Lorca continued to draft the *Tragicomedia* and *El retablillo de don Cristóbal* (which some consider

---

[3] *Obras completas* (Madrid: Aguilar, 1986), III, 791.
[4] Porras Soriano, 68.

two versions of the same piece). There were plans for staging in Madrid, in Cadiz and in New York, but neither piece was performed until 1934, when *El retablillo* was presented in Buenos Aires. This programme was introduced by a moving dialogue between Don Cristóbal (operated by Lorca) and Lorca himself. Don Cristóbal reminds Lorca of their first collaboration in 1923: 'I still remember the smiling faces of the children' and of the fact that on the stage 'I live for ever and never die' (Porras Soriano, 104).

On Lorca's return to Spain, *El retablillo* was finally performed on several occasions in Madrid and Lorca continued to plan performances for *Los títeres de cachiporra*. He told a friend in December 1935 that he was considering leaving Spain for America again but would not do so until *Los títeres de cachiporra* had been staged in Spain. This piece was not, however, performed in Spain until 1937, after Lorca's death. A note by Marcelle Auclair cites Lorca talking to one of his fellow-prisoners just before leaving for Viznar: 'We'll make a puppet show' (Porras Soriano, 434). Clearly Lorca had an ongoing passion for the puppet theatre throughout his life and career.

Carnival and theories of the carnivalesque have become the site for many discussions of identity, hierarchy and notions of ownership. From Bakhtin's seminal work *Rabelais and his World*, which analyses mediaeval carnival, to postmodernist debates about perception and authorship, the term 'carnivalesque' has been employed to denote a number of significant characteristics of situation, drama or text. Carnival, whether we perceive it as revolutionary celebration or as an authorised letting-off of steam which in fact reinforces the status quo, embodies within the event itself the ritual or symbolic inversion or subversion of figures of authority, official social mores and customs, and predominant hierarchies. It is a festive and seasonal event linked to agrarian and agricultural renewal rites; it is characterised by popular participation in open spaces, accessible to all. The text, or narrative, of carnival is polylogic: that is, many voices of equal value are heard in determining its progression. In other words, it is an 'open' text with no prearranged beginning, middle or end, but consists instead of a series of interactions and relationships which take place *in situ*. There is thus no single author and there are no heroes. It follows a non-linear structure where events, or dramas, spring from themselves. The participants are masqueraders who—in a confusion of identity—perform other identities, often self-referentially. Carnival is connected to both the spiritual and the material within the rhythms of nature, and Bakhtin shows that the material body is particularly evident, in the exuberant consumption of food, drink and other bodies, while these same things are just as exuberantly ejected from the body: 'The limits between the body and the world are erased.'[5] Thus carnival itself embodies both 'refuse' and the 'ideal'. Emphasis is placed on the orifices of the body where cyclical regeneration takes place, drawing attention to this regenerative aspect which symbolises the constant battle between life and death. Bodies threaten to break their boundaries as they manifest both excess and fantasy. There is a constant sense of exceeding limits, as chaos threatens to rule.

Finally, within the carnivalesque there is a proliferation of the grotesque and the grotesque body. The term 'grotesque' is believed to derive from the discovery around AD 1500 of fantastic murals in the grotto excavated among the ruins of Nero's Domus Aurea in Rome. The *grotte* (caves) lent their name to the outlandish images they revealed and the noun, *la grottesca*, became 'grotesque' in the English language by the end of the sixteenth century. The Roman writer, Marcus Vitruvius Pollio, expressed his revolt and confusion at the 'monstrous forms rather than clear images of the familiar world'.[6] The murals depicted humans and animals in various states of growth and metamorphosis. The overriding feature of these paintings is that none of the figures stands separately, complete and self-sufficient. All of them grow into and from each other. Bakhtin identifies the salient features of these murals as their state of incompletion, transition and openness. During the nineteenth century, the term 'grotesque' became associated with a menacing and sinister aspect; the positive celebratory qualities of the popular grotesque came to be seen as part of a dark underworld. At the same time, horror and disgust with the grotesque became associated with desire. The menacing thus became fascinating. This prevailing attitude coincided with the development of the freak show in the fairground or carnival context, and indeed the rise of popular puppet

[5] Mikhail Bakhtin, *Rabelais and His World*, trans. Helene Iswolsky (Indiana University Press, 1984), 310.
[6] Philip Thomson, *The Grotesque,* The Critical Idiom, 24 (London: Methuen, 1972), 12.

theatre throughout Europe. The grotesque became associated with the representation of the human body—the known element—in combination with excess, fantasy, exaggeration and the animalistic—the unknown. The grotesque body also implies a state of co-dependence on other, surrounding bodies and encourages free and familiar contact. Bakhtin argues that the key elements of the body are those at which it outgrows itself and transgresses its own limits. These definitions are significant when considering the glove puppet, and, in particular, the figure of Don Cristóbal within the carnivalesque.

Lorca wrote several drafts of plays and a number of plays with their roots in puppetry. Here I intend to discuss: *La niña que riega al albahaca y el príncipe preguntón*, the incomplete draft *Cristobical*, *Los títeres de cachiporra*, and *El retablillo de don Cristóbal*. There is a constant sense of development through these plays and his final piece, *El retablillo de don Cristóbal* is, although brief, the most complete and the most carnivalesque.

All of these plays are comic; they are located within the framework of festive ritual and comic tradition. Rhythm, repetition and rhyme are more important elements than complexities of plot. This links them to the notion of ritual. Luigi Allegri, in his discussion of popular puppet theatre, notes that for everyone to participate in ritual it is necessary for all the participants to know the execution of the ritual.[7] Thus, in theatre, both performers and spectators must have a complicit understanding of the performance. Lorca's audiences would have certainly been familiar with the characters of Don Cristóbal, Rosita and Currito. The tale of a young, sexually aware woman being married to an old man for money was also well known in popular narrative. (The story of Don Perlimplín, for instance, came from a popular ballad.) *La niña que riega la albahaca* is derived from an old Andalusian folk tale (although Francisco Porras has also identified it as a Catalan story, so there may have been multiple sources). Ritual aspects are suggested in *Cristobical* by the action taking place on the feast of San Juan (24 June) and symbolic references to midnight. In *La niña que riega la albahaca* the negro's speech introducing each frame points to the ritual of the event:

---

[7] Luigi Allegri, *Per una storia del teatro come spettacolo: Il teatro di burattini come forma di cultura subalterna* (Parma: Università di Parma, 1978), 55–77.

'One sunny morning, at the hour when one cock crowed and another cock crowed, and another and another'.[8] This sense of ritual also links these plays to festive regeneration.

The strongest and most pervasive image of the carnivalesque in Lorca's puppet plays is that of the grotesque body. This, as I have suggested, is a body which is incomplete; one which mixes binary opposites and merges incompatible images. Bakhtin identifies the life of the grotesque body as being marked by three crucial moments of spasm: birth, orgasm and death. The use of the word spasm creates the image of violent, excessive, frenzied, involuntary motion dominated by the body. In *Los títeres de cachiporra* the body of Don Cristóbal literally bursts its boundaries: '*(The club falls from his hand and a great grinding of springs is heard.)* Oh my little belly! Oh I'm dying! Oh!'[9] In *Cristobical* there are references to the fragmentation of the body and sawdust. In *La niña que riega la albahaca y el príncipe preguntón* bodily functions are referred to early on when the prince cannot come onto the stage until he has finished peeing (a device which is used in *El retablillo de don Cristóbal* later on). We find, however, the best example of the grotesque body in *El retablillo de don Cristóbal*. Rosita experiences all three spasms in a few short pages: she (presumably) experiences multiple orgasm in her meetings with her lovers; she experiences the spasms of five births in quick succession and shortly afterwards the spasms of death as Don Cristóbal beats her. Don Cristóbal himself is caught in a continual spasm. His comic violence and exchanges with first the patient, Rosita's mother and finally with Rosita herself are run through with almost constant sexual innuendo in a to-and-fro rhythm of dialogue and action which reflects sexual activity, culminating in a violent paroxysm at the end of the play where Rosita and her mother are treated to beatings with his big, hard club.

There are further examples of the grotesque body in the whole style of performance. In popular glove puppet tradition the link between puppeteer and puppet is intimate; the puppet is indeed an incomplete body, incapable of standing alone. The puppeteer has his/her hand in

---

[8] Federico García Lorca, *The Basil-Watering Girl and the Prying Prince*, trans. John London (London: Atlas Press, 1996), 33.

[9] Federico García Lorca, *The Billy-Club Puppets*, trans. James Graham-Luján and Richard O'Connell (London: Secker & Warburg, 1976), 53.

direct contact with the body of the puppet, inside it. The analogy is made more interesting by the fact that glove puppets are operated from below; the puppeteer's hand finds entry to the puppet body through the lower body. The glove puppet body cannot, by nature, be a closed, static body as without the 'growing out of' another body or other bodies it does not exist (at least in terms of performance). The image of a glove puppet suggests incompletion, as traditionally the limits of its body are unseen (the puppeteer is hidden inside the booth). That part of the body which is unseen is, moreover, the lower bodily stratum which in imagination could extend indefinitely. Attention is drawn to the bodily functions of the puppets, their 'orifices and protuberances': Don Cristóbal and the prince urinate, Rosita copulates, food and drink which enter through the mouth are of prime importance; the prince in *La niña que riega la albahaca* exchanges grapes for kisses, thus suggesting oral satisfaction. The eye is drawn to the exaggerated bellies, humps and breasts of the puppets, and the *porra*, or club, is a phallic symbol. Even *La niña que riega la albahaca* which at first glance is a simple folk tale, is told through considerations of the body: kisses, food, disease and suggestions at the end of the piece of future sexual (and thus regenerative) activity: 'In the mornings, will you show me the little cockerel who sings everything?'[10] The puppets are disproportionate and unbalanced in appearance, which further challenges the notion of the classical, closed body: Don Cristóbal has a huge belly and hump; Don Leñador-Corazón in *Cristobical* is a hunchback; Cristobita in *Los títeres de cachiporra*, referring to Rosita, says 'She looks about three feet high';[11] the patient in *El retablillo de don Cristóbal* has a ridiculously long neck. We are reminded of the freak show.

Michael Bristol suggests that 'carnival is put into operation as resistance to any tendency to absolutise authority'.[12] This challenging of hegemonic structures and hierarchies is an integral part of Lorca's puppet plays. Throughout the plays, the narrative and judgments on the action are discussed. The plays do not exist as single units presenting a single story. Instead, they are presented as fictions with possibilities of

[10] London, 38.
[11] Graham-Luján and O'Connell, 20.
[12] Michael Bristol, *Carnival and Theatre* (London: Methuen, 1985), 213.

varying response. *La niña que riega la albahaca* is introduced as one of several 'stories for sale'; the action which ensues is of a fragmented nature; the characters are introduced before their appearance, which doubly reinforces the fiction of the story (doubly as they are already represented as puppets and not humans); furthermore, the characters refuse to conform to the requirements of the story and refuse to come on stage until they are ready. The negro and the shoemaker engage in a discussion on the narrative and argue over the progression of the story:

Negro:	We ought to explain that the shoemaker is a widower.
Shoemaker:	And has been for going on four years.
Negro:	Come on, Don Gaiferos, don't open that little drawer of sad memories![13]

The audience are involved in the action by being asked to call Irene. The suggestion in the piece is therefore one of many voices contributing to create the performance. The notion of a single, invisible author is thrown out and all the characters are involved in the creation. In *Cristobical*, Cristobica refers to the Director, again drawing attention to the theatricality of the convention. The character Mosquito in *Los títeres de cachiporra* sits outside the action, commenting upon it and moving it on. Again, in *El retablillo de don Cristóbal* this idea is elaborated upon and the Poet and the Director engage several times in discussion about the action of the piece and the character of Don Cristóbal:

Director:	Don't I pay you?
Poet:	Yes sir. It's just that deep down I feel that Don Cristóbal is good.
Director:	Fool! ... Who are you to put an end to his trademark? ...
Poet:	I've said my piece. I'll say no more.
Director:	No, sir. You'll say what's required, and what the audience knows to be true.
Poet:	Distinguished audience. As the writer, it's my duty to tell you that Don Cristóbal's bad.

[13] London, 33.

And, later:

Poet: If the Director really wanted to, Don Cristóbal could see the water nymphs and Miss Rosita could fill her hair with frost when in Act Three the snow falls on the innocents. But the owner of the theatre has the characters kept in an iron box and only lets them be seen by ladies with silk bosoms and stupid noses and gentlemen with beards who belong to a club and are always saying 'jolly good!' But Don Cristóbal and Miss Rosita are not like that.
Director: Who is it saying such things?
Poet: I was saying they're about to get married.
Director: Stop poking your nose in.[14]

Like the Prince in *La niña que riega la albahaca*, Don Cristóbal refuses to come on stage until he has finished urinating; Rosita is not ready as she is putting her shoes on. Once onstage, Don Cristóbal further refuses to participate in the story as he prefers going to the bullfight. So the hierarchy is challenged at all levels: the idea of authorship is challenged in the discussions about action and character; the Director himself is questioned in his approach; Don Cristóbal, the rich, powerful figure of patriarchy, is shown to be a fool, cuckolded and ultimately prevented from killing off the characters; Rosita's mother is forced to obey Don Cristóbal and Rosita herself challenges all norms of social and sexual behaviour by trickery, insatiable sexual appetites and the ability to reproduce at a startling rate. Don Cristóbal kills her at the end but she has already produced five children. She is, moreover, only a puppet and as such cannot be killed at all, a point to which I will return later.

The means of communication in Lorca's puppet plays is anti-logical and anti-linear, a further feature of the carnivalesque. The language derives its own impulse from itself; situations are resolved through illogical means or the rhythm of the language itself. Rhyme and childlike language are used in place of reason. In *La niña que riega la*

---

[14] Federico García Lorca, *The Puppet Play of Don Cristóbal*, trans. Gwynne Edwards (London: Methuen, 1990), 68, 76.

albahaca, for instance, we hear that the magician 'has a hat of stars and can cure lovesickness'.[15] This *non sequitur* of associations has no place in the adult world of cause and effect but would sound entirely natural said by a child—or a puppet. Less romantically, Don Cristóbal in *Los títeres de cachiporra* says to Rosita: 'Are you sick? I thought you sighed! But that's because I please you so.'[16] And in *El retablillo de don Cristóbal* he responds to the Director's instructions that he is to play a Doctor with equal lack of logic:

Director:	Remember, Don Cristóbal. You need money to get married.
Cristóbal:	I know I do.
Director:	Then get it quick.
Cristóbal:	I'll get my club.[17]

The patient, when faced with Don Cristóbal's club (referred to by Don Cristóbal as a 'brandy flask') responds illogically:

Patient:	Good day to you.
Cristóbal:	I fancy you mean good night.
Patient:	In that case I'll say good evening.
Cristóbal:	Good night, good night!
Patient:	I think I might manage good night.
Cristóbal:	You'd better manage good night.
Patient:	I can see from all you say you're a very fine doctor. I'm sure you'll cure me. Good day to you. (69)

Later, Rosita's mother instructs Don Cristóbal to give Rosita a kick to make her obey and yet weeps at Rosita's wedding. In the following extract it is the rhythm, not logic, which defines the scene:

[15] London, 37.
[16] Graham-Luján and O'Connell, 49.
[17] Edwards, 69.

Rosita: On such a night the stars shine bright
Up there above the houses,
On such a night the kids count stars
While old men sleep on horses.
But as for me, I'd like to be
On the divan
With Juan,
On the settee
With Pepe,
On the sofa
With Saldivar,
Across a chair
With fair Enrique,
Upon the floor
With Antonito,
Against the wall
With strong Pascual. (73–74)

The rhymes often refer to children's songs and folktales from the streets of Granada; Cristóbal's vulgar retort to Rosita's mother comes directly from the street:

Cristóbal: You, good lady, are a hag.
Sorry. I meant to say old bag.
I expect you wipe your backside with an old rag. (72)

and this exchange between Cristóbal and Rosita is derived from a popular folk tale:

Rosita: Oh Cristóbal, I'm frightened! What are you going to do to me?
Cristóbal: I'm going to mmmmmmm...
Rosita: Oh no, don't frighten me.
at twelve o'clock tonight, what are you going to do to me?
Cristóbal: I'm going to aaaaaaa... (76)

and so on. The folk tale goes:

> Little cockroach, little cockroach,
> will you marry me?
> And at twelve o'clock tonight,
> what will you do to me?
> I'm going to guau, guau, guau...
> No, you're frightening me.[18]

Thus language in the puppet plays has more to do with alliterative sound, familiar rhyme and—often sexual—rhythm than the expression of a linear idea.

One feature of the carnivalesque is the idea of masquerading, or playing out of other identities. A popular notion of carnival is that masking conceals the true identity of the wearer of the mask, enabling them to play an 'other'. I believe that in carnival masquerading the reverse often takes place, and that masqueraders, through dressing up as their apparent 'opposite', for instance, men dressing up as women, actually draw attention to their 'normal' or social self. In Lorca's puppet plays we are constantly drawn to the fiction of the performances. The puppets are called upon to play 'parts' in the masquerade, but are unable to leave their true natures behind. Thus both Don Leñador-Corazón and Cristóbal in *Cristobical* draw attention to the puppetness of the characters:

> Don Leñador-Corazón: Some people are full of sawdust! Ha, ha, ha![19]

In *Los títeres de cachiporra* the barber makes the discovery of Cristobita's wooden head:

---

[18] Tadea Fuentes, *El folklore infantil en la obra de Federico García Lorca*, (Granada: Universidad de Granada, 1991), 137.
[19] Federico García Lorca, *Cristobical*, intr. Piero Menarini (Society of Spanish and Spanish-American Studies, 1986), 35.

Figaro: This is amazing! Just what I suspected. ... Don Cristobita has a wooden head. Poplar wood! Ha, ha, ha! ... And look, what a lot of paint.[20]

Cristobita eventually breaks the boundaries of his puppet body and, quite literally, explodes, demonstrating the illusion of his existence.

In *El retablillo de don Cristóbal* this theme is taken further. Don Cristóbal, called upon by the Director to play a part in a play, is unable to play anything other than himself. He masquerades as a Doctor, but in fact plays Don Cristóbal. The Poet masquerades as a story-teller but is unable to play anything other than a poet:

Poet: Laugh, cry, do as you like. I'm off to get myself a piece of bread, ... and then to iron the company's costumes. I want to tell you I know how roses are born, and how the starfish develops and grows.[21]

So the 'players' in these pieces in fact never play anything other than themselves. They exist as performers within the piece, but also exist dynamically outside the piece, which challenges the very idea of life and death. In *Los títeres de cachiporra*, Cristobita explodes and dies; we know, however, that he is a puppet and as such cannot die. The tension implicit in this illusory treatment of life and death is a crucial feature of puppet performance. The puppet lives in the moment of performance but cannot die. Don Cristóbal himself appears several times outside performance: once as Master of Ceremonies for Lorca's famous 'evening of puppets' on 6 January 1923, where he improvises with the children in the audience; and again on Lorca's hand for the 'Dialogue between Don Cristóbal and the Poet' in Buenos Aires in 1934:

Cristóbal: I feel sad.
Lorca: What is this?

---

[20] Graham-Luján and O'Connell, 41.
[21] Edwards, 67.

Cristóbal: Nothing. ... After all, I cannot shed tears ...[22]

It is this capacity for defying death which is Don Cristóbal's most exciting trait. He is a defiant roar against the tyranny of death. In this he is the supreme carnivalesque performer, invoking the forces of cyclic regeneration whilst remaining faithful to his tradition.

Lorca's puppet plays, therefore, are much more than comic diversions; they challenge authority and sterility through subversion and laughter. Noisy, rude and discordant, they are the carnival procession with Lorca leading the way. Full of 'refuse', they nevertheless seek the 'ideal'.

---

[22] Porras Soriano, 104–105.

Learning from the Master: Lorca's homage to Picasso

Jacqueline Cockburn

When Lorca arrived at the Residencia de Estudiantes in Madrid in 1919, he had already been exposed to modern painting, but during his years there he went to a number of lectures about issues that were at the forefront of critical debates at the time, and his great friend, Salvador Dalí, introduced him to new concepts of modern art.[1] It is clear from Lorca's lecture entitled 'Sketch de la nueva pintura' (1928), given at the Athenaeum in Granada, that he was passionate about what he called New Painting and that this had an enormous influence on his own graphic work.[2] During this lecture Lorca paid homage to Picasso at several points and it seems clear that he knew his work intimately. The two Andalusians never met but they shared similar family backgrounds and a certain nationalism born out of a sense of alienation. Picasso lived much of his life in France as a displaced Spaniard and constantly alluded either overtly or covertly to affinities with the country which nurtured him. Lorca lived as part of a society which would not tolerate his sexual proclivities; and anxious as he was to be part of the Madrid *avant-garde*, he was proud and perhaps self-conscious of his Andalusian roots. He consequently anchored his identity in the comforting notion of Spanishness. In this paper I intend to explore Picasso's influence on Lorca's graphic work in order to situate him within a Spanish art-historical context. I shall begin by analysing Lorca's lecture, and attempt to show the extent to which it is possible to see echoes of Picasso in much of Lorca's work. I am not suggesting that we should

---

[1] The lectures were published in the college's magazine, *Residencia*, between 1926 and 1934. Facsimile edition: *Residencia: Revista de la Residencia de Estudiantes 1926-1934* (Madrid: Publicaciones de la Residencia de Estudiantes, 1990).

[2] Federico García Lorca, *Obras completas*, III (Madrid: Aguilar, 1986), 272-81.

dismiss Lorca as a copyist. It seems clear that his work perpetuates part of a Spanish pictorial tradition.

In the lecture Lorca began by claiming that the Impressionist preoccupation with light had drowned the beauty of form and annihilated the object: 'El río fugitivo sirve de canon contra el plinto de mármol' (272) ('The rushing river serves as the model rather than the marble plinth'). He referred to Impressionism as a drunken orgy and felt that painting was on its deathbed. He hailed the advent of Purism, then later Constructivism, but it was clearly in his opinion the arrival of Cubism—which he likened to Perseus killing the dragon of 'conventional' painting—which meant most to him.

Lorca hailed three Spaniards, Picasso, Juan Gris and Joan Miró, as the great revolutionaries of modern painting, while also likening Picasso's painting to Goya, Fragonard and Mantegna. Lorca maintained that the First World War had destroyed 'reality'. After the war it was felt that it had become impossible to trust one's own observation, so the painter became forced to discover a new kind of reality. Pure representation no longer had a place in this world, so it was necessary to find 'su expresión geométrica o lírica' (274) ('its geometric or lyrical expression'). Painting, he said, became autonomous out of pain and suffering. He quoted Juan Gris, who in a lecture at the Sorbonne said that it was no longer interesting to paint a bottle in a realistic way because the glass-maker could make the real thing. Now what was needed was pictorial expression, not visual reality. He compared the poet's image, which defined, with the painter, who creates a plastic image which fixes and directs the emotion. When referring to Cubist paintings in the genre of still life, he said they were created 'con una guitarra o un violín, una manzana, una mano de yeso y una pipa de lobo marino' (275) ('with a guitar or a violin, an apple, a plaster hand and an old sea dog's pipe'). Lorca had a very clear image of a new direction for art and although he was scathing about artists who earned their daily bread from copying the masters, I hope to show that he appropriated many of the classical genres.

In his lecture Lorca showed two Picasso slides, referred to rather cryptically as 'The Old Lady' and the 'Aragonese Girl'.[3] 'The Old

---

[3] For copyright reasons, it has unfortunately been impossible to reproduce

Lady' is clearly 'La Celestina' (1904). It is not clear what the other painting is, but Lorca's comment about it is most illuminating. He referred to what he called the deepest essence of Spanish painting as *'pintoresca y, gracias a Dios, ahora agonizante'* (273) ('picturesque and, thank God, now in its death-throes'). It is of vital importance to understand *his* definition of the Spanish tradition. If we take 'pintoresca' to mean not just picturesque but painterly, colourful, enlivening, it is important to remember that within the context of Romantic writing it also meant *suitable to be painted*, that is, the sort of painting that would be admired on the Grand Tour. The demise of this kind of painterly art paved the way for the experimental freedom sought by Picasso, yet it was a mixture of a classical notion of academic genres and a syncretic or folkloric quality that enabled Lorca to be part of the *avant-garde* and yet nationalistic at the same time. The shock of the new was, after all, the reworking of the old, and much of Lorca's work borders on pastiche as he reworks classical genres.

References to Spain abound in Picasso's still life pictures. In 'Bottle of Anís del Mono, Wine Glass and Playing Card' (1915) he represents the three objects within a Cubist framework. The Anís del Mono bottle reappears frequently with its distinctive diamond pattern. In the 1909 version, 'Still Life with Liqueur Bottle' the bottle itself was initially identified as a tube of paint but, in 1971, Picasso explained to William Rubin what it actually was, and added that the object above it was a *botijo* (a traditional terracotta jar with a spout for drinking water), but in the shape of a ceramic rooster. Robert Rosenblum comments that the Anís del Mono bottle, with its decorative Harlequin pattern of diamonds, appears as an 'almost clandestine symbol of Picasso's Spanish identity'.[4] Other expatriate painters such as Diego Rivera, Juan

---

Picasso's paintings here. Most of the works referred to are reproduced in Carsten-Peter Warncke, *Pablo Picasso, 1881–1973* (Köln: Benedikt Taschen, 1995), vol. 1: *The Works 1890–1936*. A large number of Lorca's drawings are reproduced in Mario Hernández (ed.), *Libro de los dibujos de Federico García Lorca* (Madrid: Tabapress/Fundación Federico García Lorca, 1990).

[4] Robert Rosenblum, 'The Spanishness of Picasso's Still Lifes', *Picasso and the Spanish Tradition*, ed. Jonathan Brown (New Haven and London: Yale University Press, 1996), 78.

Gris and Rafael Barradas were to appropriate it later.[5] The Spanishness of the bottle is further reiterated by the red, yellow and black dots that appear like bubbles at the top of the bottle and fill the glass.

Naturaleza muerta con botella de ron "Jamaica" (1925)

---

[5] See William B. Jordan and Peter Cherry, *Spanish Still Life from Velázquez to Goya* (London: National Gallery/Yale University, 1995).

In Lorca's 'Naturaleza muerta con botella de ron "Jamaica"' (1925) ('Still Life With Bottle of Rum') he chose Jamaican rum but echoed the bubbles in the glass and at the top of the bottle, angling his objects to suggest a Cubist vocabulary. The notion that what a nation imbibes can become a symbol is interesting, particularly in the light of class distinctions. Both Jamaican rum and Anís del Mono are cheap alcoholic drinks: the Spaniards associate the Anís del Mono bottle with Christmas, when the empty bottle is used as a musical instrument by scraping a knife along the patterned surface to make a musical sound to accompany the *villancicos* (carols). It is interesting to note that the Anís del Mono image was a product of industrial capitalism but has been absorbed into popular culture. It forms part of the cultural *bricolage* which fascinated both Picasso and Lorca, who both appropriated labels in order to confirm stereotypes.

The bottle also has anthropomorphic elements, similar to the emerging guitar in Picasso's image. The guitar is a symbol that runs the risk of becoming a cliché or a folkloric image of Spain but it cannot go unnoticed. It, too, is part of a Cubist vocabulary, both evocative and anthropomorphic. While traditional still life pictures were filled with allegorical meanings, often alluding to Christian themes such as the transience of life, the Cubist vocabulary, in contrast, stresses the moment and the notion that any symbolism is fluid and constantly changing. Picasso's 'Guitare' (1916) is just one of his many images of this instrument: Picasso portrayed the guitar obsessively, often alluding in its shape to the female nude. He had probably read 'La psicología de la guitarra', an outrageous article that appeared in the April 1901 edition of *Arte Joven*, a journal to which he contributed. In *La casa de Bernarda Alba* La Poncia refers, with a mixture of horror and delight, to a certain Paca la Roseta who was carried off by Maximiliano on a horse: 'La llevaba cogida como si tocara una guitarra' ('He carried her in his arms as if he were playing a guitar'). Lorca's use of yellow in 'Guitarra' (1927) is evocative and vibrant and he, like Picasso, focuses on the central body of the instrument. The guitar is potentially an expressive extension of man and a potent source of both sound and rhythm. Picasso came from a world where the guitar can be a symbol of suffering humanity and of love. It is frequently seen in Cubist still life pictures where instruments are sometimes a musical reminder of abstract form.

Lorca's 'Composición con instrumentos musicales' ('Composition With Musical Instruments') (1927) has a drawing by Dalí on the back (a female nude with a hat on in the form of a tree) and he gave this drawing to Ana María Dalí. He fused the themes of musical instruments and masks, exploring the notion of performance by masking the identity of the performer. We will look at his use of masks later. He is once more referring to Picasso, who frequently portrayed masked musicians in paintings such as 'Musiciens aux masques' (1921).

If we look back to a key work by the Spanish master of still life, Meléndez, 'Still Life: oranges, watermelon and jar, and box of sweetmeats' (1760), we are aware of the fact that every object seems to carry its own luminosity and, within the arrangement, all the objects seem to jostle for a foreground position. It is this juxtaposition of sombre, austere colours, suggestive of a monastic starkness, and the riotous, celebratory, acidic oranges which makes the particular flavour that I am calling Spanish. This dialogue between the garish and the stark, the folkloric and the sacred, sets up a particular tension that I intend to explore. The pungency of those oranges contrasts wildly with the solidity of the wooden table or the boxes which seem precariously balanced in a Cézannesque fashion. It is this juxtaposition of sentiments that is particularly idiosyncratic, like the liqueur bottle used as part of a Christmas celebration.

Picasso picks up this passion for colour in his still life 'La Desserte' (1901): the yellow and orange dance across the canvas, and the contemporary ceramics called *azulejos de oficios* are further evidence of Spanish flavour. In some of his work the presence of the drinking vessel (*porrón*) is almost anthropomorphic, although in 'The Harem' (1906) it is suggestive of something more genital. He included a drinking vessel in one of his preliminary sketches for 'Les Demoiselles d'Avignon' (1906) but it is not in the final version.

Lorca's lemons can be interpreted in the same way as Picasso's oranges. If we look at 'Nocturno frutero con limones y naranja' ('Nocturne with Lemons and an Orange') (1934) or 'Nocturno frutero con dos limones' ('Nocturne with Two Lemons') (1934), we can see a reworking of the notions of still life within a theatrical framework. Traditionally fruit has religious overtones: angels brought baskets of fruit to Christ in the wilderness and the orange is sometimes a substitute for an apple in the hand of the Infant Christ and in representations of

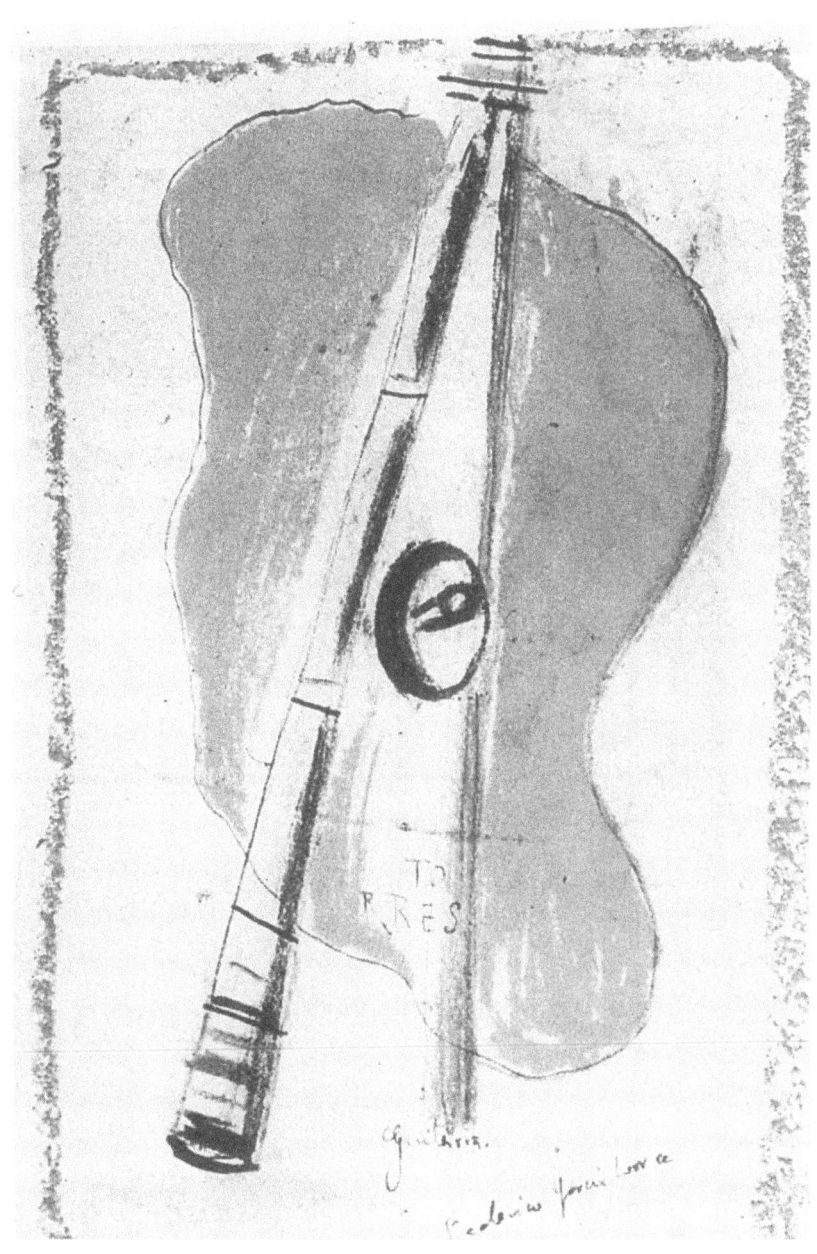

Guitarra (1927)

Composición con instrumentos musicales (1927)

the Tree of Knowledge. Here we see the fruit presented in a theatrical way, with colour used in a highly focused fashion. The fruit is presented in a cosy world screened off from the neighbours by chintzy curtains, yet it can be seen by a moonlit world. We will explore this notion of an inside and an outside world when we look at women on balconies. The decoration on the jug in Lorca's pictures echoes Picasso's pottery and the salt cellar on the side serves to counteract the acidity of the fruit.

Lorca considered his drawings as gifts and both his letters and his book covers such as 'Copy of "Romance de la luna luna"' are frequently accompanied by a drawing which he thought might enliven the letter. Here it is almost as if he saw the lemon as a personal logo or as a reminder of his Spanishness.

If we look at Lorca's 'Teorema de la copa y la mandolina' ('Theorem of the Wine Glass and the Mandolin') (1927), in the light of Picasso's 'Mandolin and Guitar' (1924), an echoing of certain shapes and colours is evident, although Lorca's image is more theorised, and therefore more abstract. Lorca seems to be exploring still life within a Cubist theoretical framework as outlined in his speech at the Athenaeum, working with shapes and picture planes in true Cubist fashion as he saw it. He is schematising the act of looking and analysing objects in relation to one another and to the space around them, along the lines of Picasso's declaration that 'I paint forms as I think them, not as I see them.' In 'Teorema de la copa y la mandolina' he adds the equivalent of the Venn diagram in order to explore use of space and mixings of primary colours, just as he used numbers in his poetry to create tension, as in the prose poem 'Suicidio en Alejandría' ('Suicide in Alexandria'). The general effect is of flatness, as if objects have been splayed, and yet they are fragmentary and abstract. The numbers also suggest the kind of abstract quality found in mathematics which obviously fascinated Lorca.[6] The appearance in 'Teorema' of the equation $A=A$ suggests an awareness on Lorca's part of Niels Bohr's theory of complementarity

---

[6] For an interesting account of scientific debates around this time see Adriana Bergero, 'Science, Modern Art and Surrealism: the representation of imaginary matter' in C. Brian Morris, ed., *The Surrealist Adventure in Spain* (Ottawa: Dovehouse, 1991), 19-39.

Nocturno frutero con dos limones (1934)

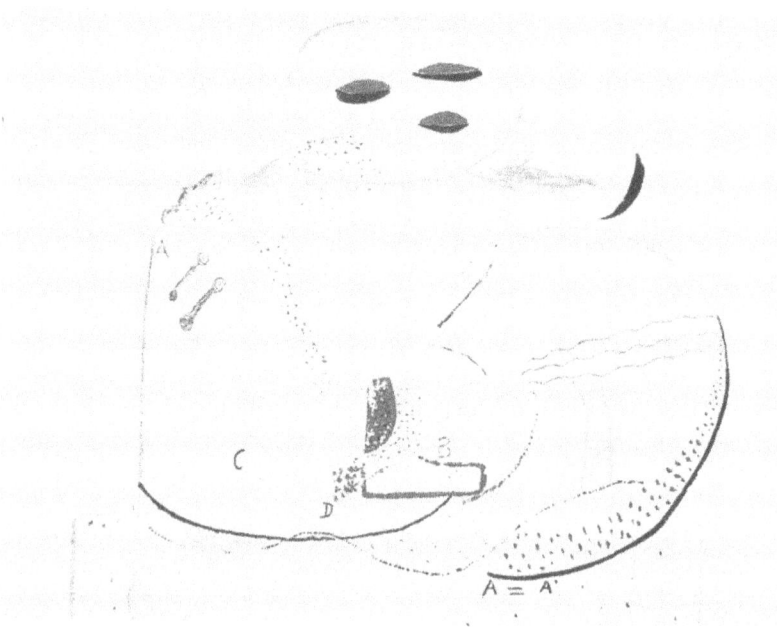

Teorema de la copa y la mandolina (1927)

and an interest in the notion of a binary opposition between reality and absence.[7]

What gradually becomes most interesting in the drawings of Lorca is the reworking of traditional genres within the context of the twentieth-century *avant-garde*. It is perhaps tempting to see Lorca's drawings as simplistic because he could do no more, but once we begin to explore his artistic awareness and cultural heritage it becomes clear that the childlike element is there to stress notions of the primitive or the syncretic. The apparent simplicity belies the sophistication of his thought processes and the seriousness of his artistic apprenticeship.

Picasso stated that he strongly identified with the character of Harlequin, and he frequently used him as a third-person-narrative technique in order to explore issues indirectly. Although Harlequin is represented as dying in the 1906 painting 'Death of Harlequin', he appears in many later works and was ultimately transformed into Paul, one of Picasso's children. The embodiment of the outsider, Harlequin travels alone and can only really exist within the confines of his costume. Trapped within a limited set role, his job is to entertain. Picasso used another clown figure, Pierrot, in a similar way, as in his 'Pierrot with a Mask' (1918). For an artist this notion of performance is inevitably pertinent and Lorca presents us with the clown with whom he also claimed to associate himself in his earlier poems. Lorca's clown figure, as we can see in 'Payaso del guante' ('Gloved Clown') (1925), is plucked from the circus he belongs to and put in an alien environment. The bar and the glass suggest sociability, yet the clown does not belong in this world. He is as displaced as the pear reminiscent of the still-life paintings of Picasso. He wears melancholic make-up and his eyes are listless and unseeing. The costume covers every inch of his torso and the fact that he is also gloved transforms the body entirely into costume. The creative hands and face must be protected. They are also cut off by the ruffle and the head seems separated from the neck. He is a clown taken away from his own world and displaced. Propped up against the bar, his role is made clear by his costume, yet he is

---

[7] It is also interesting to note that the philosopher Henri Bergson gave a lecture at the Residencia on 1 May 1926, which was published in *Residencia*, Year 1, no 2 (1926), 174–6.

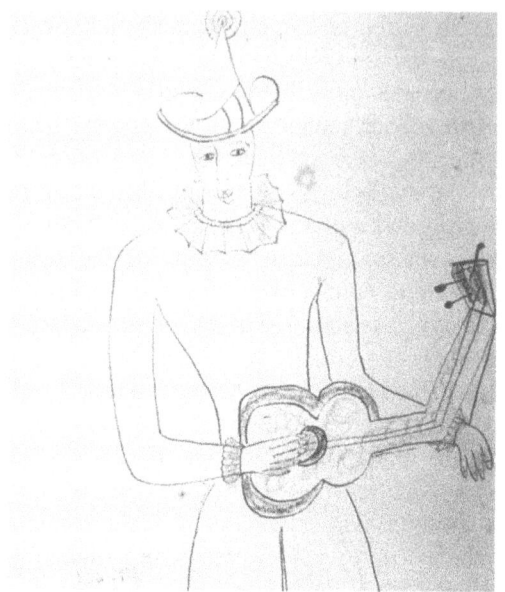
Payaso con guitarra (1925)

Payaso del guante (1925)

decontextualised. Picasso's Pierrot is equally melancholic and, unlike Lorca's, who wears the required 'mask', he has momentarily taken it off either to read or to adjust the ruffle.

Picasso often depicted Harlequin playing the guitar. In the image 'Harlequin Playing a Guitar' (1918) he stresses his own notion of Spanishness. Lorca gave his clowns musical talents which traditionally they probably did not have. But it is important to mention that Lorca himself was a performer. He was an accomplished composer who at one time felt that it was his destiny to become a musician. In 'Payaso con guitarra' ('Clown with a Guitar') (1925), we see a clown with no fixed gender, but he/she is once again taken out of a familiar environment and given another role to play. The clown has the costume but is never seen in the role of making people laugh. Lorca's clowns seem displaced and decorative.

Picasso began 'Harlequin' (1915) a few months before his beloved Eva (Marcelle Humbert) died. The diamond pattern is reminiscent of an Anís del Mono bottle and, indeed, the bottle-top head is dehumanised like a De Chirico dummy. Picasso could have been thinking of the playful figure of the *Commedia dell'Arte* but also the legendary medieval figure of Herlequin: a soul escaped from hell. He has merged two characters and all that is left of one of them is the shadow. Harlequin's tiny mouth is eerie and the eyes are beady; the hands are like tiny paws and they hold up a rectangle, onto which, according to John Richardson, the painter's face is portrayed in profile in the unpainted area.[8]

If we accept that Lorca's clown drawings express an idea of performed emotion symbolising the mixture of tragic and comic in human experience, a concept that takes us right back to the *Commedia dell'Arte*, we have to address his repeated images of clowns with double faces. 'Payaso de rostro desdoblado' ('Clown with a Doubled Face') (1927) is one of Lorca's many images of mask-like doubled faces. If you look at the titles you will see that he always refers to a single 'rostro' which is 'doblado'. In January 1933, when Lorca gave a young

---

[8] John Richardson, *A Life of Picasso, 1907–1917: the painter of modern life* (New York: Random House, 1996), II.

friend, Manuel García Vinolas, a drawing of a double face, he said 'I give you my self-portrait'.

Payaso de rostro desdoblado (1927)

His repeated images of clowns, masks and double faces are surely linked with his work as a dramatist, problematised in words in his plays such as *El público* and *Así que pasen cinco años*, and suggest the idea that to perform an identity gives it the freedom not to be tied down in terms of meaning. The one who is masked is in need of protection, but masquerade could suggest a prior being that might be disclosed. Lacan argues that 'the function of the mask dominates the identification through which refusals of love are resolved'.[9] So the mask is part of the incorporative strategy of melancholy, the taking on of attributes of the object/other that is lost, where loss is a consequence of a refusal of love. The mask has a double function: one inscribes and wears a melancholic identification, and the refuser becomes part of the identity of the refused.

In Freud's 1917 essay 'Mourning and Melancholia', it is the experience of losing another human being whom one has loved that leads one to incorporate the other into the structure of the ego, even taking on attributes of the other and 'sustaining the other through magical acts of imitation'.[10] Lorca himself used the word 'real' but any notion of a reality behind the mask is problematic. The real can only elude us and be replaced by performance and masquerade. An image is essentially a *trompe l'œil*; it does not shift with the gaze, so it is a performance, a disguise, a masquerade and any sense of anything real is translated into absence.

It is interesting to look at Picasso's 'Harlequin with a Mirror' (1923) and compare it with Lorca's 'El beso' ('The Kiss') (1927). The mirror is not held up between the viewer and the object. It is the object itself which is mirrored or doubled and serves to shut out the viewer or perhaps to retain a certain intimacy inside the image. The 'real' thus stands for what is neither symbolic nor imaginary. It is that which always returns to the same place. Lacan calls it 'the umbilical cord of the symbolic' or 'that which can be approached but not grasped'. Perhaps the double is expelled or rejected from the original and hence becomes alien. As the body is seen as a vital and sacred enclosure

---

[9] For an interesting reading of Lacan see Judith Butler, *Gender Trouble: feminism and the subversion of identity* (London: Routledge, 1990), 43–57.

[10] This is also taken from Butler, *Gender Trouble*, 57–71.

lacking a soul, it presents itself as a signifying lack. In Lorca's 'El beso' he shows his own outline and that of Dalí as an ominous shadow. The painting was originally called 'Beso en el espejo' ('Kiss in the Mirror').

There is a vital link to be made between Picasso and Dalí, enabling us to begin to explore Lorca's work within a Surrealist context. In 'Studio With Plaster Head' (1925), Picasso used a classical sculptural bust as a self-conscious image of the notion of painting. Dalí echoed this in 'Still Life By Mauve Moonlight' (1926) and presented the head of Lorca fused with his own as a still life set in Cadaqués, a place which Picasso visited, Lorca loved and in which Dalí lived. We see the boats of Cadaqués and the moon, Lorca's moon: the moon which brings death and insanity yet also creativity. This is not a romantic moon but it brings a cold sunless world and reaches out to the realms of instinct. Lorca said 'to be an artist one must see with the eyes of a child and ask for the moon'. Dalí represented Lorca in his images many times, confirming, at the very least, a remarkable personal closeness. Dalí also seems to have acted as a kind of filter of influences, so that Lorca received the influence of Picasso (and to some extent the Spanish tradition) mediated by the work of Dalí.[11]

In 'Retrato de Dalí' ('Portrait of Dalí') (1927) Lorca took the familiar oval face and presented it with a mask-like palette falling to one side. Just as Dalí chose to link his own identity with that of Lorca's by using a double image incorporating features of both men, Lorca performed the issue of identity through the filter of the mask. In this painting the man and the painter gently overlap. The scene is conventional, a bar. The stippled title is echoed by stippled smoke. Dalí inhales the smoke from the bowl, not from the mouthpiece—as if he is inverting direction. The caricature of Dalí is similar to the one Lorca presents of himself. Only one half of the jacket is coloured: one half of him smokes and the other half drinks. The symbolic palette with its words for colours and palette hole for mouth allows us access to both sides of the man: the man who is a painter and the man who enjoys other pleasures in life.

[11] Much has been written about the relationship between Lorca and Dalí. See, for example, Antonina Rodrigo, *Lorca-Dalí: Una amistad traicionada* (Barcelona: Planeta, 1981); and Salvador Dalí, *Salvador Dalí escribe a Federico García Lorca* (Madrid: Ministerio de Cultura, 1978).

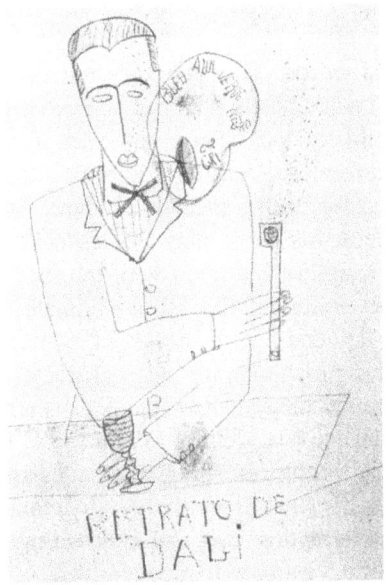
Retrato de Dalí (1927)

Dama en el balcón (1927)

This notion of inside and outside echoes synthetic Cubist practices, where the viewer reorders the image to construct a reality somewhere between painting and words. Thus the very notion of representation is questioned. Identity can be paraded: it can be seen as a façade.

Although it is unlikely that Lorca had seen Picasso's preliminary sketch for 'Les Demoiselles d'Avignon' in which the naked women are accompanied by a sailor and a medical student, the appearance of a sailor and a student in his short play *La doncella, el marinero y el estudiante* is another sign of his interest in the motifs characteristic of Picasso's work. The notion of the sailor—homeless, rootless, on the margins of society—abounds in the work of both Picasso and Lorca. The student and the prostitute are also characters without a fixed identity. In Lorca's play, the *doncella* (maiden) is tempted by both men and is prepared to change her identity to suit them, but decides to take cover behind maternal protection. Picasso decided to remove the sailor and the student from his final aggressively all female cast and the still life is altered to show tempting fruit and a melon in a shape that echoes the moon that takes the Virgin up to Heaven in El Greco's 'Assumption of the Virgin' (1577). One wonders whether the fruit is a phallic image or a moon that can 'save' the women and bear them aloft.

The *doncella* of Lorca's play is protected by a balcony which keeps her under surveillance or within the boundaries of domesticity. This convention is once again predominant within Spanish tradition. Lorca's 'Dama en el balcón' ('Lady on the Balcony') (1927), bears a close resemblance to Goya's 'Women on the Balcony' (1811), but Goya's *majas* are shadowed by the sinister presence of men in the background. The women on the balcony are part of an Andalusian ritual of courtship seen frequently in literature. In *La doncella, el marinero y el estudiante*, the balcony itself enables a woman to be seen within controlled circumstances. It is all part of the *disimulo* (ritual of concealment), just as a fan or a mask enables a performer to create an identity which is in flux. There is no doubting the Spanishness of the women on the balcony, with mantillas on their heads. In both works the mantilla is shaped by a comb keeping it in place. Goya depicts the Spanish woman with her veil as a sign of her religious fervour yet the slightly arrogant beauty is quite apparent. Lorca's 'Dama' is protected not just by the veil, but also by the balcony which keeps her aloof and unavailable in time-honoured tradition. She can be seen, she can look but she cannot be touched. Picasso, too, retained this mixture of innocence and worldliness. We have only to look at 'Portrait of Benedetta Casals' (1905), in which the woman is on the one hand vulnerable yet also posing and seductive.

Retrato de dama española sentada (1929)

Lorca's 'Retrato de dama española sentada' ('Portrait of a Seated Spanish Lady') (1929) takes the woman away from her balcony, sitting outside yet still, in a sense, inside, within the walls of a patio, gripping onto the cross around her waist. The gushing fountain in the background contrasts with her demureness and the heaviness of her attire. In this image the familiar stage-set backgrounds are reminiscent of Picasso's stage set for Manuel de Falla's *El sombrero de tres picos* (*The Three-Cornered Hat*), prepared for the Russian Ballet in 1919. Lorca would have seen Picasso's set and costume designs at the house of his fellow Granadino Manuel de Falla, who kept them in his hall, having been given them in 1921 by Picasso. They were even dedicated to him. The critic Enrique Díez Canedo in *El Sol* (Madrid, 26 December 1930) commented that for the première of *La zapatera prodigiosa* the costumes were based on drawings by the poet, Lorca, which in turn were influenced by Picasso's costumes for Falla's *El sombrero de tres picos*.

Lorca was Picasso's silent apprentice. He drew from Picasso, he learnt, he experimented and he finally appropriated. In the magazine *Gallo,* edited by Lorca, we see, in the first edition which came out in April 1928, an article about Picasso by Lorca's mentor, Sebastiá Gasch, accompanied by three untitled paintings of 1914, 1921 and 1924. In the same issue Lorca chose to publish two plays, *La doncella, el marinero y el estudiante* and *El paseo de Buster Keaton*.

What do Lorca's drawings teach us about the man? That he was, on the one hand, bred in the culture of *cante jondo*, steeped in his own folkloric and syncretic roots, but that he was also wildly *avant-garde*. In his homage to Picasso, he identified with the master's primitive modernism. He learnt from Picasso and appropriated his themes as part of a search for his own notion of Spanish roots, paying homage with echoes and reverberations in pictures that were forms of communication. Whether his drawings represent a reworking of Picasso, a pastiche or simply an admiring nod in his direction, they undoubtedly reveal a shared set of cultural references.

2

Creative responses

The Death of Lorca
Merryn Williams

Most of them are dead now, members of the 'black squads'
whose cars raced off down darkened streets, that summer of '36.
All died violently, one way or another.
The names are lost. The old are afraid to speak.

The poet's books come off the presses in thousands,
translated, carried in students' pockets
down the highways of Paris or Buenos Aires;
his plays sung over the air; his picture goes round the world.

Some died in exile. Picasso painting
horse, bull and naked lamp in raging black and white.
Or the English housewife recalling her childhood trauma:
Send me a ghost writer. Make them hear my story.

He lies with the obscure. 'Give him coffee!' the general
joked. The gravedigger found four of them at dawn,
roped together, Lorca by the one-legged schoolmaster;
dug a new trench in the olive grove.

The moon reveals a landscape with no shelter,
women wringing shirts by an icy mountain stream,
and heaped bones in the ossuary white as jasmine;
the juicy oranges lead globes, discoloured by moonlight.

Yet the poetry, bound in olive and khaki,
spreads wide, and the fountain gives good drinking water.
Still it murmurs, half a mile from the place
where Lorca fell. His death unjarred a door,
disclosing more killings, and then more.

the night journey
john clifford

I had a dream I'd died.
It was great.
No more Millennium Dome. No more self-assessment tax returns.
No more getting angry at Ian Paisley.
No more being afraid for India and Pakistan.
No more living in this repulsive country.
No more living through this shameful time.
I was so happy.
What made it better was it wasn't the first time I'd tried to do it.
When I took an overdose, they pumped out my belly.
When I hung myself, they cut the rope.
When I cut my wrists they stitched them up again.
And not out of love of life or feeling for me:
Simply out of bureaucratic cowardice.
So I felt so happy for a while I didn't notice how dull it was.
There was no blue light. I'd been expecting a blue light. I'd read about it
in *Hello*.
Someone's after death experience.
Perhaps it was lady Di. Or maybe a mother of two from Bromsgrove.
And perhaps it was in *Good Housekeeping*.
Whatever. She'd seen this blue light, this beautiful blue light,
And in that blue light were all the people she'd ever loved
And knew she would be able to meet again.
Only I never had a blue light. I'd ended up in a car park.
Or at least what looked like a car park.
Looked like the car park in Disney World.
And I remembered when we arrived, looking out the car window, and
                                              thinking
Christ! Have we really paid good money to end up in a place like this?
Full of parking places
Full of parking places with numbers and names
Like Goofy or Mickey or Snow White.
I wanted to be in Snow White but we ended up in Grumpy.
We were Grumpy 21.

And we were meant to remember that to help us find our way home

And that's when I understood.
There's no way forward. There's no way back.
There is no way home.
And that's when I started to be afraid.
And then I saw a man, or something,
Walking in the distance
Walking a little strangely
All muffled up in some medieval thing so I could hardly see his face
And I said: 'Who are you?'
And he looked at me with pity in his eyes
And touched me on the forehead, there...
And I remember...
I remember a book. In verse. A big one. 3 volumes.
Inferno. Purgatorio. Paradiso
And I remember how I never got to paradise
I just got stuck half way through purgatory
And then I remember again, and I understand
I understand that every word is true
I am in the middle of the path of life[1]
I have lost my way
And when I look around
I find I'm on a hillside
A bare hillside. A wild and savage place
The sun is setting
Darkness is closing in all around
And then, all of a sudden,
I see ahead a lion,
Terrible of aspect,
That makes the air tremble in terror. And behind me a she wolf
A she wolf so ravenous and lean
She seems as if charged with all cravings
I cannot go forward
I cannot go back
I want to go up high in the mountains
To catch the last shreds of sunlight

---

[1] Dante, *Inferno*, I, 1.

But the creatures drive me downward
Down to where the sun is silent
That's when I see you, see this figure on the distant slope
And I call out to you, and you can barely reply
Your voice is hoarse
Hoarse with long silence
And so it hurts. It hurts to speak.
And I know in a minute I'm going to recognise you,
and I'll call you a fountain
A fountain pouring forth so rich a stream of speech!
Glory and Light of Poets,
I'll say,
Let the long study and great love
That made me read you over and over again
Let it be of help to me.
You are my author. You taught me what I know.
And I hope I'm not really in the book
And that you're not really Virgil
I thought Latin was so dull
But instead you say:
There's a song[2]
whose words I'll never speak
a song that's sleeping on my lips.
The song whose words I'll never speak!
There was a glow-worm
high in the honeysuckle
and the moon pricked the water
with a moonbeam.
That was when I dreamed
the song
whose words I'll never speak.
A song full of lips
and faraway river-beds.
A song full of hours
lost in the shadows
A song of a living star
shining in perpetual daylight.

[2] Lorca, 'Verlaine' in *Canciones*.

A song
Whose words I've come to speak

And you're taking off your cloak
And underneath it there you are
In a beautiful suit, silk shirt,
and floppy tie,
of the kind that poets wear
Federico!
And it's true! Every word of it is true!
You are my poet
And the deep study and great love I bore you
Did help along the way
And suddenly I'm remembering
verde que te quiero verde
Preciosa y el aire
Córdoba
Lejana y sola
And the Guardia Civil hammering on the door[3]
A las cinco de la tarde
a las cinco en sombra de la tarde
And how they spoke to me,
those poems I didn't really understand
and yet which touched my heart.
Poems which somehow came from where I was
poems which came from a deep dark desperate place
poems coming in spite of a certain knowledge
that the person you really were
could only be hated
and never truly understood.

And when you wrote:
I cannot condemn[4]
The boy who writes a girl's name on his pillow
Or dresses up as a bride
Deep in his closet's warm darkness

---

[3] Lorca, *Romancero gitano*.
[4] Lorca, 'Oda a Walt Whitman' in *Poeta en Nueva York*.

I think you saved my life.

And here you are
in this dead place
and you look at me and smile and say:
'Time to go'
'Where?'
'Where we're going'
And we walk. Arm in arm we walk.
Walk along the deep and savage way
Walk through an empty and uncertain land
a place where the sun does not shine,
and neither does the moon
a place where the sky is empty of stars
Until we come to a gate.
And behind the gate is weeping.
And above the gate it says:
'Through me the way to the despairing city
Through me the way followed by the lost
Through me the way to suffering that lasts for ever
Anyone who enters here lose hope'[5]

And I don't want to go in there, but you say:
This is the time to abandon fear
This is the time to leave mistrust behind
This is the place where we shall see
The sad people, the woeful people
Those who have lost the use of the thinking mind

And you look at me with pity in your eyes
And I'm inside
This place, where it's sticky
everything seems covered in slime
there's people there, though I can't see their faces
there's the men who touched me up
the men who wanted to beat me
the man who got me drunk and stroked my hands

[5] Dante, *Inferno*, III, 1-9.

the man who got me stoned and tried to rape me
there's all the lies I told
there's all the wishes I could never express
all the dresses I longed to wear and never dared to
all the tears I wanted to weep and was too ashamed

Memory
Help us
understanding
Enlighten us
Determination
Give us strength!
And if you still live
High in the mountains,
Strong and beautiful spirits
Of poetry and song
Inspire us
Give us courage
Give us power
Help us in this feat of madness and of memory
This ordeal of imagination and of strength

And all of a sudden
I'm in Scunthorpe!
It's raining and it's Sunday and I'm bored out of my mind!

And you, Federico,
you're in Fuente Vaqueros
and you're a boy again!
Surrounded by lizards. Strange blue flowers.
And the heat.
Crickets rubbing their legs.
Drily.
In the dust of the dry afternoon.

We've got the local park
And a clock made out of flowers
And a miniature railway that runs
On alternate Sundays
But you live in a village where it's always warm

A village that's watered by an everlasting spring.
A fountain of pure water
That bubbles up from the ground
And has flowed there for ever and ever!
Scunthorpe used to have municipal baths.
But they closed them down in 1955.

Your village is a special place
Where special people live
People who aren't like anyone else.
Anarchists. Freethinkers. Artists.

We've got seaside landladies.
Fish and chip proprietors.
The people who empty the slot machines.
There's the man who runs the miniature railway,
He collects match box labels in his spare time.
Then there's the people who sell hats.
Hats that say
Kiss me stupid
And then there's the Rotary Club.

You dress up in costumes from a chest in the attic
And pretend to hold services for the whole family
And I sit in my room and I play by myself
Making houses with my Bayko construction set

You enter the church and you're lost in adoration
Before our Lady in the corner in a lovely frock
The Virgin of Good Love
With sparkling jewels and a silver crown
Holding her baby son and laughing
Laughing in the incense filled darkness
I go to matins in the parish church
and we sing hymns ancient and modern

And you have the most amazing festivals
pilgrimages and pagan rites
and when people speak
their speech full of poetry and infused

THE NIGHT JOURNEY

with the spirit of the dark and pagan earth

And Betty down our street does her clog dances
And everyone laughs behind her back
And then we've got
Thought of the Day on the Home Service

Your mother gathers everyone around
And reads aloud the most amazing poetry and plays
My mum used to make the tea
And when she expressed an opinion
My dad would make fun of her.
My dad also likes to watch the boxing and sometimes
I'm allowed to stay up late to watch
The Black and White Minstrel Show

Your mother is a teacher
Who gives free lessons to the poor
And your father rides a big white horse
And is loved by everyone!

My father admires the works of Winston Churchill
Whose speeches, he says, are the greatest works of literature
That anyone has ever written
And my mum ... my mum's died
My mother. My dead mother.
My mother fading
My mother fading from my mind.
I can't remember the shape of her nose.

I can't remember the colour of her eyes. I can't remember her smiling!
I want to stop her going
But there's nothing I can do
She's fading
She's an old photograph
Vanishing in the grey waves of the cold dark sea.

And Federico's right beside me
Telling me of the death of his beautiful friend
And he looks at me

Raising his arms to bless

Bless the timid and the shy
For they shall be shameless.
Bless the lonely and misunderstood
For she shall have everyone she wants.
Bless the poor
For she shall be rich.
Bless the chairman of the board
For she shall lose everything!
Bless the boy in the closet in the silk wedding gown
For he shall come out
Bless the prostitute
For she shall be honoured
Bless the frigid and the impotent
For they shall have sex for ever and ever!
Amen! Amen!
And bless the fathers who don't care because they've never been cared
                               for
For they shall be loved
Bless the mothers who hit
Because they cannot still their children's tears
For they shall be comforted
Bless the bully and the criminal
For they shall lose all fear
Bless the inadequates who go into government
For they shall lose their power
Bless the gangster who boasts of the women he's raped
and victims he's robbed and the enemies he's killed
For he is them
And they are him
And shall be for ever and ever.
Amen amen.
And bless this boy who's been frozen in terror
Remind him he is not alone
Remind him there are others who are crying in the darkness
With their heads in the pillow so that no-one can hear

Remind them that one day we will hear each other
And on that day the earth shall be changed forever!

And when I look down I discover I'm the Virgin
High in the church looking down on the worshippers
Looking down on the supplicants from my beautiful niche
I love it.
Love the frock.
Love the niche.
I've got a little ledge to rest my bum on
And my halo lights up when someone puts a coin in the slot
And when I look down I see I've got a supplicant
Down on his knees with his face in the dust
And ... it's you, Federico,
Full of guilt and defilement
Begging me to set you free
Take the heart's bitterness from me, you're praying,
Lift this curse from me.
Deliver me from my shame

And I can't do that, Federico.
You've got the wrong virgin
You want the other one, the respectable one,
The virgin of perverted love.
The one with the tears
The one who's carried on the backs of men
Who beat their wives.
The one that'll tell you it's your duty to resist
Resist your sinful longing
Marry a good catholic girl and make her miserable for ever.

But I can't tell you that. I'm the Virgin of Good Love,
Remember?
Federico. Listen.
They say my son once took a boy into his arms.
A little boy the disciples wanted to send away
Because they thought he would disturb him.
And my son said 'No. Let him stay.
Be like him.
Be like a little child.
But if anyone destroys the faith of a little one
Perverts the faith of a child who believes in me

It would be better for him to have a millstone hung around his neck
And be thrown into the depths of the sea.'[6]

Oh Federico. How many millstones would it take
To hang round the necks of everyone
Who's ever misled a little child
And told them they have to be ashamed?
Not enough millstones, Federico.
Not in the whole wide world.
Not enough sea!

And Federico's running out the church
Federico's sailing away in an ocean liner
Sailing. Sailing away to a new world!
To a city that has no walls
Not like cities in Europe
Walled. Guarded. Imprisoned
But open. Open to the sea!
Guarded by a lady with a torch
Offering freedom to the outcast
Shelter to the oppressed
A welcome to the rejected and forlorn! An open city
A city of the free!

On the Titanic's sister ship
With electric lights and luxury staterooms. And six square meals a day!
And you play the piano and recite
And make eyes at a beautiful steward
Who is devastatingly attractive in his dazzling white uniform
And the ocean is smooth as glass!

And then you reach New York
A city made of ash
A city made of death and copper wires.
Where each day they kill
4 million ducks
5 million pigs

---

[6] Matthew, 18.

THE NIGHT JOURNEY

Two thousand doves
And they drink 8 million litres of milk.[7]

And I'm there, the Virgin,
Standing on a street corner on the Lower East Side
Selling my body for petty cash
Though nowadays I also accept credit cards
It's the American way
And I can see you
You're high up there
On top of the Chrysler Building
The highest building of New York
And you're shouting at the Pope[8]
You're threatening him with arsenic sharks
And shards of silver pointed glass
Shouting across the ocean
To the man in white in his tower in Rome
In his golden tower and his gleaming dome
The great dome
which anoints the armies with holy oil,
which greases all their military tongues
shouting because there's no-one now
No-one to give out bread and wine
No-one to make grass grow on the mouths of the dead
No-one to spread out the linen of final repose.

Just millions and millions of blacksmiths
Forging chains for the children who haven't even been born.
Millions and millions of carpenters
Making coffins that have no cross.
Just a huge crowd of lamentations
Unbuttoning their clothing to make it easy for the bullets.

The man in white should be speaking
The man in white should be screaming
He should weep with so fearful a mourning

---

[7] Lorca, 'Nueva York (Oficina y denuncia)' in *Poeta en Nueva York*.
[8] Lorca, 'Grito hacia Roma' in *Poeta en Nueva York*.

That it dissolves his rings and diamond telephones.

But he's just a man. A man in white.
Who knows nothing of the mystery of the ear of wheat
Nothing of the groans of the woman giving birth
Who doesn't even know that Christ can still give water
Or that money burns away the most marvellous kiss

The schoolteachers tell the children
Of a wonderful light coming down from the mountain
But what really arrives is a meeting of sewers

Look say the teachers, pointing with reverence,
Look at the enormous cupolas filling with incense;
But there is no love beneath the stone statues
No love behind their cold definitive eyes.

Love lives in flesh torn by thirst's talons
Love lives in the tiny thatched hut defying the flooding
Love lives in ditches where they're fighting the serpents of famine
Love lives in the sad dead sea where dead seagulls rock slowly;

Love lives in the secretest kiss you can imagine
Pricking amongst dark pillows.

But the old man in white who wants light in his fingers
Still says: Love, love, love,
Applauded by millions of corpses;
Still says: Love, love, love,
With gold vestments that tremble with tenderness; still says:
Peace, peace, peace,
While the knives' teeth are chattering
And he blesses the muzzles of the guns.

And he'll keep on saying
Love, love, love,
Until his lips have all turned into silver.
And all the while, all the while, oh all the while
The blacks are taking out the spittoons
Boys are trembling under the pale terror of executives

Women are drowning in industrial oil
And the whole crowd with their hammers, their violins or their clouds
Have to scream till their brains are exploding,
Have to scream at the huge church domes
Scream in a madness of fire
Scream in a madness of snow
Scream the scream of every night's screaming
Scream with so fierce and heart-rending a voice
That the cities all tremble like little girls
And break their chains of music and gasoline.
Because we want our daily bread
Because we want and we demand it,
The alder tree in flower and the perpetual germ of tenderness,
Because we want and we demand
That the will of the earth be done
And that she gives her fruit to everyone

And I see you, Federico,
Walking down Wall Street
Watching all the criminals
Watching them deal in millions
Their hands are shaking
Their hands are shaking
Because they're holding money[9]
There's a beggar without legs
Pushing himself down the street on a trolley
And you and him and me are the only honest men
The only honest men on this street of thieves

Because neither of us has any money
There's a man threw himself out the window
Because he lost ten million dollars
Threw himself off the forty-third floor
Of the Astor building
And they say
That's class!

---

[9] Lorca writing home to his parents, August 1929.

His hands.
I see his hands.
His hands are white on the cement of the sidewalk
His white floury hands
And I think I understand
I think I understand the logic of America

This system of values, this way of being
That if we allow it will destroy us all

As all of us
living working breathing seeing
living under the shadow of advancing death
doing what we can
to defy the approaching darkness

And I'm with you now
Now this night in the railway station
now that the war's beginning and you're on your way home
All the crowds are hurrying,
They're all rushing past
It's bedlam. Everyone's afraid. Everyone's afraid of the war.

It's the last train south
I beg you not to take it.

Don't take it. Don't go home.
They hate you there.
And it's not your home.
Not any more.
Your home's with me.
In my arms is home.
Not there. You won't be safe there. They hate you.
Rancid little city.
With its rancid little minds.
Stay with me.
Let me protect you.
Let me keep you safe.

It can't be helped!, you say,

It's where I belong.
Let go my hand.
Don't embrace me.
We must not kiss.
I could not bear to cause a scandal. Don't cry.
We will meet soon.

And you walked away
You held your mouth rigid.
You held your back stiff.
It wasn't the body I knew any more.

The crowd swallowed you
And I never saw you in this life again

And this is the place, Federico,
This is the place where traitors live.
It's where they make those fragmentation bombs
The ones that explode on impact
And send little plastic pellets flying everywhere
That are invisible to x rays
It's where they make the powdered milk
That they know will poison babies
It's where they dump the nuclear waste
and if a bit leaks out then what the hell
it's where the cowards and the bullies live
the ones addicted to violence and hatred
the ones who shot you that dark night and boasted afterwards
they'd shot you twice up the arse for being queer

And Federico in the old amazing story
of the lost sad soul and his poet guide
When they come at last to frozen heart of hell
There they find a secret hidden stair
Which they climb up until they find
The sweet fresh air of earth
And see once more the shining stars

And I say shall we climb
Federico, shall we climb

the secret stairway out of hell
let's climb, Federico, hand in hand, together
let's climb let's climb

and I know deep in my stomach's pit I know
this is the moment I wake up

and I'm lying in a hospital bed
and I feel so ill
and my throat's so sore
and I know I know
I'm still alive
they've pumped my stomach out again

I'm in a cubicle, there's curtains all around
and when I poke my head out
I can see all hell has broken loose
it's like a war
late this night in the casualty ward

and very slowly I get up
and I put on my clothes
and a nice nurse pops her head in
and to my surprise
she wants to be nice but she hasn't the time
and I say: Don't worry I'm just fine
don't bring me trousers
I'm happy in the dress

and when she's gone
I very quietly slip outside
there's rubbish in the streets
a cold wind and dirty paper blowing about
up in the sky I can still see Venus.
It's almost dawn.
Federico's left me now and I walk alone
past the cardboard houses and the broken rubbish bags
and high above me, hidden behind the clouds
the secret hidden harmonies of the revolving stars
it's love, they say,

THE NIGHT JOURNEY

love that moves the stars

so why can't we see them?
why can't we see the stars?

edinburgh, 28 may, 1998

Ode To Federico García Lorca[1]
Pablo Neruda

If I could weep with fear in a lonely house,
if I could pluck out my eyes and eat them,
I would do it for your grieving orange-tree voice
and for your poetry which leaps out shouting.

Because for you they paint hospitals blue,
and schools and ports grow,
and wounded angels are clothed in feathers,
and wedding-day fish are covered with scales,
and hedgehogs take to flight:
for you tailor-shops with their black membranes
fill up with spoons and blood,
and swallow red ribbons and kiss each other to death,
and dress in white.

When you fly dressed as a peach tree,
when you laugh with a laugh of hurricaned rice,
when to sing you shake arteries and teeth,
throat and fingers,
I could die for how sweet you are,
I could die for the red lakes
where in the midst of autumn you live
with a fallen steed and a bloodied god,
I could die for the cemeteries
that pass like ashen rivers
with water and tombs,
at night, among drowned bells:
rivers thick as dormitories
of sick soldiers, that suddenly swell
toward death in rivers with marble numbers
and rotten crowns, and funeral oils:

---

[1] 'Oda a Federico García Lorca' from *Residencia en la tierra*, 2 (first published in 1935). Pablo Neruda, *Obras completas*, I, 3rd ed. (Buenos Aires: Losada, 1967), 240–3.

ODE TO FEDERICO GARCIA LORCA

I could die to see you at night
watching the drowned crosses go by,
standing and weeping,
because before death's river you weep,
deserted, wounded,
you weep weeping, your eyes filled
with tears, with tears, with tears.

If at night, lost and alone, I could
gather oblivion and shadow and smoke
above railways and steamers,
with a black funnel,
biting the ashes,
I would do it for the tree where you grow,
for the nests of golden waters that you gather,
and for the vine that covers your bones,
and tells you the secret of the night.

Cities with smell of wet onions
wait for you to pass, singing raucously,
and silent sperm boats pursue you,
and green swallows nest in your hair,
and also snails and weeks,
furled masts and cherry trees
sway decisively
when your pale, fifteen-eyed head
and your mouth of sunken blood appear.

If I could fill mayoralties with soot
and, sobbing, tear down clocks,
it would be to see summer
come to your home with broken lips,
come many people dressed in agony,
come regions of sad splendour,
come dead ploughs and poppies,
come grave-diggers and horsemen,
come planets and maps soaked in blood,
come divers covered in ashes,
come masked men dragging damsels
run through by great knives,
come roots, veins, hospitals,

springs, ants,
comes night with the bed where
a solitary hussar is dying among the spiders,
comes a rose of hatred and pins,
comes a yellowish boat,
comes a windy day with a child,
come I with Oliverio, Norah,
Vicente Aleixandre, Delia,
Maruca, Malva Marina, María Luisa, and Larco,
La Rubia, Rafael Ugarte,
Cotapos, Rafael Alberti,
Carlos, Bebé, Manolo Altolaguirre,
Molinari,
Rosales, Concha Méndez,
and others that slip my mind.
Come, let me crown you, youth of health
and butterflies, youth as pure
as a black lightning flash, perpetually free;
and between the two of us,
now, when there is no one else among the rocks,
let us speak simply, you as you, I as I;
what is verse for if not for the dew?

What is verse for if not for that night
when a bitter dagger discovers us, for that day,
for that dusk, for that broken corner
when the battered heart of man prepares to die?

Above all at night,
at night there are many stars,
all within a river
like a ribbon next to the windows
of houses filled with the poor.

Someone of theirs has died, perhaps
they have lost their positions in the offices,
in the hospitals, in the elevators,
in the mines,
human beings suffer stubbornly wounded
and there is intent and weeping everywhere:

ODE TO FEDERICO GARCIA LORCA

while the stars flow in an endless river
there is much weeping at the windows,
the thresholds are worn away by weeping,
the bedrooms are soaked by weeping
that comes like a wave to bite the carpets.

Federico,
you see the world, the streets,
the vinegar,
the farewells in the stations
when the smoke lifts its decisive wheels
toward where there is nothing
but separations, stones, railway tracks.

There are so many people asking questions
everywhere.
There is the bleeding blind-man, and the irate man, and the
disheartened man,
and the wretch, the tree of finger-nails,
the brigand with envy on his back.

That is life, Federico, here you have
the things that my friendship can offer you,
the friendship of a melancholy manly man.
Already you know many things;
other things you will come to know slowly.

Translated by Sebastian Doggart

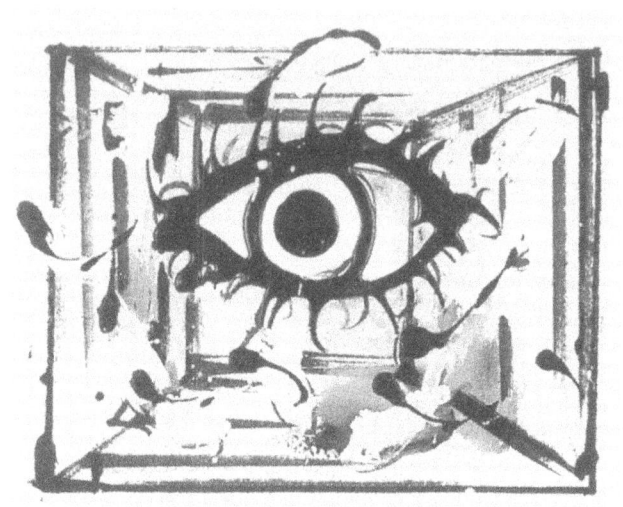

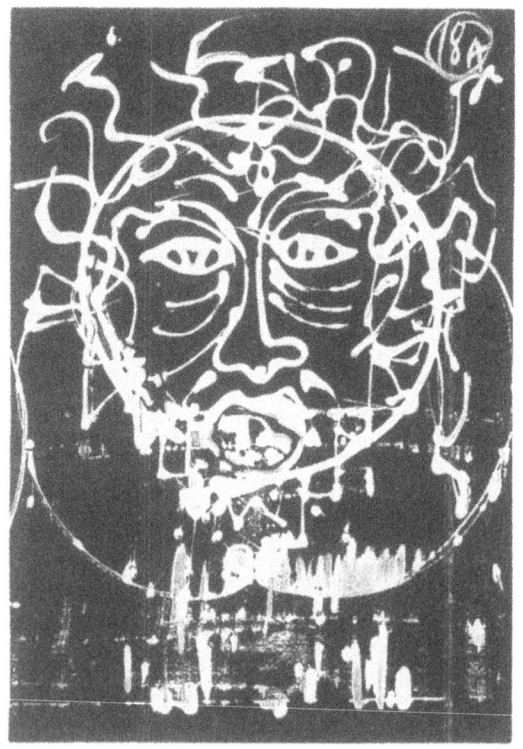

Images from Viage a la luna *by Frederic Amat*

Notes on *Viaje a la luna* (*Voyage to the Moon*)
Frederic Amat

One hundred years after the birth of Federico García Lorca, and following mishaps and failed attempts to produce it, the time has come to screen publicly the poet's only film script: *Viaje a la luna*.[1]

Written in New York, *Viaje a la luna* is a silent film that speaks for itself, a transformation of poetry into moving images which defy narrative discourse. Lorca's script finds its meaning in the succession and contrast of scenes. It invites the viewer to reinvent a mosaic of allegorical images, a 'theorem of the moon'. In this unique project of medium-length film-making we find resonances with two other works which, together with *Viaje a la luna,* make up the trinity of Lorca's New York writings: the book of poems *Poeta en Nueva York* and the play *El público*. As well as these three literary works, there is a constellation of drawings which illuminate the poet's American writings with elegant and unnerving expressiveness. Joan Miró wrote of these drawings that 'they seem to me the work of a great poet, which is the greatest praise I can give to any form of expression.'

Eyes recur in Lorca's drawings like flying fish. One portrays a landscape of pyramids; at the centre a young man stands on a pedestal next to a grave. Threads of wiry blood emerge from his heart, dance, and form a 'panorama of open eyes and bitter wounds on fire'. The title evokes the temperature of the coloured crayons: 'Desire of dead cities'. In his screenplay for *Viaje a la luna*, the poet brings in another of his New York drawings to develop a tension between his lines on paper and the bars that he superimposes, thus creating a space of immediate phosphorescence: 'Sequence 38: double exposure of bars passing over a drawing: *Death of Saint Radegund*' (68).

---

[1] The first complete edition in Spanish based on Lorca's manuscript is edited by Antonio Monegal (Valencia: Pre-Textos, 1994). Page references are to this edition. The manuscript had earlier been translated into English by Greg Simon and Steven F. White: in Federico García Lorca, *Collected Poems*, ed. C. Maurer (New York: Farrar Straus Giroux, 1991), 631–9.

Poems, theatre, cinema and drawings are woven together in a kaleidoscope of influences and echoes. These help us unravel the poet's profound suggestion: his 'truth of a man of blood' as 'a wounded pulse courting things on the other side', a visionary state of methodical creative delirium in which scenes and characters progress with apparent unease, but reveal a deep poetic logic. *Viaje a la luna* is not a tour of the unconscious; it is consciousness in anguished lucidity, it is the will to unmask a reality imposed as a monolith. The poet's attitude mirrors the spirit of surrealism, that last academy of revolution and rupture. It takes a brazen stance against reason, scandalises bourgeois morality, and plays a bloody joke on mean and stunted ways of thinking. Lorca shares the boldness of the *avant-garde* and its indignation towards institutionalised hypocrisy, but in his New York work we are not in a dream of surrealist reason, but in a dialogue between dream and wakefulness, which takes place through an awareness of how living is like dying and of how death is an extreme form of love. The fish biting its own tail; love and interruption implying death as episodes of accidental destiny. In Juliet's tomb, love does not conquer death; but 'in the last resort', do Romeo and Juliet necessarily have to be a man and a woman for the scene to be produced in a cold and heartbreaking way? Lorca makes this point through one of the characters in his play *El público*: 'Romeo may be a bird and Juliet may be a stone. Romeo may be a grain of salt and Juliet a map.'[2] There are no questions; there is desire. Reconquest of love in its original state of innocence, far from any moral which might turn it into stagnant water, anchored instinct.

The poet's personal situation, woven in the threads of homosexual love, is a paradigm of both anguish and identity: 'seed and ladder' of his poetic art. It cannot be reduced to a simple vindication of homosexual rights. His intention goes much further. It is an exaltation of love that is free, a love confronted by the values which repress instinct and which still graze and bleat through our valleys with masks of tolerance hiding faces of intransigence. *Viaje a la luna* is not just a trip inside the poet; it is also a universal journey. Through theatre, poetry and cinema, Lorca shows us a world of disguises, appearances

---

[2] *Obras completas* (Madrid: Aguilar, 1986), II, 602.

and masks, manifested in its true identity, naked and raw. The face in its final grimace: the skull.

At the crossroads of love, we are the victims of our own passion. We do not possess it; it possesses us. The mystery of love as exorcism of death. There is no other God than god made man, he who turns his anguish into transforming sacrifice. The voice of the poet is plural; he takes the presence of that god which is mask-less, humanised, moved by amorous desire, a god who takes on bodily form, dies and revives. 'Centre stage, a bed, upright and facing downstage, like a primitive painting; on it, a red naked man, wearing a crown of blue thorns.'[3] This is how the fifth scene of *El público* begins, with an image that recurs in *Viaje a la luna*: 'The man with the veins appears in the street and freezes as if crucified with his arms outstretched. He moves forward by jump cuts' (71).

We are in a cinema and a theatre ruled by symbols as a store of knowledge: a cinema and a theatre in which Lorca glimpses a new form of stage performance which at the same time drinks from the fountains of the Spanish *auto sacramental*.

The images of *Viaje a la luna* begin and end with a white bed, a kind of biographical allegory. At the start we see a 'white bed against a grey wall. A dance of the numbers 13 and 22 takes place on the bedclothes. From two figures, they begin to multiply like tiny ants' (59). In the final scenes 'a bed appears and hands covering a dead man' (75). The numerology is not random: 'Love, love, love', neigh the three horses in *El público*. 'Love of the one with the two and love of the three which is suffocated by being one between two.'[4] Thirteen and twenty-two are two ages of adolescence and youth which are represented in two of the film's scenes. As in many of García Lorca's drawings, we contemplate characters with split identities. The *Viaje a la luna* is not a spatial voyage; it is a journey through the poetic mirror of time and light that is the moon of cold silver and the hidden shadow of water.

For years, a sombre curse has hung over attempts to locate Lorca's American manuscripts. Specialists and scholars have written pages and pages of doubts, approximations and brilliant ideas on the subject. In

---

[3] García Lorca, *Obras completas*, II, 647.
[4] Ibid., 639.

the case of *Poeta en Nueva York*, the mystery began with the first publication of the work in 1940, through José Bergamín in Mexico and the Norton edition in New York. Who has the manuscript which Lorca gave Bergamín in 1936 and today is thought to be in Mexico? Did Bergamín alter the order of poems? Many other mysteries surround his play *El público,* unedited until publication in the 1970s, through the lucid studies of Rafael Martínez Nadal, the friend to whom Lorca entrusted the manuscript before embarking on his last trip to Granada, where he was assassinated a few weeks later. This piece of theatre, 'impossible' though not unperformable, was finally premiered on 12 December 1986 in the Piccolo Theatre in Milan under Lluís Pasqual's direction, with costumes and set created by Fabià Puigserver, and with my collaboration. 'Theatre in the theatre' was our approach to the set, with the trapdoors open to show 'beneath the moon the fake goblets, the poison and the skull of theatres', curtains turned to stone-like fossils stranded in an orchestra pit of blue sand.

Three years later, in 1989, there appeared in Oklahoma, forgotten at the back of a drawer, the original script for *Viaje a la luna*. Until then, only inexact translations had been known. Seventy-two scenes were found, written by Lorca on small diary pages for the painter Emilio Amero, whom he got to know during his stay in New York. Spurred on by the experiences of the *avant-garde*, Amero invited the poet to write a film script. Lorca was certainly aware of the poetic, dynamic and psychoanalytical possibilities of the camera and must also have felt stimulated by seeing many prodigious works created in the then innovative medium of cinema. The script for *Viaje a la luna* shows awareness of the ideas of Eisenstein about montage as a collision of confrontational sequences; of the visions of Buster Keaton, Friedrich Murnau, Vsevolod Pudovkin, Erich von Stroheim, and Abel Gance; and of the visual rhythms of 1920s *avant-garde* film makers like René Clair, Man Ray, Marcel Duchamp and Fernand Léger. In that decade, painting and film found a fertile communion through techniques of revealing time through light and composition. Cinema made it possible, through movement, to visualise the convulsive acceleration of a new technological and urban society. Machines appear on the screen as abstract automatons, confronted by the human, rural world to which Lorca had always felt attached.

On his return to Mexico in the 1930s, it is known that Emilio Amero started shooting *Viaje a la luna*, but there is no evidence that he completed it. He also contributed photographs to a poetry journal, *Contemporáneos*, which was unfairly ignored in Spain. But did Amero shoot Lorca's original script? Does the filmed material exist somewhere? Or did it perhaps disappear in the fire at the Mexican film library in the early 1980s? Who knows. For the moment, my Mexican investigations have failed.

During Lorca's stay in New York, his friends Buñuel and Dalí presented in Paris the film *Un Chien andalou*, an extraordinary and innovative combination of poetic and filmic images. The poet probably never saw the film, but we know that he was angry at what he considered to be a personal slight, through a remark that Ian Gibson quotes in his invaluable biography of Lorca: 'Buñuel has made a tiny little shit of a film called *An Andalusian Dog*—and I'm the Dog.'[5] This explains an ironic letter that he sent Dalí from Granada on his return from America in 1930, after more than one year of letter-writing silence. In this letter, the poet tells the Catalan painter about the riches and successes that he has achieved in New York and invites him to spend some time in a city that was 'totally inverse and opposed in its form and dream to the now rotten neo-romanticism of Paris.' He finishes with a line destined to make Dalí green with envy: 'I want you to know my news, like the short film I've made with a black New York poet, which will be premiered when I return in a wonderful cinema on Eighth Street where they screen all the Russian and German productions.' But Lorca never returned to New York.

Beyond veneration for the film as a relic, disentangling the glittering enigmas of *Viaje a la luna* by recreating its images has been a fascinating task for me. An undertaking to distil its essence, to silhouette its poetic suggestions, to apply different filmic processes to let the script itself reveal Lorca's own conception, secretive and inexplicable, but in no way unintelligible. Making the poet's idea visible allows us to see pictorial, filmic processes of virtual reality and of image editing. His unusual approach makes it appropriate to use,

---

[5] Ian Gibson, *Federico García Lorca: a life* (London: Faber and Faber, 1989), 229.

without anachronism, both the virtual technology of the late twentieth century and more traditional forms. It is a representation of representations in which the drawn is juxtaposed with the filmed. The powerful text makes Lorca's suggestions contemporary, for they transcend the decline of surrealist iconography, now made obsolete by the visual saturation of advertising imagery and cybernetic virtuality. A literal interpretation of the surrealist instructions would diminish the film and Lorca's vision. His magnetic images must be allowed to flow to an exact rhythm, to reveal the underworld of desire and its frustration, on a voyage that takes us from the microcosm to a reflection of the stars: the freedom of man to 'build his desire through coral vein or heavenly nude; tomorrow, loves will be rocks and time a sleeping breeze through the branches.'

Translated by Sebastian Doggart

Irish ReLorcations

Colin Teevan

The first half-way decent play that I wrote, and some might say the last, was entitled *The Murder of Federico García Lorca*.[1] This play was based firmly in my own fancy and spurious whim. It told the story of Lorca's last night alive, spent under the armed guard of Franco's troops. To pass the hours before the inevitable, Lorca encourages his guard to act out the story of Don Quixote with him. With Lorca as the dreaming knight, the young Francoist as Sancho, this was a love story spiced with politics, death, intrigue and a detective who, on a mission to root out subversives, discovers that he himself is his own subverter and arrests himself. No doubt it would have been a masterpiece had I known a little more about writing plays at the time.

Although I do hope to someday return to the material, the reason I am relating this story now is to both ask and, of course, supply possible answers to the question of why a then young and aspiring Irish writer like myself would choose to write his first play about the apparently Spanish writer Federico García Lorca?

You will have noticed that I said 'apparently' Spanish. For Lorca is one of the few truly great playwrights who, in reaching the zenith of his profession bilocated, or in this case 'bilorcated'; one self remaining a Spanish poet, the other self going on to achieve that state of playwriting perfection known in the business as Irishness. Thus, there were in fact two Lorcas; one Spanish, one Irish.

Not many playwrights have achieved this feat. We Irish are an insular, xenophobic bunch. We distrust people who do not come from the same side of a city as ourselves, let alone the same side of the water. In fact, in my family we distrusted siblings who sat on the other side of the dinner table. When the Irish do embrace foreigners, it generally has a negative causality; we only embrace the European

---

[1] 'The Murder of Federico García Lorca', never published, produced at the Bedlam Theatre, Edinburgh (December 1989) by E.U.T.C.

Union as a way of avoiding embracing the more proximate Britain; we embrace all things American because they're not English ... I'm not sure I should go further with this line of reasoning, but you get the drift. Irish peoples' appreciation of foreign playwriting is equally xenophobic. I can think of only two other foreign playwrights whose work has been so admired that they have been granted an Irish self, let alone held in such esteem that they are regularly produced; they are Liam O'Shakespeare and Antony O'Chekhov. That is the Liam O'Shakespeare who wrote tragedies about doomed mythical Celtic leaders such as Macbeth and Lear. He is nothing to William Shakespeare, Tudor propagandist and general peddler of bawdiness and smut. Similarly Antony O'Chekhov was a member of the fading landed Irish Ascendency and nothing to the socially concerned Russian doctor who wrote wickedly subtle comedies about human aspiration and self obsession. No, Antony O'Chekhov wrote moving plays about his doomed Anglo-Irish class and these plays are absolutely adored by the Dublin middle-class Catholics who would simply die to be a doomed Anglo-Irish Protestant.[2]

As you can see, when it comes to granting a playwright Irishness, we Irish are also very selective as to the bits of a writer's *œuvre* we wish to adopt and the bits they can keep. In this way, when it came to dividing up the opus between the Spanish Lorca and the Irish Lorca we see that the Spanish Lorca could keep the poetry (we've more fecking poets than we know what to do with), the experimental drama (we're more meat and two veg. when it comes to de 'tee-ay-ter') and the surrealism (sure God love the poor beggar); socialism never milked a cow, and as for the homosexuality—well, the less said ...

No, the Irish Lorca was author of just three plays, honest to God rural plays, in the manner of the great John B. Keane—only with fewer funny bits: *Bodas de sangre*, *Yerma* and *La casa de Bernarda Alba*. And these plays owe their very existence to the work of the writers of the Irish National Theatre Society.

The influence of the works of John Millington Synge on the emerging young Irish playwright Federico García Lorca has long been identified

---

[2] The celebrated comic actress, Roaleen Lenihan, epitomised this mindset in revue in the early 1980s with her song, 'I wish I was a Protestant'.

and has received much attention. The first act of cultural acquisition in the name of Mother Ireland came as far back as 1939 when the Argentinian-based Irish academic, Patrick O. Dudgeon, first wrote on the similarities between Synge's *Riders to the Sea* and Lorca's *Bodas de sangre*, after seeing the latter in Buenos Aires.[3] The extent of that influence has since been elaborated upon by critics from Edwin Honig and Alfredo de la Guardia in 1944 to (more recently and more circumspectly) the one Irish and now Spanish critic, Ian Gibson, in his biography of Lorca.[4] Jean J. Smoot in her *The Poets and Time* compares the work of the two writers in question directly. Briefly summarising her evidence, it is clear that in 1920–1921 Lorca and his friend, the poet Miguel Cerón Rubio, spent much time studying and discussing *Riders to the Sea*. Lorca himself is believed to have contemplated doing his own translation of *The Playboy of the Western World* and producing it with his 'Club Teatral de Cultura'. Further to this there is the evidence of the plays themselves. The world of Lorca's three rural tragedies and the plays of J.M. Synge have several striking similarities: both set their plays in poor, rural, almost pagan communities far from the affectations of urban bourgeois society, close to what Honig calls the 'elemental passions'.[5] The storylines of *Riders to the Sea* and *Bodas de sangre* are at first glance very similar—mothers who have lost husbands and all but one son, lose that son—and the characters of these mothers are very similar in both plays; and, as Ian Gibson points out, on the realisation of their final son's death they utter almost identical lines, Maurya in *Riders to the Sea* saying 'They're all gone now' and the Mother in *Bodas de sangre* 'They're all dead now.'[6] When these last remaining sons are gone, we sense that for both women the functions of their lives are over. It is arguable, though, that the reason the mothers are similar is that they are both archetypal mothers, without any function beyond being mothers, so it is in their

---

[3] Jean J. Smoot, The Poets and Time: a comparison of plays by John Millington Synge and García Lorca (Madrid: José Porrúa Turanzas, 1978), 1.
[4] Ian Gibson, *Federico García Lorca* (London: Faber and Faber, 1989), 339–41.
[5] Edwin Honig, *García Lorca* (Norfolk, Connecticut: New Directions, 1944), 214–15.
[6] Gibson, 340.

lack of character rather than psychologically verifiable character that they are similar.

Smoot, in what is a thought-provoking study, goes on to tease out similarities between *The Playboy of the Western World* and *La casa de Bernarda Alba*—as regards representations of repressive societies—and between *In the Shadow of the Glen* and *Yerma*, in that both plays deal with women attempting to free themselves from barren relationships. Smoot also compares *Doña Rosita la soltera* to Synge's unfinished *Deirdre of the Sorrows*, interpreting both as contemplations on the tragedy of time. Whatever the similarities, the analogies are less exact than those between *Riders to the Sea* and *Bodas de sangre*. It is undoubtedly clear that Synge's work had some influence on the later works of Lorca—most especially *Bodas de sangre* and *Yerma*—in their depiction of a pagan, peasant world, where people, living close to nature, are involved in elemental struggles with nature itself, their own natures and the nature of the repressive society in which they live.

In terms of language there are also similarities; in these late plays Lorca discovers a poeticised version of his native South on stage.[7] Perhaps Synge's work helped convince Lorca of the theatrical possibilities of this dialect; however, Lorca had already achieved such an effect in his poetry, most noticeably his *Poema del cante jondo* and *Romancero gitano*, so such a development was also intrinsic to his own development as a writer.

While Synge is the most obvious influence amongst the Irish dramatists on Lorca, there are many other social and socio-theatrical, if there is such a thing, similarities between Lorca's Spain and the Ireland that produced the writers of the National Theatre Society. Ireland and Spain at the turn of the century had much in common: both were predominantly Catholic, agricultural, peasant societies—apart, of course, from their industrialist, separatist North Easts. Both, too, were peripheral to the progressive, industrial, urban European experience. Ibsen, Wedekind, Strindberg, Maeterlinck, not to mention the London-based Irish playwrights, Wilde and Shaw, are all, whatever their

---

[7] I think one has only to look at the Kiltartanese of some of Lady Gregory's and Yeats's peasant efforts to see how patronising and affected such an experiment could be.

politics, urban bourgeois writers, generally detailing an urban experience for urban bourgeois audiences and largely, though not exclusively, through a naturalist or 'realist' aesthetic. When the rural Irish were represented it was in terms of racial stereotypes, even by Irishmen like Dion Boucicault.

Ireland and Spain immediately prior to these respective periods also had little indigenous, innovative, creative theatrical activity. As Professor Gwynne Edwards argues elsewhere in this volume, Spanish theatre seemed content to ape the realism generally current on the European stage at the time, while Irish theatre in the 1890s was almost wholly imported from England, even when written by Anglo-Irish exiles.

It was perhaps in reaction to the presentation of alien worlds or stereotypical versions of their own world in non-indigenous forms that the writers at the centre of the Irish National Theatre movement, largely under the inspired leadership of W.B. Yeats, felt impelled to create a new theatre that reflected what they at least believed to be the reality of a largely rural national experience.[8] The writers of the National Theatre Society continually sought to develop a non-bourgeois aesthetic which might reflect the society which they wrote about. Synge's classical background has been well documented in several works[9] and stressed in recent productions such as The Abbey's *Well of the Saints* of 1993 which, in Joe Vanek's design was played out on a tatty, Irish peasant version of the Greek σκηνη. Similarly, Sean O'Casey, whose early, perhaps more famous works adhered to a naturalist style, continually pushed the aesthetics of his own theatre away from this starting-point towards expressionism. Yeats himself continually experimented, working his way through a myriad of international collaborators—Ezra Pound, Edward Gordon Craig, Michio Ito and Ninette de Valois,[10] to name but a few—and repeatedly making use of classical, non-bourgeois

---

[8] Though, ironically, under Yeats in the early years they remained generally urban-based bourgeois writers presenting the works to the Dublin and London bourgeoisie.
[9] Not least in Smoot, 13-63.
[10] Coincidentally, Dame Ninette de Valois celebrated her 100th birthday in the same month as Lorca and celebrations for her birthday coincided with the Lorca Fiesta.

forms such as dance, mask, abstract design and movement. Yeats, a poet-playwright like Lorca, shared with the Andalusian an interest in pushing the boundaries of theatrical representation. And quite separately from each other, it would seem at least, it was in the 1930s that they achieved their clearest theatrical vision. The political intention behind this restless search was to create a new, distinctive and indigenous theatrical aesthetic,[11] and found expression in a style or styles that drew heavily upon folk and classical forms rather than bourgeois traditions.

While Spain, unlike Ireland, did have a great and distinct theatrical tradition,[12] by the time Lorca was born in 1898, the Golden Age of Spanish Theatre was long gone, the family silverware long pawned and the Spanish were being relieved of the last vestiges of the empire by the United States. Lorca's work both as a playwright and a producer, most especially in his time in charge of La Barraca, drew enormously on Spain's various theatrical traditions.

Furthermore, while well versed in the classics of the Spanish Golden Age—as his choice of repertoire of Cervantes, Calderón and Lope de Vega for La Barraca's first season in 1931 demonstrated—Lorca's early plays seem to be more influenced by Spain's vulgar theatre traditions— puppet theatre, bawdy comedy and musical theatre.[13] Throughout the 1920s he toyed with traditional Spanish forms, often trying them in new or strange styles as in *Don Perlimplín* and *Don Cristóbal*, culminating in the two most formally and stylistically elaborate experiments—*El público* and *Así que pasen cinco años*. After working on these, however, he seems to have set about realising on stage a representation of the peasant world he had grown up in (albeit, like the writers of the Irish National Theatre Movement, as a privileged *voyeur* of that world).

[11] This said, the management of the Abbey Theatre in terms of direct engagement with politics always remained aloof.
[12] While Ireland had produced many of the finest playwrights in the English canon between 1700 and 1900, including Congreve, Farquhar, Sheridan, Boucicault, Wilde and Shaw, the traditions they tended to draw on are the traditions of the English stage. If they have anything in common it is their subtle subversion of these traditions rather than the forging of a distinct separate aesthetic.
[13] Lorca's use and development of characters, styles and technique from traditional Spanish puppet theatre is excellently demonstrated by Cariad Astles elsewhere in this volume.

This thematic departure led to a formal and stylistic departure. Both of these developments could be viewed as a result of his increasing politicisation as the left and the right began to square up to each other, and as Lorca himself began to be increasingly identified not only with leftist thinking, but also with the Republican government through such government-funded schemes as La Barraca.

Both Yeats and his fellow writers in the 1900s and Lorca and his fellow practitioners in the 1930s were therefore engaged in a political project, not only in the world they chose to represent on stage and how they sought to represent it, but also in the agendas of the theatrical movements they spearheaded. Both Yeats and Lorca found that the theatre in their respective countries was largely socially irrelevant and decided to create and produce theatre that was relevant. They saw theatre as both for and representing the community, rather than the individual—that is, they politicised the medium.[14]

The final similarity, and most tragically for Lorca, between Irish and Spanish society, was that both Lorca and the writers of the Irish National Theatre Movement were writing at times of huge civil ferment in their respective countries, and they were, whether they embraced the role or not, part of that civil ferment. These were times when the very identities of these countries were constantly and heatedly under debate. Repeatedly, in both the Irish and the Spanish plays, we see small communities where the prevailing orthodoxy is challenged and brought to a state of potential if not actual explosion. As can be seen by the Playboy riots in Dublin and the fact that the Francoists saw fit to murder Lorca, these plays were read as state of the nation addresses whether their authors intended them as such or not.

It is not hard, therefore, to see how the Hibernicisation of Lorca occurred; so much does he have in common with the writers of the Irish National Theatre Movement, you can almost see the Guinness moustache on him. Indeed, J.B. Trend in an essay on Lorca, argued that:

---

[14] It is noticeable that characterisation in Lorca, Synge, Yeats and Lady Gregory tends to be at the level of archetype, rather than the idiosyncratic individual of the more naturalist bourgeois theatre of Ibsen, Chekhov and Shaw. This would seem to echo the feeling that their works seek to represent communities rather than individuals.

The proper language for translating Lorca's plays is Anglo-Irish. Yet one looks in vain for that beautiful choice of simple words, and those appealing Anglo-Irish cadences, in the translations of Lorca's plays that are printed and performed.[15]

The Spanish Lorca, however, while undoubtedly influenced by the theatrical project of Yeats, Synge and company, differs fundamentally from these writers in three broad areas: in the interests of alliteration, they are sun, sex and socialism.

The first of these is self-evident. Sun pervades the work of García Lorca. It is an elemental force of nature; on the one hand, nurturing and life-giving, but also, if trapped inside an airless house, for example, it is suffocating, parching and relentless—which sounds more like what the rain represents in Ireland than sun. The director Lynn Parker's adaptation of *La casa de Bernarda Alba*[16] attempted to transplant the play to Cavan. From the moment it began, it had a hard job selling us the idea that there was a blistering heat wave outside. And it stretched the bounds of the suspension of our disbelief to believe that seven young Irish girls and their mammy included would not be rushing out of the house to offer up their white and freckled skin for ritual burning by the sun regardless of who'd just passed away.

Flippancy aside, the sun's role as life-giver and life force is intimately tied up in Lorca's work with the whole theme of sexuality, reproduction and regeneration. In *La casa de Bernarda Alba* the blotting out of the sun echoes the enforced repression of the daughters' sexuality. In *Yerma*, it is in Juan's house that Yerma is trapped, but out in the sun that she meets the two people who offer her potential means of escape—the Old Pagan Woman and her lover Víctor. The final scenes, between magic and reality, are set at daybreak, echoing also the tension between the absolute despair and absolute release of the situation. In *Bodas de sangre*, the Bride's relationships are suggested by her relationship to the sun. She lives in a 'cave' at the outset when she is clearly still yearning for her secret, hence dark, love, Leonardo. The marriage scene takes place in the sunshine to her socially acceptable

---

[15] J.B. Trend, 'Lorca', *Lorca, a collection of critical essays*, ed. Manuel Durán (Englewood Cliffs, NJ: Prentice-Hall, 1962), 47.
[16] Charabanc Theatre Company, Belfast, 1993.

Bridegroom, but her secret desires overcome her and she elopes with Leonardo to the dark, night-time forest where the two men will duel it out for her.[17]

I'm sure it is no mistake that in Freudian theory the forest has long been associated with sexuality. The pulsating sexuality of these pieces is unmistakable, as is the politico-sexual agenda. There is a very clear message concerning sexuality in these plays: the repression by society of sexual desire, which is associated with the individual's freedom, leads to tragedy. Perhaps it was his experience as a homosexual in an oppressively homophobic culture that led to the recurrence of this sexual subtext in the work of Lorca. So well had Irish society succeeded in repressing sexuality, that desire is hardly evident in the early work of Yeats at all; his version of romantic love seems quite divorced from elemental sexual passion. Indeed, these works are quite aphysical. Later works, such as *King of the Great Clock Tower*, do suggest far greater sexual desires; though these desires are detailed through the symbolism of the piece and no explicit passionate interchange occurs between the characters of the Queen and the Stroller. I think Yeats's idea of love was too ideal and rarefied for his characters ever to be driven by a physical sexual imperative. Even in his later years as he dabbled in monkey glands and hermaphroditism, evident in such work as the Crazy Jane poems, most of his sexual encounters still seem to take place in his head and are full of regret rather than physical urgency.

As regards Synge, it is perhaps here, most of all, that the comparison between his and Lorca's work falls down. While the recurring motivation for action in Lorca's work is sexual/reproductive desire, in Synge's work it is most often grubby money. There is little sexuality in evidence at all in *Riders to the Sea*;[18] Bartley insists on going to sea so soon after his brother Michael has died on it and breaking his mother's heart to boot because: 'This is the one boat going for two weeks or beyond it, and the fair will be a good fair for horses' (21). The only

---

[17] In Jacqueline Cockburn's paper on Lorca and Picasso, she highlights the influence on Lorca of extreme contrast between light and dark in Spanish still-life painting. It would seem that this extreme contrast is something which he also seeks to achieve in his theatre.

[18] All quotations from John Millington Synge's work are from *Plays, Poems and Prose* (London: J.M. Dent, 1941), pp. 301.

thing he shows any interest in, in his brief appearance, is money. It is true that Lorca's Bridegroom and the Bride's father do view marriage as a financial transaction. They talk about the size of their respective estates and their relative value. This is, however, in contrast to Leonardo's great and reciprocated passion for the Bride. Passion and sexuality are motivations so strong they will override all financial prudence. In the work of Synge, money is such a strong passion, it will lead men to risk their lives for it. Interestingly, the sea, in Freudian theory, is associated with the mother and the mother's womb. Thus, while Lorca's men die in the forest of sexuality, Synge's men drown in the amniotic fluid of their Irish Mammy's womb.

In the Shadow of the Glen would appear to be about the intended and eventual adultery of Nora Burke in the light of her loveless marriage to the old farmer Dan Burke. However, we should be warned, there is no sunshine here; the Tramp indeed speaks of the 'great rain' outside. This is adultery Irish style—it's all to do with money and nothing to do with sex. Nora makes clear why she married the old Dan: 'What way would I live and I an old woman, if I didn't marry a man with a bit of a farm and cows on it, and a sheep on the back hills' (11). It only struck her after her marriage that she might like a few kids. This is in stark contrast to Yerma, who sees children as the actual fulfilment of her marriage. Michael Dara states his love for Nora only after he has counted the presumed-dead Dan's money, and his chat-up line is, 'And they were saying at the fair my lambs were the best lambs and I got a grand price for I'm no fool now at making money' (12). As for the Tramp, with whom she eventually leaves, while Nora admires his fine words, she does not seem driven by an overwhelming passion, the like of which drives Yerma to do such dreadful deeds. True, Nora realises that she would be better off anywhere other than with Dan Burke, but Michael Dara is not interested in her now that she has no money, so there's nothing for it but the Tramp, and his fine talk is all very well, but she is worried about her material comforts: 'Thinking it's myself will be wheezing that time with lying down under the heavens when the night is cold' (16).

The Playboy of the Western World is about the romance of Christy Mahon and Pegeen Mike. But while Pegeen's love for the supposed parricide is undoubtedly sincere, at least as long as his story holds, Christy is repeatedly impressed by the size of her jugs—beer jugs, that is—and the number of bottles behind the bar: 'Well, this'd be a fine place to be my whole life talking out with swearing Christians, in place of my old cat and dog' (128). It puts one in mind of the old joke: 'What's the definition of an Irish homosexual? Someone who prefers women to Guinness.'

What romance there is in *The Playboy of the Western World* is based on the fantasy of Christy's parricidal deeds, not on a sexual and emotional imperative as in all of Lorca's later work. For instance, compare the steadfastness and depth of passion with which Doña Rosita clings to her fiction compared to Pegeen's rapid dismissal of Christy when he is found out to be spinning her a yarn. Christy too is quick to drop Pegeen and blithely romps off into the sunset with his Dad at the end. Pegeen and Doña Rosita have both fallen in love with fictions but whereas Doña Rosita's tragedy is the tenacity with which she clings to that fiction, even after she knows it to be untrue, Pegeen's tragedy is that she was had and knows she was had. At the end of *Doña Rosita* one is left with the feeling that love is something even bigger than people; at the end of *The Playboy of the Western World*, I cannot help but feel that Synge is suggesting that love is intricately bound up with the suspension of disbelief.

Another Hiberniciser of Lorca, Katie Davis, compares Lorca's work to O'Casey's in *Federico García Lorca and Sean O'Casey*.[19] I do not have the space here to go into the many flaws in this thesis, but suffice it to point out that O'Casey is another writer whose dramas hinge upon money rather than sexual passion. In *Juno and the Paycock*, for instance, Mary might have had a moment of passion with Bentham, but it is money, not sex, that will tear the family apart.

One Irish playwright of that earlier period who did write about passion and sexuality as a major motivating force was, of course, Oscar Wilde, at least in *Salome* and *The Importance of Being Earnest*. But it is noticeable that he chose to write *Salome* in French and whatever passion there is in *Earnest* is evident largely only in code and quite often that code dictates that the characters express the opposite of what they are feeling. Lorca, identifying Wilde's coyness about passion, claimed in

---

[19] Katie Brittain Adams Davis, *Federico García Lorca and Sean O'Casey: powerful voices in the wilderness* (Salzburg: Universität Salzburg, 1978).

1930 that he was going to write a play, the never-completed 'Destruction of Sodom', which would make Wilde appear 'an out-of-date, fat and pusillanimous old queen.'[20] (Though how Lorca intended that a play could make someone appear fatter than they already appeared to be we will never know.)

The final major difference between the works of Lorca and those of the writers of the Irish National Theatre movement was in both the politics within their plays and their attitude to their audiences. It would take a far longer work than this to discuss the politics of each of the plays mentioned here; however, it does appear to me that in his three rural tragedies, Lorca represents an 'everyperson' individual whose fundamental passions are at odds with the prevailing orthodoxy. These are plays about injustice and most often a society's injustice to an individual's justifiable and authentic passions. The conflict results in tragedy—as it was to end for both Lorca and Spain.

The work of the National Theatre writers is far less clear, but one prevailing motif does appear to run through the works of Synge, O'Casey, Lady Gregory and Yeats: if Lorca's work posits a kind of Us against Them, the work of the Irish dramatists suggests an Us against Us. They portray communities divided against themselves, scrabbling for pennies while the evils of real poverty, injustice or colonialism rage on. Perhaps all these writers, as Protestants, and all somewhat alienated from the society in which they lived, felt it was the very exclusivity of the new Catholic nationalism that was the flaw at the heart of Irish society. Lorca, it must be remembered, was of the same religion as his peasant subjects, something that comes through not only in his sympathy and understanding of their beliefs, however pagan, but also through the very Catholic symbols and sentiments at work in his plays.

Furthermore, under Yeats, The National Theatre Society maintained an aloof attitude towards its audience. When the first production of the National Theatre, *The Countess Cathleen*, for example, was booed and Yeats's friends urged him to defend and perhaps even explain his work, Yeats's telling reaction pointed towards the direction in which his

---

[20] Luis Cardoza y Aragón, 'Federico García Lorca', *El Nacional* (Mexico, 1936), quoted in Gibson (1989), 293.

politics would lead him by the 1930s 'Literature is always justified and needs no justification'.[21]

Whatever the justification for Yeats's outrage, he always considered himself superior to his audience. In his verse 'On Those Who Hated *The Playboy of the Western World*', he characterised the Dublin theatre audience as eunuchs not fit to touch the garments of J.M. Synge. This is in stark contrast to Lorca's principles in founding La Barraca, stated in *El Sol* in December 1931: 'To help educate people who for centuries had been deprived of seeing plays.' While this might appear patronising, Lorca did not tell his audience what they should and should not like. He programmed plays that he thought they might respond to rather than plays he thought good for them. As Gibson argues, his programming of Calderon's *Life is a Dream* in his first season is testimony to that.[22] The Church objected to what they saw as a 'Catholic' work being presented by a 'Marxist' group and organised protests against the production throughout La Barraca's first tour. Lorca did not pander to his audience, often putting contemporary twists on such revered classics, most famously Lope de Vega's *Fuente Ovejuna*, where all references to Ferdinand and Isabella, symbols of Catholic Law and Order, were cut.[23]

La Barraca was a collective. Everyone, even Lorca, dressed in boiler suits and helped out with all aspects of production, not only acting and set construction but also driving and catering. After we have tried to imagine Yeats in a boiler suit, I think we can safely say that the National Theatre Society which emerged from the Irish Literary Theatre and went on to become the Abbey Theatre, was founded by members of the élite, middle and governing classes, and always remained a hierarchy, an institution through which writers largely from one class could address the nation. Most importantly, it was an institution through which Yeats himself could address the Irish people. And after the founding of the Free State, the government, realising the propaganda

---

[21] Quoted in Adrian Frazier, *Behind the Scenes: Yeats, Horniman and the struggle for the Abbey Theatre* (Berkeley and London: University of California Press, 1990), xiv.
[22] Gibson, 323.
[23] Ibid., 354-55.

potential of such an institution, contributed towards the running of it and soon appointed a former Minister of Finance, Ernest Blythe, as Artistic Director.

Auden once said that 'each Nation fashions Ancient Greece in its own likeness', and perhaps this is also true of Lorca: perhaps we have been guilty of fashioning a Lorca in the image of an Irish writer. It has been traditional amongst many critics and happily accepted by Irish critics and theatre practitioners and theatregoers alike that Lorca's finest works for theatre are so good they could be Irish. I hope I have made a case for some aspects of their Spanishness. To fashion Lorca as voice of any marginalised situation is to obscure the uniqueness and idiosyncrasy of his work.

However, if they are so un-Irish and idiosyncratic, how does one explain their extraordinary popularity in Ireland in the last ten years, both to prospective Irish translators, Irish critics, such as Ian Gibson, and at the Irish box office. *Bodas de sangre* alone has been translated by the poet Brendan Kennelly, the novelist Dermot Healy, David Johnston, writer and broadcaster Aidan Matthews, playwright Frank McGuinness, not to mention comedian and actor Owen O'Neill. These are the few that I have been able to unearth. There have been at least five separate productions of the play in the Republic of Ireland alone in the last ten years—a country with a population of three and a half million. *La casa de Bernarda Alba* and *Yerma* have received several productions and translations each, though admittedly fewer than *Bodas de sangre*.

While, of course, some of this interest is explained by the fact that, like several other writers, Lorca's work briefly came out of copyright in the late eighties and early nineties, it must be observed that there was no similar rush to produce Yeats's plays, nor even Joyce's play *Exiles*, all of which similarly came out of copyright, let alone plays by some Johnny foreigner.

I suppose part of the appeal must be that these three great plays offer an Irish audience a fully recognisable world—there is hardly an Irish person I know who is more than one spit from the bog. And even if we are more inclined to live in towns, we have transplanted the gossiping, in-fighting, *fiestaing* from the bog to the town. And Ireland today, despite the marauding Celtic Tiger, remains a tribal rather than a class-divided society. Lorca also offers the Irish audience a recognisable theatrical world—we know this world from Synge, Yeats and Lady Gregory down through J.B. Keane to Brian Friel. Hence there is a certain security in these works.

However, Ireland, both North and South, has been undergoing radical social transformation in the last twenty years. In the South the authority of the Church has crumbled in a succession of debates, referenda and scandals over issues most often to do with sex—abortion, contraception, divorce, homosexuality—as well as the almost daily revelation of child abuse. The long suppression of discussion, let alone action, on such issues by the Catholic Church has finally been thrown off. Most often these debates have centred on the roles and the rights of women. On all these areas of intense debate, these plays of Lorca speak to us in a way the writers of the National Theatre Society do not.

In the North the repression has been of a different sort—it has been the repression of social progress by, on the one hand, an ultra-conservative Calvinism and, on the other, by an ultra-conservative paramilitary nationalism. These forces have been completely male-orchestrated, to the near obliteration of the female voice from public debate. Lorca's plays allow us to see both these repressed emotions and what happens to them, often through marginalised female characters. Yet again, he speaks to Irish people but with the aptness that is perhaps only allowed or digestible from a foreigner. Perhaps in reality, it is the Ireland of ten years ago that resembles the Spain of the 1930s.

So, by roundabout ways I arrive back at my start—why was the first serious play I chose to write about Federico García Lorca? I suppose my motivation in writing a play about Lorca and his murder by the forces of reaction could be seen as my own reaction to both my upbringing in Ireland and living away from it for the first time. I suppose, in throwing off the prejudices and internal repressions of the conservative Catholic society I had grown up in, I chose to write about a writer who depicted the unconscious of a society's doomed attempt to throw off its own forces of repression. I am thankful to say that the two Irelands' subsequent attempts have not been so doomed and that Lorca's Spain is in a state of rude good health. W.H. Auden, a poet whom I have quoted, wrote an elegy for W.B. Yeats, whose name has also arisen. It concludes:

> Follow poet, follow right
> To the bottom of the night,
> With your unconstraining voice
> Still persuade us to rejoice;
>
> With the farming of a verse
> Make a vineyard of the curse,
> Sing of human unsuccess
> In a rapture of distress;
>
> In the deserts of the heart
> Let the healing fountain start,
> In the prison of his days
> Teach the free man how to praise.[24]

Lorca was another such poet. A man for all nations. *Slainte*, Federico.

---

[24] W.H. Auden, 'In memory of W.B. Yeats' (1939), *Collected Poems* (London: Faber and Faber, 1976), 198.

Looking for Lorca: a legacy in the Americas
Caridad Svich

birth of a poet

>Cien años.
>Hace cien años
>nació un poeta
>con una corona de rosas
>sobre su cabeza
>y unas espinas aterciopeladas. El poeta cantaba
>en su cuna.
>El poeta lloraba.
>Y su grito, su canto
>se oyen
>este día de mañana. Esta mañana de cien anos
>desde que nació
>el poeta.[1]

In 1898, a year that would give us George Gershwin and Bertolt Brecht, Federico García Lorca was born in Granada. In 1998, on the centennial of his birth, and sixty-two years after his death, Hispanic playwrights in the Americas celebrate his legacy as they search for his spirit in their work.

Contemporary United States-based Hispanic dramatists like María Irene Fornes, Migdalia Cruz and José Rivera, along with their counterparts in Central and South America, have regarded Federico García Lorca's work as a seminal influence and inspiration for the re-visioning of a new theatre. Drawing on Lorca's experimental work, in

---

[1] 'A hundred years. / A hundred years ago / a poet was born / with a crown of roses / on his head / and velvety thorns. The poet sang / in his cradle. / The poet cried. / And his cry, his song / can be heard / still today. On this morning a hundred years / since the birth / of the poet.'

particular, a new generation of playwrights has sought to extend the vocabulary of dramatic writing, and expand on 'Lorcan' fusions of time and space, realism and symbolism, poetry and prose, music and masque. Whether directly acknowledging García Lorca's influence or not, these dramatists have taken elements and ideas from his work and forged a 'hybrid' theatre that is both Hispanic and American, and that is still very much in the making, thus developing Lorca's 'theatre for tomorrow' into a theatre for today.

alphabetical Lorca

Alma, grito, duende. Fluid time: past, present, and future. Compressed time: raging against the elements, hurling against walls. Blood, fire, and sand. A theatre of elements. A theatre of song. Exasperated clowns, wooden swords, and merciless violence. In Lorca, death is always real, resurrection is not possible. A Catholic theatre. Of priests and satyrs. Ceremonies and crimes. A theatre of images where green walls, white roses and black wedding gowns appear out of the air and talk to the moon. A theatre of women. Destroyed, destroying, triumphant, and wilful. Where men are complex, and weak. Virile and mysterious. An erotic theatre which places sexuality at its centre, denouncing cruelty and the contradictions of society's basic institutions. Authority be damned. A theatre of nature. Hell and Spain. A theatre for the world.

The first time I heard Lorca's name was in my Spanish class in high school in Charlotte, North Carolina. My teacher told us there was a poet whose work we should read. His name was García Lorca and he was born in 1898. 'Read this', he said as he tossed a slim volume into our eager hands, 'and report on it tomorrow.'

It was a collection of poems entitled *Romancero gitano.* I looked at this slim book with a mixture of fear and awe. 'Oh odd-shaped moon against a silver sky,' I thought, 'what am I to make of you?' They were 'ballads', our teacher told us, 'songs'. Did we know what 'cante jondo' was? I had heard bits of flamenco when I was a child. My grandparents were from Spain—Galicia. And, of course, I had seen the Saturday morning cartoons on television, animated figures stomping and clapping and throwing their voices, but no, I did not know deep song, where the throat reaches back into a place unknown and produces a sound that has no name, except for 'the blues'. Yes, I had heard the blues. And the Gypsy ballads went into me, and ignited something in my brain.

'Lorca was a poet,' our teacher said, 'one of the greats. And a playwright, too'. Is it any coincidence that I started writing plays shortly after reading Lorca's work for the first time?

origin: imprint

From this early contact with García Lorca's work and subsequent personal rediscoveries of his work over time, certain elements began to make themselves manifest in my own writing for the theatre: inscriptions on the body, the public versus the private, the elements versus human nature, beauty as aesthetic and form, dream as structure, locating the elemental in the strange and the fantastical in the commonplace, the art of burning yourself through until there is no trace.

With each Lorca play I have translated into English—*Don Perlimplín, Así que pasen cinco años, Quimera, El paseo de Buster Keaton*—the struggle and responsibility of the translation process illuminates the difficulty of negotiating not only Spanish and English but also the dilemma of how to interact with a mystery over time—how a text can give you only a phantom memory, whereby one is always constantly in the shadows, chasing after Lorca.

vision

'SELAH: Spirit is vision: fragment and memory reflected in the mind's eye. You got to see it. Inside you. It's in the heart where we see things. It's in the heart where we lay to rest trouble and joy'.[2] Lorca's ghost came to visit me as I wove together the tapestry of scenes which would become *Alchemy of Desire/Dead-Man's Blues*, which premiered at the Cincinnati Playhouse in Ohio in 1994. After years of writing and exploring different themes in my work, it was Lorca, and the memory of how I felt when I came upon his work for the first time in high

---

[2] Caridad Svich, *Alchemy of Desire / Dead-Man's Blues* in *Out of the Fringe*, María Teresa Marrero and Caridad Svich, eds (New York: TCG Publications/Nick Hern Books, 1999), 58.

school, that made me return to a place in my writing of 'deep song', and allowed me to rediscover the joy of creating a text which could incorporate poetry, song, ritual, image, and traditional Western narrative—the kind of text that is still considered 'alternative' today in some circles, even though its roots go beyond Lorca to the *autos sacramentales* of medieval Spain and the work of Euripides and the Greeks.

A story about a grieving war widow, and the four neighbourhood women who console her, *Alchemy of Desire/Dead-Man's Blues* is 'Lorcan' in spirit, owing a small but significant debt to *La casa de Bernarda Alba* as well as other works by Lorca. As Maria Delgado has noted in her eloquent introductory essay 'From the UK: A European perspective on Latino theater' in the anthology of Latino plays and performance texts *Out of the Fringe*, the play *Alchemy of Desire/Dead-Man's Blues* has a 'female chorus that evokes [...] the washerwomen of *Yerma*. [...] As with the female protagonists of *Bodas de sangre*, for the women of the play the loss of lovers, husbands, and children is a brutal fact of their existence.' However, this play does not merely acknowledge its debt to Lorca, it is also part of an emerging body of Hispanic performance literature that is 'hybrid' in nature and slowly changing the face of American drama.

That Latino playwrights have drawn blood from Lorca's work to create their own is important to the understanding of a theatre whose history is only beginning to be fully documented. Hispanic drama, which encompasses the work of United States-born or -based Latinos and its relationship to the work of their colleagues in Central and South America, as it responds to or diverges from the Spanish dramatic tradition, has taken Lorca at his word and broken free of mainstream theatrical constraints. However, especially in the United States, this has been achieved without access to stage representations of Lorca's work outside of the primarily academic arena. García Lorca's theatre remains unknown to the general public. The major theatrical institutions have, for the most part, neglected to stage his work, refusing to acknowledge his importance as a world theatrical figure. This lack of access to the experience of witnessing Lorca's work in the performance arena has made his influence on United States-based Hispanic playwrights a purely literary one. As Lorca's work has been marginalised in the United States, it has also caused writers of Hispanic origin to be marginalised. Thus, it has left Hispanic playwrights looking for Lorca, and has made his legacy all the more poignant.

poet in the United States: where is Lorca?
'There's this code of honor that we all seem to be struggling with,' playwright José Rivera has noted, 'being Latino in the US is like being caught in the middle between tradition and non-tradition. But we have come to feel comfortable with contradiction.'[3] In a country with its own rich indigenous and Spanish colonial history, and an ever-increasing Hispanic population, mainstream culture, and therefore mainstream theatre, which encompasses United States regional theatre and the Mecca of New York, persists in de-valuing the works of the great Spanish dramatists from Calderón de la Barca to Valle-Inclán, Buero Vallejo and García Lorca, and today's adventurous playwrights like Paloma Pedrero and beyond.

If one were to look at a record of any given season over the last ten years, one would be hard pressed to find more than five major productions of García Lorca's work, and by 'major' I mean a production by a theatre which has considerable impact on its specific regional community and/or the national cultural radar, such as it is.

As critic Lindy Zesch as recently observed, 'The fact that the US is itself the fourth-largest Spanish-speaking country in the world has had little impact on our theatre and festival repertoires. Latin American plays are infrequently translated and produced, [and] theatres from Latin America rarely tour the US'.[4] The bulk of the presentations of Lorca's work can be found in the university arena, fuelled by students and academics eager to test the theatrical concepts posited by Lorca, especially in works like *Así que pasen cinco años* and *El público*. The rest of the presentations of his body of theatrical work have been shouldered by the nation's Hispanic theatres like Repertorio Español and Intar in New York, and Bilingual Foundation for the Arts in Los Angeles, companies which are regarded by the press and the larger 'official' theatrical community as theatres which exist merely to 'serve' the Latino community, as social work 'serves'. Thus, these brave

---

[3] Ed Morales, 'New World Order', *American Theatre* (May–June 1998), 43.
[4] Lindy Zesch, 'Viva Teatro!', *American Theatre* (May–June 1998), 24.

professional companies, which have spent as much as twenty-five to thirty years building an audience and struggling to solidify their reputation, are marginalised by their very existence.

To a generation of Latino dramatists raised in the United States, García Lorca's isolation has offered a curious kind of solace. His literary example, and thus his legend, have made him a banner figure, a totem, representing all those who have been artistically marginalised: queer Lorca; feminist Lorca; Lorca of Spain, the 'invisible' European country; Lorca of the strange.

geography: New York—Fornes, Cruz and Rivera

Cuban-born, New York-based dramatist María Irene Fornes' substantial body of work has made her a pioneer not only in Latino theatre but in American theatre as well. From her loose experimental works of the early 1960s, which include *Tango Palace* and *Promenades* to the flourishing of her mature period which begins with *Fefu and Her Friends* and continues with *Sarita* and *Abingdon Square*, Fornes has staked her own unique claim on the forging of a new theatrical identity in Hispanic theatre. Although she often cites Ibsen and Chekhov as her models, there is the undeniable stamp of Lorca's influence in her fluid dissection of time and space and of her characters' private and public personas, in the struggles her female heroines face, and in the hauntingly fatalistic endings she chooses for her plays.

Fornes draws less on Lorca's 'theatre of tomorrow' and more on the sense of repression, horror, blood and beauty of his rural tragedies. In Mae's struggle to define herself in *Mud*, for instance, there is an echo of *La casa de Bernarda Alba* and Adela's desire to break free of her tyrannical world. In *Sarita*, Fornes' titular heroine struggles against her own sexual desire and the forces of machismo which ultimately, as in *Bodas de sangre*, determine her fall. While this may be interpreted as reflective of a writer focusing on a specifically notorious aspect of Hispanic culture—its prevalent machismo and women's continuing difficulty to break free of its pervasiveness—Fornes is canny enough as a playwright to draw on a tradition of writing that has come before her, and use that tradition to continue to explore women's roles in society and women's roles in theatre.

FELA: A woman like me
loves a man,
only one,
and he must
run away.
He must forsake her.
He must forget her.
He must betray her.
And he must drink
And die alone.[5]

Fornes also uses particularly 'Lorcan' elements of image and song to propel a variety of her plays. In *Sarita*, Fela sings 'A Woman Like Me' to ironically describe her social situation. In *The Danube*, Fornes' image of the garden with its 'dried leaves [...] and cement pillar, the top of which is cut at a slant with a cloth sculpted over it. The word 'True' engraved on the base' (ibid., 53), recalls the garden of Lorca's *Don Perlimplín*. And as young Marion hangs perilously from a rope in *Abingdon Square* reciting Dante to strengthen her spirit, the force of the image recalls Yerma's defiant 'Que mi boca se quede muda' ('May I never speak again').[6]

In fact, Fornes' *Abingdon Square*, with its story of thwarted passion and self-discovery set in pre-World War I New York City, is the most 'Lorcan' of the plays in her œuvre. With the impending changes of the women's movement as a backdrop, Fornes reconnects to a political sensibility that is powerful but never didactic or self-conscious. As Marion, the central character, searches for her identity in other men, she slowly comes to terms with her own sexuality and individualism. Despite the confines of corsets and social codes, a society constricted by its own norms, the characters in *Abingdon Square* maintain a refreshing frankness of tone and spirit while speaking a language bold and

[5] María Irene Fornes, *María Irene Fornes: plays*, preface by Susan Sontag (New York: PAJ Publications, 1986), 104.
[6] Federico García Lorca, *Yerma, La casa de Bernarda Alba, Doña Rosita la soltera* (Madrid: Ediciones Novelas y Cuentos, 1974), 79.

delicate. There are sharp echoes of Lorca in Fornes' work, and in her now trademark cutting of scenes into indelible snapshots—poems—of different moments in her characters' lives, she is able to dissect both literary time and theatrical time in a manner Lorca was only beginning to explore in *Así que pasen cinco años* and *El público*.

Another writer based in New York who has been inspired by Lorca is the Bronx-born-and-bred Migdalia Cruz. She, along with José Rivera, is part of a generation of writers influenced by Fornes. Of Puerto Rican descent, Cruz explores with candour, feeling, and shocking intimacy the workings of characters at odds with life on the street, or characters who are caught in worlds that mirror or refract the world of fairy tales and historical novels. Moreover, she allows her characters to express their desires with an erotic fullness that allows for all taboos to be broken.

The gay and lesbian sensibility which is usually silenced in Latino culture comes to the fore in Cruz's work, as well as the work of an entire wave of Hispanic dramatists, who in looking for icons have found in Lorca the perfect gay 'martyr' to fetishise and idolise. That Lorca's homosexual sensibility was more complex than simple coding will allow seems to be a small point to a gallery of writers who have taken up his name for a political and literary cause. Migdalia Cruz, however, does not fully belong to that gallery. She is more interested in what Lorca repressed in his writings, what was underneath the surface of his texts, and in making these subterranean forces take centre stage in her work.

In her free adaptation of García Lorca's *La casa de Bernarda Alba* entitled *Another Part of the House*, which premiered at Classic Stage Company in New York in 1997, Cruz sets the action in Cuba in 1895 and makes the characters of Poncia and María Josefa the focal points for this re-telling of Lorca's story. Poncia and Bernarda have an overtly homoerotic relationship, and there is an incestuous feeling in this Alba house as the sisters play their desires against each other. 'For *Another Part of the House* [...] what I wanted to do was write all the unspoken stuff that Lorca didn't write—what I thought was underneath the play', Cruz has said; 'I felt that I wrote around the subtext and its viscera as opposed to its outside world form'.[7] Although this approach may strike

---

[7] Daedalus Howell, 'Play Right', *Sonoma County Independent* (30 October–5 November 1997), 3.

purists as crude, Cruz's exploration of *La casa de Bernarda Alba*'s subtext is a genuine reworking of Lorca's classic by a writer deeply influenced by his work. By making Poncia an Afro-Cuban slave, Cruz also heightens the class and racial divisions between servant and mistress, and thus makes their erotic union cross more than sexual boundaries.

> BERNARDA: Who taught you such a soothing touch? My fingers don't know how to move like that. You steal the pain right out of me.[8]

Migdalia Cruz offers her tribute to Lorca in the manner in which she builds on his characters' ignited passions and desires, and throughout her work, as she pushes her characters to confront each other in startling ways. Fusing her own sense of lyricism and beauty with Lorca's, she has created an emerging body of work that explores the savage and dark elements of the human psyche, creating a link to the brutal nature in much of the Spanish tragic canon.

Born in Puerto Rico but raised in New York, José Rivera has established his theatrical voice at the intersection of the Old World and the New World, at the juncture of the Americas. Freely admitting to drawing inspiration from the magic-realist tradition as well as Lorca, Calderón de la Barca, and American pop culture, Rivera's work is at its core syncretic, romantic and poetic.

Juxtaposing the suspended time of dreams and fantasy with the 'real' time of average daily life, Rivera finds an elastic way to contain multiple realities on a single plane in his plays. Nowhere is this more evident than in his chamber piece *Cloud Tectonics*. Premiering at the Actors Theatre of Louisville in 1995, *Cloud Tectonics* is a play about a mysterious pregnant young woman named Celestina del Sol and her encounter with a young man named Aníbal de la Luna, who may or may not be her future son. Evocative of Lorca's *El amor de don Perlimplín con Belisa en su jardín* and *Así que pasen cinco años*, Rivera creates a contemporary fable of romantic love that transcends time, even as it comments on it. Celestina is a character that functions as

---

[8] Migdalia Cruz, 'Another Part of the House', unpublished playscript (1997), 67.

mother, lover and sister in one. She is an echo of an echo of herself and of others' image of her.

> CELESTINA: How do you know what time feels like, Aníbal?... Is the organ for 'time' the heart? Is it the spinal cord, that silver waterfall of nerves and memories... Does 'time' have a sound? What bells, Aníbal, what vibrating string played by that virtuoso accompanies the passage of time?... Or is it just the invisible freight train that runs over you every single day... pieces so small they can't hold your soul to the earth anymore, and that's why you die? [9]

Rivera turns the question of time as it relates to the moments of conception, falling in love, even finding one's own language into a philosophical construct that holds his comic and tender play together, much as Lorca does in the masterful and more ambitious work *Así que pasen cinco años*.

While Lorca was expansive and playful in his visual sensibility, and in his ability to combine ceremony with action, Rivera as a younger, though established, Hispanic dramatist seeks to contain his worlds, even when they become nightmarish, as in his oft-produced play *Marisol*. A breakthrough of sorts for Rivera, *Marisol* is the play in which he allows himself as a writer to fully investigate the presentation of a world out of orbit. After early plays that toyed with notions of fluid time, ritual, and eroticism, *Marisol* uses the language of cyberpunk fiction to revitalise the Hispanic-American dramatic genre. Abandoned by her guardian angel, Marisol is caught in a Manhattan that is going up in flames, where a celestial Armageddon rages in the skies overhead. Recalling the more surreal elements of Lorca's work, the play is contained by the totality of its commitment to the nightmare into which Marisol falls. A hellish picaresque, *Marisol* is kin to *Poeta en Nueva York* as it presents an illuminating contemporary meditation on the perilousness of human existence in a fractured, garbage-ridden world.

Fornes, Cruz, and Rivera represent different imaginative territories where the spirit of Lorca's work resides. Separated by generation and

---

[9] José Rivera, *Cloud Tectonics* (New York: TCG Publications/Nick Hern Books, 1997), 21–22.

temperament, these dramatists have pushed at the walls of mainstream theatre in the United States, demanding, that Lorca's theatrical experiments of the 1920s and 1930s in Spain not be ignored. In so doing, they have encouraged a promising wave of younger Hispanic dramatists to seek their space both within and outside the margins set by mainstream culture. Performers and playwrights like Luis Alfaro and Nilo Cruz are breaking free of theatrical constraints levelled at them for being 'Hispanic' and are taking their inspiration not only from Lorca and his uniquely literary presence in the United States but from the dramatists who have made the breaking down of structural, formal, and content-specific taboos a necessary endeavour for the creation of a Hispanic-American performance literature.

It can also be argued that generations of non-Hispanic United States dramatists influenced by Lorca have allowed for the development of a Latino theatrical sensibility. Tennessee Williams, Edward Albee, Sam Shepard, Adrienne Kennedy, and to a lesser extent, the self-styled 'wordsmiths' like Mac Wellman and Len Jenkin, bred by the provocative explorations of the 1970s and 1980s performance art scenes in New York and San Francisco, have incorporated 'Lorcan' concepts and references into their works, offering Latino writers an opportunity to decode these references and seek out their origin, making of them what they will.

In a country where Lorca is virtually absent from the stage and relegated to the bookshelves and halls of universities' 'ivory towers', transformation and transmutation have been the method by which Lorca's work has found a way to be seen and heard. Acts of ventriloquism and sleight-of-hand can be detected in the works of many a Hispanic and non-Latino playwright. It is credit to Lorca's genius that these acts of homage only deepen the search for his work to be truly represented. In the United States, Lorca waits to be discovered.

a view from the Americas

If Lorca is the great known/unknown presence in Hispanic-American performance literature, the rest of the Americas have been embracing his work and building on its foundation for a long time. García Lorca's trips to Cuba and Argentina in the 1930s and the performance history of his plays there and elsewhere in Central and South America, spurred in part by Margarita Xirgu's theatrical ambassadorship of his work, have left an indelible mark on much of the theatre that has emerged since the untimely death of the poet.

In Argentina, where the theatrical tradition has been linked to the erratic politics of the country as well as the strong influence of the European *avant-garde*, Griselda Gambaro has distinguished herself as one of the world's pre-eminent theatrical voices. Like her United States counterpart, María Irene Fornes, Gambaro uses an episodic, 'snapshot' structure to tell her stories of women abused by and triumphant against authority.

Although her work is deeply rooted in Argentina, she is markedly influenced by Lorca, Ionesco, Beckett and Pinter. While her work hardly calls to mind Lorca's magic and delicacy, it does recall his poetry, heightened theatricality, unapologetic emotional power, and pre-feminist sensibility. As Lorca's work has been championed by various groups of political and intellectual thought, feminism has been linked to the 'Lorcan' vocabulary since at least the early 1960s, before the word was codified and integrated into contemporary culture. The women in *La casa de Bernarda Alba*, *Doña Rosita la soltera*, *Bodas de sangre* and *Yerma* have served as radical models for discussion and debate in feminist theatrical theory.

Playing at the intersection of Eros and Thanatos, Gambaro's theatre not only places women at the centre of the feminist question but moves beyond that to examine, as Lorca did, how ingrained social roles have determined women's plight in relationship to the patriarchy. Whereas Lorca sent out a defiant cry, Gambaro beats down the opposition, submitting it to her impassioned, idiosyncratic, will. In a play like *Antígona furiosa*, written in 1985-86, the first image is of Antígona hanged. As the play progresses in a timeless space, Antígona is both interrogator and interrogated. The members of the Chorus are two *porteños* sitting at a Buenos Aires café, and the play shifts between Antígona's moments of fury, usually in soliloquy, and the Chorus's mocking ironic banter at her expense. It is a disconcerting play, as is most of Gambaro's work, and it is one that fits squarely in a tradition of work by writers from the Americas that examines not only the question of the 'woman in society', but also how one country's history can be inscribed into that of the world. Like Lorca's touchstone play *Bernarda Alba*, *Antígona furiosa*, though small in scale, is constructed around the paradigm of will versus desire, action versus action, violence versus passivity. Gambaro wants her audience to bear witness to the cruelty that her characters suffer on stage, but she also wants to implicate her audience in the acts of cruelty. No one is exempt in Gambaro's theatre. Not even the audience.

In one of her early plays from the 1960s, *Las paredes* (*The Walls*), Gambaro focuses on a Young Man, not unlike Lorca's Young Man from *Así que pasen cinco años*, who is abducted upon returning home from a day in the country, and brought to an 1850s-style room, even though the time is the present. There are occasional screams offstage, and the Young Man is kept by an Usher and a Functionary in a room which is clearly a prison of some sort, and, as the play progresses, begins to vanish. An eerily prescient play about the dilemma of the *desaparecidos* in Argentina, *Las paredes*, which critic Diana Taylor has called exemplary of Gambaro's 'theater of crisis', is a seductive, brutal play suffused with a feeling of death. *Las paredes* uses space and time in as fictive a manner as Lorca and creates a world where past and present are as fluid as they are in memory.

While Gambaro explores violence, politics, and women's roles in society, poet/novelist/dramatist Ricardo Massa, who shares with Gambaro a long history in Argentine theatre, works in a more surreal manner with similar subject matter. Less interested in creating roles for women, Massa explores the dream state as it relates to memory and the body politic.

In his performance text *La trama de sogas* (*Rope Plot*), presented in Buenos Aires in 1988, Massa uses puppets, a complex multi-layered sound score, and a dislocated scenario where hats and ropes speak with a clown, a man, and his lover to present an anguished universe where the only solution to the erosion of a society's historical record vis-à-vis the public's personal memory is madness. Reminiscent of the more 'impossible' theatrical notions posited by Lorca's *El público* as well as the *commedia dell'arte* elements in *Los títeres de cachiporra*, *La trama de sogas* is a tender, bitter and hallucinatory piece of theatre that is delicate and extreme, and very much a piece of 'whole theatre'—where the text is only an element of the *mise en scène*.

Chilean dramatist Inés Margarita Stranger belongs to a young generation of theatre practitioners and also works within the notion of 'whole theatre'. Often developing work collectively with a group of actors, Stranger is interested in the liminal space where the real and the symbolic collide and in placing the female body at the centre of the theatrical experience.

There is little doubt that Margarita Xirgu's arrival in Chile in 1938, and her stay in Santiago, where she founded her Academy of Dramatic Art, awoke in the Chilean public a love for the magic and poetry of García Lorca's theatre. Xirgu's vital presence invigorated a theatre that in the early 1930s was floundering, and which, subsequent to her arrival, and that of other visiting artists like Louis Jouvet, flourished. Inés Margarita Stranger belongs to a new tradition of artists who are building on this vigorous foundation. A philosophical writer by nature, Stranger, in her play *Cariño malo* (*Bad Love*), presented in Chile in 1990, creates a fluid theatrical environment where the private, interior space is presented as 'real', and the public, exterior one as 'surreal'. Three women—Eva, Victoria and Amapola—enact the various roles assigned to women in society as perceived by the male gaze. Ironic and poetic, *Cariño malo* uses elements of song, cabaret, role-playing, melodrama and detailed sequences of visual action and image to explore the 'bad love' of its title, the rage that women carry, and how passion and desire can trap but also liberate women from trying to be 'what they're supposed to be'.

Suffused with a homoerotic subtext, Stranger's work, which is firmly situated in the world of performance art in its sensibility, nevertheless bears the imprint of Lorca's influence in its use of signs and metaphors to tell its story rather than adhering to a more traditional nineteenth-century model, and its focus on women's identity in society and the roles that they are asked to play in service of the patriarchy. Like the work of her contemporaries in the United States, Stranger benefits from Lorca's experiments to re-envision a 'hybrid theatre for tomorrow'.

If Lorca found in Cuba a measure of solace and joy, Cuban playwrights have paid considerable homage to him in their work over the years. Expatriate dramatist Eduardo Manet's extensive body of work both in Cuba and Paris have established him as one of the leading dramatists of the Americas. His ritualised theatrical worlds, which explore the idea of metatheatre or role-playing within a role, his dark wit and Catholic sensibility, link him inevitably to Lorca, as does the work of José Triana, another Cuban expatriate who found in Paris a place where he could put into perspective his sense of the Latin-American experience.

The varied and provocative work that has emerged in the Caribbean and Latin America owes much of its debt to the presence of García Lorca's work on their stages. The theatre wrought in blood, fire and sand in the 1920s and early 1930s has become a part of the theatrical language in Central and South America and its vocabulary continues to expand while retaining its own elemental mystery.

the past contains the future

The slim book with the pencil-thin lettering that captured my imagination in the white-grey room of my high school days remains a constant source of inspiration and pleasure as I write today. The great poet who opened a window in my work and offered me a glimpse of 'deep song' sends his spirit shouting into the night. The words begin slowly, rising out of my throat: *alma, grito, duende*. And a hundred years of white roses and velvet thorns look down on me, withered petals in bloom on the head of a new-born poet. A new page begins. Another curtain rises. Where is Lorca this morning?

Editions of plays referred to

Cruz, Migdalia, 'Another Part of the House', unpublished playscript (1997).
Fornes, María Irene, *María Irene Fornes: Plays*, preface by Susan Sontag (New York: PAJ Publications, 1986).
____, *Promenade and Other Plays* (New York: PAJ Publications, 1987).
Gambaro, Griselda, *Teatro 3* (Buenos Aires: Ediciones de la Flor, 1995).
Massa, Ricardo, *La trama de sogas* (Buenos Aires: Ediciones Teatro Istituto di Antropologia di Milano, 1988).
Rivera, José, *Cloud Tectonics* (New York: TCG Publications/Nick Hern Books, 1997).
Stranger, Inés Margarita, *Antología bilingüe de dramaturgia de mujeres latinoamericanas*, eds Graciela Ravetti and Sara Rojo (Belo Horizonte: Armazem de Ideias, 1996).
Svich, Caridad, *Alchemy of Desire/Dead-Man's Blues* in *Out of the Fringe*, eds María Teresa Marrero and Caridad Svich (New York: TCG Publications/Nick Hern Books, 1999).

Directors' Panel

Saturday, 30 May 1998, Newcastle Playhouse

Panelists present:

David Johnston	Chair
Alison Andrews	University of Northumbria, director of *The Billy-Club Puppets*
Hayley Carmichael	Member of Told By An Idiot theatre company
John Clifford	Writer, translator of *The House of Bernarda Alba*
Sebastian Doggart	Festival organiser, director of *A Poet in New York*
Paul Hunter	Member of Told By An Idiot theatre company, director of 'I Weep At My Piano'
Alan Lyddiard	Artistic Director of Northern Stage, director of *Blood Wedding* and *The Moon Comes Out, Federico*

David Johnston I'll start by simply asking our colleagues to tell us how they approached a play by Lorca. If they haven't directed any Lorca yet, how they would go about it. Sebastian Doggart is largely responsible for setting up this conference, so I'll start off with him.

Sebastian Doggart As a director, what I find most exciting about Lorca is his openness. He allows responses in so many different fields and calls for so many different creative resources to be used in a production. His words and drawings, evoking dreams, flamenco, puppets, theatre within theatre, open up so many visual possibilities. Unlike a playwright like Beckett, who rigorously prescribes actions and movements on the director, Lorca gives only sparse stage directions. As a result, he's as liberating to direct as Euripides, Shakespeare, Calderón or Chekhov.

It also means that all of a director's creative tools have to come into play: naturalistic tools are vital for the director and performers to develop motivations and relationships, and to choose actions.

Associative tools like music and dance can create a counterpoint to the text. Interpretive techniques can focus a production on a particular time or place, like the Irish spin that Brendan Kennelly gave to his translation of *Blood Wedding* or the feminist reading of *Yerma* that seemed to underpin Fabià Puigserver's womb-like trampoline of a set.

These three lines of approach informed the production of the dramatic monologue, *Poet in New York*, which involved a very intimate relationship between the performer, Gabrielle Jourdan, and the audience. In a naturalistic sense, we tried to imagine the impact that Lorca would have had on his New York audiences through his lectures and poetry: what would they have seen and felt in his presence? What effect was Lorca looking to achieve? How did the rejection he felt from Salvador Dalí and Emilio Aladrén influence his bitter attack on New York society?

In the associative approach to directing the piece, Gabi and I looked at how to dramatise the parallel and contradictory relationship between the text, the drawings he made during the period, and 1920s photographs of New York and Cuba. Lorca said that there were some things that he couldn't express through words, which only images could express. We played with that idea, both in the images shown to the audience, and in Gabi's physicality.

In an interpretive approach to the play, I made the decision to cast a woman as Lorca, not to be fashionably gender-blind, but because I feel Lorca's work communicates profoundly in both male and female dimensions. In a unique and transcendent sense, he is as much a man as a woman. In addition, Lorca talked about the complicity the audience feels when seeing Juliet played by a boy in *The Audience*, and we found a similar complicity in our performances.

As with the infinite elasticity of Shakespeare's texts, Lorca's openness to new readings means that his plays are premiered with every new performance. It's that endless iterability that inspires me to continue working with him, and which I think will be responsible for his endurance.

David Johnston I think the idea of Lorca being played by a woman is something that Hayley might like to comment about later on. But out of loyalty to the Playhouse I'll go to Alan next.

Alan Lyddiard I used to live in a little place where I was an actor, and a very prejudiced one at that—I would roll my own cigarettes, get bored, and do plays about motorway service stations and ketchup bottles. I found that very, very exciting and I used to think that was what theatre was all about. I was living next door, at the time, to a dance company and I happened to go and see a piece they were creating. It was a new experience for me and at first I thought it was rubbish. But I sat there and watched it and it completely changed my life. I found myself thinking, 'this is extraordinary, this is amazing—people aren't speaking to one another, they're not rolling cigarettes, they're not getting bored and there's no ketchup. It's fantastic, it's beautiful'. So my prejudice changed from then on.

When I came to Lorca for the very first time, coming out of the rolling-my-own-cigarettes period, this playwright seemed completely impenetrable to me. Then I went to Andalucía for a conference. At the very same time, someone handed me a script of Brendan Kennelly's *Blood Wedding* and I read it all the way through. When I came to the moon speech, I read it four times. The reason I read it four times was because it started with a line (which is not a Lorca line, but a Brendan Kennelly line): 'I shine with loneliness and am looking for love.' It just hit me as an extraordinary way for the moon to come in and search for the lovers and bring death to those lovers: 'I shine with loneliness and am looking for love'—it just inspired me tremendously.

One night I was in a bar in Triana where I saw these people around a table just sitting there drinking. Then all of a sudden, one of them started clapping rhythmically and somebody else then burst into song while another stood up, joined in for a while and then sat down again. It was extraordinary, the power that was in that room. It was then that I discovered this thing called flamenco. Later on that night I saw a flamenco show which was also extraordinary. The man who was singing in this performance was wonderful: an old man with a wrinkled face, wearing a white shirt. He had no teeth, but he sang from somewhere that I had never heard anyone sing from before. It kind of came up right through him and out of his mouth.

When I got back to England, I read Lorca's poetry and tried to find ways of relating it to the plays I was producing in Newcastle. I wanted to find a way into *Blood Wedding* that would bring together what I had found—the poetry of Kennelly, the dance company next door and the singing in Triana. The closest I could find to get near the feeling of Triana was in Scottish ceilidhs. Because I'd been living in Scotland for a long time, I was very familiar with ceilidh; instead of having people clapping and playing guitars, you would have someone with a fiddle and a squeeze-box. Despite being inspired by Scottish ceilidh, I felt that any production of Lorca that I was going to attempt had to have a bit of Northumberland in it. So I asked a traditional musician called Alistair Anderson, who plays the Northumbrian pipes and concertina, if he would work with me on the project.

About that time, I went back to Spain to try and discover a bit more about Lorca. I went to his house, read a lot about him and discovered Gibson, Lorca's major biographer, whose work gave me great insight into the poet. While I was doing my research, I met a choreographer called Salud López and started working with her in Spain. So my initial approach to Lorca was to call upon a traditional Northumbrian musician and a contemporary Spanish choreographer.

The next stage was to do with my belief that people on stage by themselves, presenting themselves to an audience, can be extraordinary; they don't need to do anything else but just stand there, with the lights shining on them. So I started to try to find the right performers who would give me that sense that they were able to stand on a stage and do nothing but be extraordinary. Through doing the piece, the figure of Lorca gradually, slowly began to emerge. From that point onwards, I have been trying to find out more about him.

David Johnston There are all sorts of issues there that we'll pick up on afterwards. I just wonder if there are directors in Spain at the moment who are confessing to their prejudices of narrow vision against people playing guitars and clapping their hands, who want to go to the exotic world of motorway cafés! Perhaps I'll come to Alison now, who directed Lorca's *Billy-Club Puppets* for our Fiesta.

Alison Andrews In a sense I don't feel like I've been directing Lorca, but directing a bunch of students. There's a moment in the piece that we made, where there's a small puppet theatre, surrounded by a larger puppet theatre, surrounded by the proscenium that you can see here. That moment comes from a line at the beginning of the play, where the Mosquito character, who's supposed to represent the Andalusian people, talks about wanting to show the audience the little things, the littlest things and the tiniest, littlest things of this world. That's the idea that I wanted to start with. In terms of working with students, the choice of play had to be appropriate for the circumstances. I wanted to have a piece that came without too much of the baggage of previous productions: doing *Blood Wedding*, *Yerma* or *The House of Bernarda*

Alba would mean that people might come with a sense of what those pieces should be like. I thought that it was unlikely that the *Billy-Club Puppets* would excite that kind of debate.

So what we did was to look at the story. We wanted to take that as a structure from which we could hang all our ideas. Then we took a scenario inspired by La Barraca (which again we felt was appropriate for working with a group of students), and wrapped that around the central story. So we had this envelope of conceit about a group of people returning from a very, very long tour. They come in with their dirty washing and some of them haven't seen each other for a while because some of them have been back at base. We spent a lot of time discussing who these people might be—yes, they're a group of students, but they're playing this group of people who are the performers. In our scenario, they have been given a new text to try out, after having worked on a piece that now feels dead. In a literary sense, the audience here in the Playhouse are the very first people to hear that text which has been translated from the Spanish original by one of our second-year students. We spent a lot of time discussing what it is to be an actor, especially in terms of what the audience's expectations of them are, when they get up on stage with a light shining on them, as Alan said. We wanted to leave space for the audience to consider just that, by simply gazing at the performers.

The work that I do as a theatre-maker in other fields is primarily devised work, in the sense that the text is just one of the artefacts generated from the process of collaboration between design, music and performance. I don't know of any other way to create theatre. So I had to bring myself in to the process as well. Some of my colleagues have been kind enough to say to me now, 'when I picked up the text of the *Billy-Club Puppets*, I didn't know how on earth you were going to do it.' There are very human feelings that come into that process as a director, of picking up a text and deciding to produce it. One of those feelings is fear—there's a big gap between what you feel when you pick up a text and read it, and that sense of how on earth it's going to happen on the stage. But Lorca's little story was the fundamental thing that we had to go back to. All the other ideas came from that story.

We decided to use all the facilities that this theatre had to offer, the flying facilities for example. We looked at the metaphor of puppets being strung up and drew a parallel between them and Franco's regime where perhaps everyone's a puppet under fascism. We thought we'd fly the puppets in, leaving them there so you can see the wires, you can see the workings and you can see the manipulation happening. I was interested in what Sebastian was saying about the openness of Lorca, because I felt there was plenty of space in this text, there were plenty of ambiguities and gaps. Many critics have commented on the central ambiguity about whether these characters should be played by puppets or by human actors or by human actors playing puppets. We decided to have all three states and to play between them. We wanted to get a sense of 'play'. We wanted also to leave space for improvisation.

These people in our production are surrounded by the junk you would find in a theatre greenroom: washing machines, bits of old set, scenery, dirty paint jars, so on and so forth. In our production, the performers present this new text by using what's around them. I think there's great optimism in the idea that nothing is wasted, nothing is irrelevant. Whatever you want to do, you can find a way to do it, and that's important to us, considering we didn't have much money to do this piece. But what we did have was human resources and the tools of the theatre.

David Johnston There's been a remarkable flurry of Lorca productions over the last ten years, mainly of the rural trilogy: *Blood Wedding*, *Yerma* and *The House of Bernarda Alba*, so it's very refreshing to see productions like the *Billy-Club Puppets* which are so rarely done in English. The conference and the events around the conference also demonstrate a flowering of devised pieces, which either loosely or closely look at Lorca's life, in the attempt to evoke the 'Spirit of Lorca'. Paul Hunter, the joint artistic director of Told By an Idiot, devised and directed the show 'I Weep At My Piano'.

Paul Hunter I've never directed a Lorca play before and we've never done a Lorca play as a company. When Alan spoke to us two years ago about wanting to celebrate Lorca's birthday, we told Alan about a tiny little clown show that we performed in London about seven years ago about Dalí and Lorca in which Hayley played Lorca. And Alan said, 'well why don't you bring that here and do it in the festival?' and we hadn't thought about it at all. Then Hayley suggested that we introduce the character of Luis Buñuel who was also a friend of theirs at the time. We were more interested in making something that was, as you say, trying to capture the spirit of Lorca than doing a play by Lorca at that stage. Through doing this show, I've become even more interested in Lorca and we were just talking about actually doing a Lorca play, after having performed something that was inspired by him.

We made some early decisions that helped liberate us: Hayley was born in Croydon; Darren, who plays Buñuel, was born in Darlington and Dicky, who plays Dalí, was born, I think, in Stoke-on-Trent. And I'm from Birmingham. So we decided there was no possibility of us trying to be Spanish in any way whatsoever. And once we had decided that we were not going to try to be Spanish (whatever 'being Spanish' is), we felt quite liberated. We then took that one stage further, deciding not to speak any Spanish at all. Next came the decision not to discuss their work in an overt way, as we thought we were interested in the human side of their relationship. And finally we thought, 'OK, we won't mention their names either.'

Having made all these decisions, we thought 'Oh my god, what are we going to do now?' But actually, it all proved quite liberating for us because we had to use our imaginations in a very different way. Throughout the devising process, the actors, composer, designer and myself as director, all very much wrote the story together. We approached our work first and foremost from a physical starting-point; movement or action comes before anything else in our work. Which does not mean, in any way, that we don't admire text. We love Lorca's work. In fact we were so in admiration of his writing that we wanted to try and pay some sort of visual theatrical tribute to him.

I get annoyed about the fact that the physical side of Lorca's plays is not really addressed in productions in this country; there's no real physical engagement with the text or the action. And there's no real sense of playfulness. Picking up on what Alison said: all our work comes from play. On the first day of rehearsal, I asked the actors to forget about all the things we have come to associate with the figures of Buñuel, Lorca and Dalí. I like acting where I can see a lot of the actor; I like to see the actor behind the character. We always talk about finding the pleasure of being on stage as a performer, on top of which comes the character. So there's always a little glimpse of Hayley and Dicky and Darren there in our production. Because we work primarily from improvisation, we generated loads of material. A lot of it is absolute garbage, but in order to devise like that, you have to generate lots of material. The ideal atmosphere for us to work in is one of playful anarchy. We asked our designer to bring in a collection of objects to rehearsal. One night, Hayley just picked up a pair of bull's horns and started playing around with them in the course of an improvisation.

Eventually, they became an important image in our show. Everything came from this idea of play. The same goes for our music. Ian Johnson, who very much wrote the show with us, not just musically, watched the rehearsals and then dashed away and wrote the score. It feels very organic to the actors, because they're playing within something where everyone has collaborated. One of my overriding aims (and I don't know whether we have achieved this or not), was to try and make something where it didn't matter if you didn't know much about Lorca's life, or who Dalí or Buñuel were at all. We wanted to try and make a human story, a human sort of memory play, a dream-like play about three peoples' lives. Whilst obviously we drew into it things that we knew about Lorca, that was not our main concern. Our main concern was along the lines of, if my mum came to see this, who knows nothing about Lorca, she could get something out of it.

Hayley Carmichael. I felt inadequate as a performer approaching Lorca, about not having a 'Spanish passion'. But I had to make do with what I'd got, and find something in these figures, who were so 'different', so 'Spanish', that could be universal and recognizable. When you're a student and you meet people for the first time, you make friendships that you think are going to last forever. Then you go your separate ways. That is a universal feeling that I could approach as an actor; I was very much myself with the other actors, using my feelings to access those of the character I was playing and make it accessible for the audience. Rather than feeling intimidated by the idea of a brilliant Spanish poet who died young, I reached for things about those characters that everybody understands. You know, the human things that we've all felt, because the other stuff about their life and work is 'known'.

About being a woman playing Lorca, I say 'why not?' When it came to the decision to make the piece, the casting just 'happened' that way. I don't know the date when I dared to have a go at playing Lorca; it just happened. You also need to bear in mind that we had a little history of making this other piece where I played Lorca. We didn't want to say lots about sexuality, but we thought if we got our casting right on an essential level, if every man has a feminine side and every woman a masculine one, then it made sense that as a stocky little woman who's not particularly feminine, I could play Lorca. Similarly, there's a gangly bloke, Dicky, who's got a gentleness and a femininity about him, so he could be Dalí. And Darren, who also has that gentleness, but is physically a 'big fella', could easily be Buñuel. If we got the casting right, we thought we wouldn't have to say loads of stuff about sexuality. Our story would then be informed by just seeing us together and the qualities we have as a threesome.

David Johnston   Sometimes we tend to forget, when we talk about passion in Lorca, that there's also an important issue of control, discipline and precision. John Clifford is primarily a writer. Was I right when I said you hadn't directed any Lorca?

John Clifford   Oh absolutely. It's very funny to be sitting up here and be called a director—I quite like it. No, I've never directed; I look after the words. Because creating theatre is such a collaborative process, it's so important that people can work together properly. I think I'd like to talk about what I like to find in directors. Lorca is such a demanding writer—he demands extraordinary things of us, and so it's very important that there's a very good basic communication going on between everybody who's working on a Lorca play. It's not like having a drink together; you don't have to like your collaborators particularly. It has to do with a trust, a respect for each other's artistic judgement, an openness to each other. But it's also something solid, very wordless really, that's going on between me as a writer, and a director and the actors—just respect for each other's judgement. I think a love of words is crucial, and I love words. Words matter; they have to matter doing Lorca because he was such a master of words, a creator of very precise, beautiful words. Respect for those words is very, very important for everybody.

People have been talking about playfulness and I think that's very important. I do wish Gerry Mulgrew was here, because for me he represents that playfulness. I hate directors who have an agenda, who think they know what Lorca is about and want to impose that on the actors and on the play. Gerry isn't like that. He has a kind of openness and a capacity to continually invent, a capacity to be taken to places to where Lorca wants to take him. Because Lorca does take you to very dangerous places, and you have to have the courage and the inner strength to go with him into those dark, fearful places. That's important in a director. But at the same time there's the opposite of that, which is very important: focus and discipline. Years ago I was at a conference in Oxford. I met this old man there who had worked with Lorca; he played the piano in La Barraca. And I asked him, 'what was it like working with Lorca?' and he replied, 'he was a pain; a really, really difficult man to work with, a pain in the arse in lots of ways. He was incredibly demanding.'

David Johnston I think that it's important to remember that Lorca was a notable theatre director. Spain is a country where there haven't been many great theatre directors. A contemporary exception of course is Lluís Pasqual. Lorca was a very demanding but also innovative director as well, who, I suspect, respected his words as little as a number of directors and translators are accused of respecting his words in *their* versions. He was a man of the theatre who would do everything to make the performance work. That's a very important point to remember. Thank you to all of the directors and 'aspiring directors' here in the wings for their opening comments. I think at this point, I'll throw it open to the floor and let you ask whatever you want either of individuals or of the panel.

Question from the floor [*Colin Teevan*] I've long had this sense that Lorca, like Oscar Wilde, is in danger of becoming a legend above his own work. Three of the four directors here worked the story of Lorca's life into the texts that they produced. Similarly, the first play I wrote ten years ago was 'The Murder of Lorca'. Every time you see a production of Oscar Wilde in Ireland, the production tries to put a spin on the story, to put Wilde's story into it. Do you think there's a danger of losing a sense of the actual works of Lorca?

David Johnston Perhaps I can ask Paul to open up with that one because your piece was about Lorca's life.

Paul Hunter To be honest, one thing I was surprised about was that there weren't more plays by Lorca in the Fiesta. Our decision is more to do with what we are about as a company at this stage. We haven't done a written text in five years. We've done pieces that have been inspired by texts, but our decision to do the Lorca piece was really an artistic decision connected to where we are as a company. But I do find it amazing that in England, as far as I know, there has been no major production so far of a major work by Lorca to celebrate his centenary. We did see a production at the Southwark Playhouse before we came of *In Five Years Time* which was wonderful, but I do agree with you. I think that it's important that you have work like ours, but alongside the devised work, we should be seeing Lorca's plays being produced as well. I personally think that lots of English theatre practitioners are frightened of Lorca (Gerry Mulgrew is an exception, of course). The fact that you have things like the moon coming on stage—we're not used to that. English actors still want to act in plays where people argue about things like who's left the car door open or something.

John Clifford A fear of poetry, isn't it?

Paul Hunter Yes.

Alan Lyddiard I was very inspired by the Gate's seasons of Pinter and Beckett. I wanted originally to copy that, to get every play I could possibly find, bring them together so that people could see everything by Lorca. I did *Blood Wedding* two years ago. Because I wanted to make a contribution towards this festival, I wanted to revive it. I tried to get *Yerma* and tried to get *The House of Bernarda Alba* as a complete unit alongside somebody doing *The Public*, somebody doing *Five Years On*, somebody doing *Billy-Club Puppets* and so on. That for me would have been fantastic. Unfortunately it was just not possible in terms of resources and available productions. When I travelled to Spain I saw a *Yerma* which I thought was really boring and really old-fashioned. There's a wonderful director in Spain now, el Chino, who's based at the Centre of Andalusian Theatre. He is going to do a production of *Bernarda Alba* set in the desert, which I think is a really interesting idea. I would have brought that over if it had been available. It's just pragmatism, really, that made me go in this particular direction. I knew the people you see here, and I said 'I love your idea. Do it'. Alison chose the *Billy-Club Puppets* and I was very pleased that she did because it was a piece by Lorca in the Festival and in fact it is the only piece.

Question from the floor We've discussed the idea of Lorca as being strange, exotic and difficult. I'm always annoyed at the way in which British productions of Lorca try to be authentic and Spanish as a way of trying to approach the 'otherness'. These sorts of productions are always disappointing. How do you respond to the issues of exoticness in Lorca?

David Johnston Could I just say something to that as a translator? I would like to append a note to all my translations saying 'forbidden to do flamenco in this particular version'. I've seen so many productions of Lorca where characters burst into flamenco with shouts of 'Hey, toro, toro!' And that's the National Theatre doing *Blood Wedding*—mysteriously set in Cuba. I think it is as bizarre to break into flamenco in Lorca as it would be to do Highland jigs to shouts of 'Hoots, mon!' in the banquet scene in *Macbeth*. I think that that's the trouble with the exoticism of Lorca—sometimes it becomes too easy a peg for certain productions.

Alan Lyddiard I agree with this. I believe that there is a cliché that you can follow that can lead you to the wrong place. However, it can also lead you to the right place. And although you are forbidding flamenco in your particular productions, David, you cannot deny that the influence exists—you can't ignore it; you can't say that it's not there. But it's not everything. Flamenco is something that inspired me particularly, going into that bar where ordinary people were singing ordinary songs. That was their culture; that was who they were. It wasn't presented in any theatre or posh place; it was in a bar. And I think it's important that you don't throw away flamenco just because it's become a cliché.

Paul Hunter But the difficult thing is to take what you saw in the bar and put it on stage. That is the real challenge.

David Johnston You also made the point that you transformed something that was exotic into something that was culturally valid for us.

Alison Andrews I'm trying to pull what we've been talking about together in a coherent way. The fact is that, with playwrights, particularly dead playwrights, all you have left is this text. Then a lot of opinion starts to surround how that text could be or should be produced. What seems to then happen is that the gaps in that text start to get filled in and it becomes less of a mesh; the 'Marshall McLuhan' gaps get filled in—those gaps that were once really enticing. That's a general observation that you can make about theatre in this country and in the Western world generally: the primacy of the text is the thing that's bogging us down, whether it's Lorca or Chekhov or whoever it is. And I think that's a real problem. The musical has become our mainstream theatre, and yet there is so much work that is happening outside the mainstream which is addressing exactly this. We must not get bogged down by the primacy of the text. Instead we must try to acknowledge a visual tradition in all of our collective imaginations, *our* response to theatre. We need to move away from a sense of, 'Shakespeare wrote that down, so therefore it must be OK'. Companies like Forced Entertainment and Told By An Idiot to an extent, are trying to break through this proscenium arch here (which is why I wanted to use it for the *Billy-Club Puppets*) to re-negotiate this boundary that lies between us. They are trying to find out what the political problems are about an audience being out there and performers being up here with a statement, being: 'this is the text and this is what we must say'. Orthodoxies are being challenged. We have got to be careful, even with Lorca—he still left us a text, a written down text. But we have to say that's not the end of the story.

Paul Hunter The great thing about Lorca for me is that it is intensely theatrical. That's the reason why I'm drawn to him more than some other playwrights. He's incredibly visual—it's theatre and that's why I like it. I know that he's been done a lot in film and so on, but the reason why I like it, is that there's something quite mad about it, quite wild about it, which appeals to me. This can do exactly what you're saying Alison, it can make a very theatrical gesture.

Alan Lyddiard Just as 'no more flamenco' can become a cliché, you can also make a cliché out of the idea that the text is just constricting us. I'm not someone to wave the banner for new writing, but as I said, I read Kennelly's text and it was that which gave me an inspiration for Lorca. And Kennelly had changed lots of things in the original Lorca text—maybe it's sacrilege to do that, but nevertheless it was *those* words I was reading and it was *those* words that started me off. I suppose I'm agreeing with you, Alison, about filling in gaps, but not when you say that the text gets in the way of what we really want to do. Text should be seen as a contributory element of what we want to do.

Alison Andrews We're here to celebrate Lorca and we all have a great desire to do that. It's apparent that there isn't a huge Lorca following in the country. Maybe that is a good thing. Because he was somebody who was on the edge, challenging things. The work that I've been talking about, which explores different kinds of conventions rather than working within them, is also always on the boundaries and it needs to stay on the edge. It must not get absorbed into the mainstream, otherwise it will just dissipate and disappear like that. So maybe it's a good thing that Lorca is marginalised and that there's a kind of mystery about him. It's tantalising—it's over there and not quite within our grasp. If it comes into the mainstream, then it may lose something.

Question from the floor I think that what you're saying is all about making choices and taking risks. I've *chosen* to do David's translation of Lorca because I like it and you all choose to work with his texts in particular ways. Doing Lorca with sixteen-year-olds was a huge *risk*. They all found it so scary, but they will never forget doing it. So what I want to know is whether you agree with me—is it all about choice and risk?

Hayley Carmichael I agree with what you're saying and that's why we chose to do the piece we did, knowing what we're best at so far—wanting to devise a piece that bounces off reading books, seeing Buñuel films, Lorca plays and Dalí paintings. Coming from our starting-point, I now feel as though I've accessed something that once seemed strange, difficult and inaccessible to me. As a performer I'm more used to devising work: the words that come out in the text are the words that come out of our mouths in improvisations on day one or day ten. So I know that I'm a little bit afraid of not being able to find my way into somebody else's words and I love it when I work with directors who make me feel that I've made the words mine. I do have a problem with words. I know that when I've made them mine, I'm liberated. But I have a tricky patch in the middle of the process where I'm not sure whose words they are. Starting from where we did, I now feel that I want to do the next step, I would now love to do a play by Lorca.

David Johnston John, you did a version of *The House of Bernarda Alba* for the Lyceum Opera. Would you like to talk a bit about the risks that were involved there?

John Clifford I didn't choose that play; the director called me up, I don't know why. He wanted to commission me to write a new play but he didn't dare—he was too scared, so he thought, 'I'll get him to do a Lorca so I won't feel too guilty when I see him'. I don't know why he chose *The House of Bernarda Alba*, except I think there had been a big hit in London a couple of years before. So he thought it would be a big hit in the Lyceum. And it wasn't. A lot of things in theatre don't happen because you choose, they just happen by accident. People phone you up and say funny things to you and you respond to it and then you're on a path. I said yes to *Bernarda* because I thought it might be easier than *Yerma* because it wasn't written in verse. But it was far harder—you make mistakes sometimes! A text is words and they matter. But a text is far more than words: there's the most amazing energy, especially in *The House of Bernarda Alba*. Every word is like a bomb. If you mishandle it, it's going to explode. Maybe it won't kill you but you'll get covered in slime. It's very dangerous; it's a terrifying text. But once you're on that road it just draws you on and you have to follow it and do the best you can.

Alan Lyddiard I was interested in what Hayley was saying about developing her ideas—from doing a devised piece about Lorca, she would now like to try a play by him. It's like that all the time. You choose to take one step forward because of a hundred thousand steps that you've taken earlier but that you've forgotten about.

Question from the floor The focus of this debate is on content and its expression through form. We're not used to exploring epic forms; we shy away from them—that's why we shy away from Lorca. We need to find new ways of expressing ourselves—new forms to explore the epic quality of Lorca.

Paul Hunter For me, there are lots of alternatives that are not used and are hundreds of years old. We got trapped in realism in this century. Before, we embraced melodrama and much richer theatrical styles. I get angry when melodrama is used in such a dismissive way. Melodrama is a wonderfully rich theatrical style but we don't use it. The reason why we're trapped is because realism is safer; it's secure, we understand it. It's harder to play in a different style. I don't think we need to find a new style. There's lots of things we've already got, it's just that we don't use them. They're there in Lorca, in Molière and in Shakespeare—in all of our great poets. It's not naturalism, it's something much bigger and richer than that.

David Johnston Can I just ask the panel if you have any brief concluding comments?

Alan Lyddiard One of the things that I've tried to do here at Northern Stage is to take a theatre company out of a regional repertory mould, and place it somewhere else. Doing *Blood Wedding* started the process. I want to take theatre along a road where we try to create 'parties' rather than just 'plays'. Our Fiesta has brought this idea to life and I'm grateful to Lorca for helping me to achieve that.

Hayley Carmichael When I first read Lorca I wasn't intimidated by it; on the first reading, it completely made sense. I responded to everything that was there. As a performer, I find it hard when you're not allowed to look at the audience, when you're not allowed to go 'out there' and you have to stay 'in here'. Yes, you can have two people talking to each other, but it's so *normal* to talk to each other; it's the most basic thing.

Alison Andrews I refuse to get caught up in this collective guilt about naturalism. Naturalism is a proper considered form, a response to life, that theatre-makers wanted to address. What I want to join in eschewing is theatre where you do just have people talking on the stage and not talking to us. Lorca can help us to do that.

3

Translating Lorca

'Combined tactics' in translating Lorca

Nicholas Round

If anyone listening this morning has the idea that they might learn something from me about Lorca, let me swiftly disabuse them. I've said what I want to say about him in about thirty pages at the start of John Edmunds' World's Classics volume,[1] and I've nothing to add to it now. About translating Lorca I might say rather more, but even that is conditioned by the fact that, before my collaboration in that volume, I had not actually translated very much of him: perhaps half a dozen poems, published or performed. At a very early stage of working with John, I wrote to our publisher that: 'I don't want to get myself involved in being a Lorca translator. It's damnably hard graft if it's going to be done properly. What has to sustain you must be your own commitment to *this* author, *these* texts. And I don't have that sort of commitment to Lorca.'

I have (as I then went on to say) a good deal of respect for the man and his writings. I want to see these made adequately and truthfully available in English. But I do not see it as my own mission to do that. I even find it irritating that it is always Lorca—and often it is a Lorca shaped to fit the needs of this or that sub-culture of non-Spanish readers—who becomes the prism through which Spanish culture and Spanish realities are viewed. I have colleagues, I know, who feel very differently, but I do not seek to rival their work. I am aware of many non-Hispanists—often not knowing very much about Spain—who feel entitled to handle Lorca's business in the cultural market-place. I have little urge either to seek their esteem or to get in there and contest that territory with them. I welcome the chance on the other hand, when I see someone with something authentic to offer in the Lorca domain, to help them push it along.

The offer in this case consisted of the completed drafts of John Edmunds' English versions of the four plays eventually published in

---

[1] Federico García Lorca, *Four Major Plays*, trans. John Edmunds (Oxford: Oxford University Press, 1997).

World's Classics. Although I did do a certain amount of translating in the course of my work with these, my own stance towards them was not that of a co-translator, or even of a 'correcting' translator. I never undertook the immense labour of bringing over the whole of any one of these plays into English. John Edmunds did, and the achievement of their final English versions remains his and no-one else's—whatever mixture of my own promptings they may have come to contain. These promptings do, of course, include a certain number of 'corrections'. Lorca is a writer who makes prodigious demands on the sustained attention and energies of the translator; his breadth of reference is immense. There were bound to be times, then, when some point of language or of cultural background had escaped its due attention. But there were not all that many, and 'correcting the translation' was not the defining element of what I was doing.

Most of it, rather, was about putting up alternatives over which there was a case to be argued. It was important actually to suggest alternatives, because to tell translators 'That still does not sound quite right' is to tell them nothing. If they're any good at all, they know that already; what they need to know is why the problem arises and what they can do about it. In that sense it can even be useful to raise possibilities which are *not* new to the translator—versions which they have reviewed and initially rejected, or which derive from procedures which they have not felt entitled to operate. The effect, then, is to legitimise these things, making it clear that the objections to them carry less weight than had been assumed. At other times the difference between versions may reflect a largely subjective nuancing: how one reader (but not another) hears something 'in the head', or in *viva voce* reading. Yet even here, the reasons for that experience can, in principle, be discovered and articulated, and it is one of the major gaps in current theorising about translation in that it offers so little of a metalanguage in which translators can do these things. If I was not, on the one hand, 'correcting' John's version, I was not on the other, putting forward a set of mildly interesting reader-responses, from which he might cherry-pick a few bright ideas, without particularly questioning his version at large. Nor, let me say, did he ever take it like that.

What I *was* trying to do—and what John's response allowed me to do—was to augment and to focus the range of readings, ideas, revisions, hints, experiments, objections, arguments and counterarguments which, conscious or not, inform any realised act of translation. These things are the output of that many-sided working dialogue which all good translators sustain with themselves. And not with themselves only, but with their source-text, and with the target culture to whose specific demands it is mediated, and with all those other texts which are forever intervening in all this. Seen in this light, translation is a plural enterprise anyway, and I was just a rather self-conscious and hyperactive part of that entirely normal plurality. There was one other factor, though: I too was trying to conduct a dialogue with all these other elements, and with John's drafted texts, bringing together all the relevant bits of textual, linguistic and world knowledge, so that new perspectives and new renderings emerged. These then became available for his use—a use which could perfectly-well involve (and did very often involve) their eventual rejection. That did not matter: what mattered was that the dialogue and the thinking were seriously augmented.

There is a general rule at work here: the more you stir the mix, the better the cake. The more discussion of this sort that informs the translation process, the better the eventual product. This is why you sometimes get halfway decent results out of the daft procedure common in London theatres, whereby a linguistic or academic hack is hired to do a 'literal' translation—whatever, under heaven, *that* might be—and then a person of the theatre or a poet comes along and (as Adrian Mitchell was once preposterously quoted as saying) 'puts the poetry in'. Poet and pedant—even when they're not (as they usually are) the wrong people for the job—are invariably locked into the wrong roles. Yet the fruit of such misalliances is often not worthless, and it is almost always better than what either partner would have achieved unaided. It happens because they enlarge the network of cultural and linguistic interchange—absolutely, because there are two of them, not one; practically too, because when one person's energies flag, the other keeps going. As long as they refuse to observe the stultifying division of labour assigned to them, opportune solutions are that much more likely to come into play. Recognising them when they do, of course, takes an additional *kind* of skill, and an additional degree of watchfulness. But it remains, broadly speaking, true that two chimpanzees would give you a better translation than you would ever get out of one chimpanzee. The same applies at levels more advanced than either the higher primates or current theatrical norms. Precious few collaborators, though, at any level, are given the time or the scope for such massive amplification of the translational dialogue as Oxford University Press allowed to John Edmunds and myself.

Not counting the original drafts or the eventual revised texts, we exchanged almost 250 pages of hand-written comments and suggestions, covering at a modest estimate, about 1500 specific points. I cannot tell you how many of these interventions resulted in John deleting what was in his draft in favour of some wording of my own—first, because I have not counted, and secondly because it does not seem to me to be at all relevant. For a start, quite a common effect of our dialogue was for him to move to some third way of translating the passage in question, which neither of us initially had thought of. And even when no change at all was registered, that was no proof that the input into thinking had not been made. The end in view, after all, was the emergence of a *translation*—not the vindication, in some crass totting-up of points won and points lost, of one translator's approach over another's.

That end was made significantly more attainable by some of the qualities already present in John Edmunds' drafts. Asked what was the first challenge which Lorca's work presents to its translators, most people, I suppose, would refer to its imagery. In the case of the drama at least, this seems to me demonstrably not true. It is wrong, first of all, in the rather trivial sense that the language we encounter at the start of these plays is, on the whole, unremarkable in its use of imagery. It can indeed be difficult language, but it tends to be difficult for other reasons. And it is wrong in the other, more basic, sense that there are other things which the translator needs to get right first, as a necessary (though not, of course, sufficient) condition of getting the imagery right too. It is, for example, necessary not to have a 'tin ear'. I will not name names, but notoriously there have been published translators of Lorca whose ear for 'speakable' English might have earned them a small fortune if traded on the Bolivian Metal Futures Exchange, but is no use to them at all when brought to bear on the job in hand. Yet we cannot quite leave the matter there: some of these people were native speakers of English, and would neither have uttered for themselves nor let pass unquestioned in others the kind of sentence which they were willing to have Lorca's characters speak on stage. We are dealing, then, not with an incapacity peculiar to low-souled, inartistic persons, but with a suspension of competence—a willingness to rest content once the most rudimentary of moves into English has been made, instead of going back to it again and again and again, as one has to do. For Lorca *is* demanding in just that way, and translators often have to finish what they are doing in haste or else tire easily. John Edmunds does not willingly suspend competence, and that offered a platform on which much else could be built.

No doubt something more than competence is involved—more, at any rate, than competence of that rather commonplace kind. But no one is going to match the effectiveness of Lorca's dramatic writing by offering 'competence minus' as a rendering of 'competence plus', on the specious ground that at least it is not plain, boring old competence. Neither the dialogue nor the poetic sections of these plays—a more relevant distinction, perhaps, than 'verse' and 'prose'—are straightforward for the translator. This is largely because the two aspects are so inter-related: the dialogue charged with poetic intensities; the poetry driven by its dialogic and dramatic functions. But no translator will get far with either unless they can handle prose-dialogue and verse in certain essentially straightforward ways. Lines have to be credible as speech, and must register as such on first hearing (for audiences, unlike readers, cannot come back to them at will). They must be in an English sufficiently enough of its own kind to underwrite characters and settings as given, yet not so localised and provincial as to exclude audiences on one or another side of the Atlantic. Exchanges must be effectively pivoted, so that it is clear at every point why this should be drama. Theatrical speech, of course, is never the same as natural speech; yet natural language is the indispensable substratum of Lorca's dramatic dialogue. Any English rendering that aspires to be adequate must be similarly underpinned. The tension, the strangeness, the poetic inwardness, all require to be grounded in these apparent simplicities. In practice, they are not that simple. But they are things which John Edmunds overwhelmingly gets right, just as he habitually fulfils the similarly basic agenda required of any translator of verse. That is to say, he knows which rhythmic and other shapes matter in the source-text, and which are available in the target-language. He knows from this too what the limits are to any possible correspondence between them. Conscious, then, of what ranges of variation are and are not open to him, he is willing to exploit all manner of compensating devices—assonance, vowel-harmonies, alliteration—to make up for lost regularities. As a result, his verse reads like verse, and not like *ersatz* doggerel or segmented prose.

None of the foregoing begins to address Lorca's imagery; yet it must all be in place if the translation is to serve as a vehicle for that imagery. As for the difficulty of bringing the imagery across, it is, I think, widely acknowledged but none too well understood. While preparing this talk, for example, I heard a radio feature about Lorca, in which the Irish poet, Brendan Kennelly, urged translators of Lorca into English to seek a language that was 'creative and dangerous'. As a piece of advice that seemed to me gnomic to the point of near uselessness. The thing which bewilders translators about Lorca can, I believe, be characterised much better. It begins with the sheer abundance and magpie diversity of the linguistic and cultural bits and pieces which he lays under contribution. These things challenge our knowledges, but they can in principle be traced. They are then deployed to an almost equivalent variety of specific effects: the challenge here is to our reading, which has to be at once productive enough and relevant enough. Probably we shall fail on one count or another, but we can, by the same token, read Lorca better or worse. Finally—and notwithstanding the diverse character of his output—the end-product tends to declare itself unmistakably his and no one else's. We might seek to define this, in the original texts, in terms of a set of habitual practices; in translation, we are likely to be able to assess it only when we view our versions retrospectively and observe whether the effect is there or not. In general, the result of all this is to multiply the number of times when the translator must revisit each case and each crux and try again, making the translation of Lorca a special test of energy and endurance.

For just when you feel that you have something broadly equivalent to what Lorca is doing, and tolerably acceptable as a scene or a poem in English, you find that this is not at all the case—or that if it is, it is still not what was required. What you have is a sketch or a shell of the original, or worse, just a gesture towards it. You have the meanings of the words in place, but what, taken together, do they mean? Or you have turned out something that is authentically a poem in English, but which is consciously, formally striving to be one. It points to itself and says 'Look! I'm poetic!', where the Lorca poem just *is*, with the deceptive authenticity of a tree which purports to have just grown. Or you may, in the course of an otherwise credible version, have been forced to settle at times for a sort of English 'trace' of what the Lorca original is doing, so that you are merely informing your audience about something exotic and irrecoverable. It might be too much to say that you cannot win, but to stop short at any of these points is certainly to lose.

So you go back again to the text, interrogating Lorca's own words yet more closely, as your primary witnesses for the meanings and the poetic effects which are in play. And indeed, it is in general a sound strategy to trust one's author like this: imperatives to do this or do that which derive from Lorca will be more reliable than any extra imperatives which we may, in desperation or impatience, have set up for ourselves. To that extent, the translator needs to have a certain passivity before the source-text—a 'negative capability', to use a well-worn phrase. But there is also a sense in which translators have to be consciously proactive. It is one thing to trust the author, it is quite another to invite readers or audiences to take one's own words on trust as coming from the author. In practice this means that every time the audience say, 'How extraordinary to put it that way! Yet how right and consequential it was to do so! Lorca is able to do these things because he is a poet', the translator can take satisfaction in a job well done. Often, though, we will fly less high than that, managing merely to put across, without confusion, distraction or distortion, most of the things which we can identify as going on in the text. At that modest but still costly level of achievement, a decent pride of craftsmanship is not out of place. But whenever the target-audience is led to say 'What an extraordinary way of putting things! I cannot for the life of me see why Lorca should have done it. But never mind: it must be because he's that kind of poet', then too much is being taken on trust. There is an undisguised gap, which the translation is not filling. And it really would not do to leave the under-achieved version in place, as if hoping to goad audiences into the pious reflection that, being Lorca, this is bound to be good stuff, even if it registers as neither intelligible nor memorable. There is a seductive false logic about this: 'Lorca is so good he's untranslatable, and my translation is so inadequate it shows how good he is.' It was refreshingly plain from the start—and I think it emerges more plainly still from his published versions—that John Edmunds was not having any nonsense of that sort.

That is not to say that the whole of it was free from areas of uncertainty and under-working. Such things are bound to arise. A common pattern, for example, was for a given poetic sequence to begin with some really well-characterised piece of language—in terms of linguistic power or word-music or rhythmic shape, or more than one of these—but then to fall away from the regularities thus implied, or to seek to retain them at visibly more obtrusive cost. That was only natural: what, in English, addresses one nexus of functions is unlikely to address precisely the same range and sequence of other sets of functions as are addressed by its initial Spanish equivalent. It can happen, but on the whole it does not. So we cannot eliminate this loss of regularities: our only option is to manage it, so that it does not appear as a dilution of poetic necessities, and thus as a loss of energy. But there *is* a loss of energy at such points. For the translator, the initial breakthrough into a sense and a shape realised as one was a 'quantum leap' of mental energy; inevitably a reaction sets in. At this point though, the 'handling' process by which the rest of the poetic sequence is managed, will pose demands of a rather different kind. A double movement, of analysis followed by synthesis, sets in. One key question in the analytic phase will be, 'What is Lorca building up in this poetic episode taken as a whole?'. Another is, 'What means do we dispose of for pursuing a similar range of functions?'. A third is, 'How do we order them together, so that the whole effect is consequentially attained?'. These are matters in which a collaborator whose energies have not paid the initial cost of setting the broader pattern for the passage can offer a welcome contribution to the detail. But as we move into the phase of synthesis again, the primary translator, having watched this fellow-worker pick up the text, as it were, and run with it, is very likely to want it back.

That, at all events, is how John Edmunds and I set about it, bringing a sort of 'combined tactics' to bear on the mountain which all Lorca translators have to climb. On the whole, I would claim that it worked pretty well. There were few scenes which did not receive their share of actual or speculative 'blocking in'. Given an initial English account of what the words of the prose dialogues meant, one was able to concentrate on what they were doing—to spell out at length their interpersonal and 'imagistic' or thematic point. And from that sort of exposition—even when, as often, it ended in uncertainty—both the collaborators had a readier access to English speech-acts which were more fully motivated, as well as being more closely integrated with natural English speech. It is these things, I believe, which will make the Oxford University Press versions usefully accessible to actors—who will, as John's own prefatory comment implies, quite properly use them as scripts and change them again. As for the poetic sections, these do at least read as poetry—which means, in the first place, that they are sufficiently contrasted with the prose sequences in which they are embedded. They are, as a rule, not wholly typical of English verse either, relying on loosely-defined stanzaic templates rather than on stricter forms, and using more emphatic recurrences selectively, to underwrite key points and closures. In this and other respects, they tend to sound both like and unlike English poetry (not quite the same thing as English verse)—which is rather the effect one seeks in translating any poet. Yet they are not particularly like any other English translations of Lorca's poetry for the good reason that the verse passages in his plays are themselves rather different from his poems. The dramatic pretext to which their appearance responds almost always involves representing a specific, culturally colourable, use of verse. Commonly they follow a traditional or conventional sub-genre: a lullaby; the songs sung at a wedding, or by washerwomen at a stream; a drawing-room ballad; verses from a commonplace book. Equivalents have to be sought out and held in mind—and here again, the relation to the underlying English sub-genre is properly one of likeness and unlikeness together. English-language and Spanish-language folk traditions, for example, are related, but they are neither coterminous nor, as a rule, co-referential. Besides, one has to draw back from representing Lorca—knowing, as well as knowledgeable in his use of folk elements—as a 'folkloric' author at all. Here again, the right sort of balance is maintained.

So do I see no areas for criticism in the finished state of these translations? Towards the end of my exchanges with John Edmunds, I noted that there were just eleven points on which we had not yet resolved our disagreements—not a bad residue after the thousand and more which had arisen for discussion in the first place. That outcome was made possible in great part by John's openness to discussion. Like any working dialogue, ours worked better because conducted on a basis of equality. None the less, these were, as I recognised at the outset, his translations and not mine, and there were one or two wider strategies over which our emphases remained different. Left to myself, for example, I would have taken a different line with many of the longer and more complex sentences in the prose dialogue. I was for breaking these up into shorter, more manageable mouthfuls, while John maintained that actors could handle this sort of thing perfectly well. He had experience—and possibly right—on his side, but I still think there were other considerations to be weighed. First, Spanish is a more syntactic language, and English a more paratactic one, so that sentences with more subordinate clauses tend to fall less easily on the ear in the latter than in the former. It is likely too, therefore, that spoken English sentences will be a little shorter. Secondly, a desire to preserve some of the spoken rhythms of Spanish—which we may or may not want to do, according to context—need not commit us to preserving Spanish syntactic structures or sentence-lengths. We have options in these matters.

Thirdly, the sentences do not only have to be speakable by actors; they also have to be 'speakable in character', both for the actors and for the imagination of readers. They have to be imagined, that is, as speakable by the characters portrayed, in the contexts posited for them. If they wouldn't utter *that* sentence in *that* form in English, then they can't be made to say it, whatever the players playing the parts might be able to do. The matter is often one of fine judgement, but my own judgement, for what it is worth, would often have gone another way, yielding a more paratactic, perhaps more naturalistic texture.

In the handling of verse, I was again unable to convert John Edmunds to all my own preferences, or prejudices, as the case may be. We were generally agreed on the need to be wary of conventionally 'poetic' lexis, often dead in real English, in the way in which Lorca's language is precisely *not* dead. In other respects, though, John seemed to me a little too willing to elevate the diction of these passages in a non-standard sense—too given to using inversion and hyperbaton to achieve a word order closer to the original, or to some established English metrical or prosodic pattern. Adjectives which were merely epithets tended to survive in his versions where they might not have done so for me. And the filling out of lines to achieve a perceived metrical regularity was another area of occasionally unresolved dispute. It seems to me both true and important that in English verse (which, unlike Spanish verse, is not syllabically based), pauses and 'blank' syllables can function as parts of the overall rhythmic design. I don't think that John was ever quite convinced of this in principle—though I'm happy to observe that he sometimes acted on it instinctively when it came to practice. In the end, though, you don't write somebody else's poetry for them, however generously you are admitted to the places where it is made. Yet I think there are some fairly well-grounded tests of how far the repertoire of poetic 'high style'—epithets, inversions, line-fillers and so forth—can be admitted in translation of this sort. Such features, where deployed, should have a function. And this function should be clear to the translator at the moment of deploying them. If it is merely to underline the fact that this is indeed meant to be poetic language, then they are surely out of place—certainly here, because that is *not* how Lorca establishes his own language as poetic. If their function is more than that, then they may be more acceptable. But if the function is to make good a metrical regularity or a rhyme, then we have to ask whether it is made obvious that this *is* a device to that end. If so, then the effort becomes obtrusive, and the case for doing things some other way is strong. In particular, if a difficult arrangement of language is made to underwrite a relatively easy poetic regularity, there will be a sense that control is being imperfectly exercised. There are, I have to say, very few cases in John Edmunds' work where the attachment to poetic diction goes that far. I wish there were none at all. But you can't have everything, and I'm happy to set against that the massive extent to which his versions get most things right.

Translators' Panel

Saturday, 30 May 1998, Newcastle Playhouse

Panelists present:
        David Johnston (Chair)
        John Clifford
        Gwynne Edwards
        John Edmunds
        Nicholas Round
        Colin Teevan
        Merryn Williams
        Questions from the floor

David Johnston This is the session in which some translators of Lorca's theatre and his poetry are going to give a sense of their approach, and then, as in the directors' panel this morning, we'll throw it open to the audience. If I could introduce the panel first of all. Professor Nicholas Round from the University of Sheffield is well known in international translation circles as an eminent theorist and practising translator. Nick was involved as a consultant in the translation of the four Lorca plays published in the Oxford World's Classics series recently. Then we have Dr John Edmunds from Aberystwyth, who translated the plays that I've just mentioned. Beside Nick is Merryn Williams, who translated the selected poems of Lorca, published by Bloodaxe. Beside Merryn is Professor Gwynne Edwards from Aberystwyth. I'm sure you all know Gwynne as the most prolific of all translators of Spanish dramas. Colin Teevan is an Irish playwright and also writer-in-residence at Queen's University in Belfast. Colin has a long-standing interest in Lorca, but has never translated any plays by Lorca. He has translated from the classics and from Italian. We also have John Clifford, a well-known dramatist who has translated one Lorca play, *The House of Bernarda Alba*, for the Lyceum. I would like to ask each of our translators to give a view of their approach to Lorca, or how they might approach Lorca.

Nicholas Round Translation. How to do it? The answer to that, I suppose, depends on the sense of the term—how to agree a definition of it. Because it seems to be something that has, at one and the same time, hard boundaries and extremely fuzzy boundaries. As you, David, who have worked as a teacher of languages will know, there are things that declare themselves as non-translation. The boundaries of that are pretty hard; they're not always obvious but you can get to them, even define them. But when you've got a piece of language that's been brought over into something that isn't non-translation, you still haven't got something that *is* translation.

That's where the fuzzy boundaries begin—those uncertain, blurred boundaries that are so subjective: if it's a translation for you, it isn't for me. Is it a translation for this culture, this moment in time? Yes, but not for that one. Will it do in the theatre? Will it do on the printed page? Those boundaries have to be negotiated by other means.

I'm convinced that the way they are negotiated is through the management of knowledges. If you're going to translate, if you're going to present in theatrical terms, you have to have knowledges of different kinds. In the first instance, you have to have knowledge of the media involved; you have to know the languages. This means both languages—and curiously enough, the language you're translating into, which is taken for granted, is probably the more important of the two. But it's never the only important one. You can never say, 'the other language is dispensable, this one is it.'

Secondly, you have to have knowledge of the text because work with texts is what you are doing. There is no translation that does not have a source-text and is not in some way caused by that source-text; a text that does not have those things is simply not a translation. And that means you have to have knowledge of that text in as much completeness of its internal relations as you can manage.

Then, of course, the thing that we sometimes forget, integral to and necessary for the process of translation is knowledge of the world. Some of that knowledge of the world is knowledge that is predicated by the text: the Lorca poem or play or whatever it is. You've got to know these things, because if you don't know them, you miss this or that aspect of what you are doing. But some of that knowledge of the world is knowledge that you carry with you as the person you are or as a member of—or somebody mindful of—the group to which your translation is going. That kind of knowledge is not dispensable. You've got to have it and you've got to use it.

Having and using all those kinds of knowledge means in some cases ruling them out, or keeping them off and drawing the boundaries differently. In some cases, it means letting them in, looking in unexpected places for solutions you didn't know about to problems you didn't even know were there. That arraying and managing of knowledge, which happens part consciously and part unconsciously in the translator's mind, is what orders the linguistic energies, to give your translation not just the negative virtues of not being non-translation, but the positive ones of being a translation of the thing that it translates.

So for me, the key to any process of translation (whether I happen to be translating myself, or whether I happen to be involved, as I had the privilege of being, in helping another translator to bring something to the point of readiness) has to be about understanding those knowledge-processes, facilitating them, doing them, following where they lead. Is that knowledge absolute and eternal and fixed for all time? No, of course it isn't. 'Poetry,' as the greatest Spanish poet of this century said (it isn't Lorca), 'is the word in time.' And so is translation.

David Johnston I'm sure we'll come back to this whole idea both of knowledges of the translator and how the translator bears in mind the shared knowledge of his target group. Perhaps we could go on to Merryn.

Merryn Williams I'm the odd one out because I don't have a deep knowledge of Spanish as a language, but I am a poet in English and have for a long time been interested in Lorca and the Spanish Civil War—the martyrdom of Lorca and of so many other poets this century. So several years ago, when my own poetry was running dry, I amused myself by taking the Penguin translation of Lorca in prose, and seeing if I could turn any of them into acceptable English poems. I already knew this had been done with poems in other languages which read very well in English. Lorca's plays were already very well known at that time, but the poems were not really well known. And had I had access to as many inspiring translations as you can find on the pages here,[1] I don't think I would have dared to attempt it. However, that was what I always wanted to do, to produce poems which read well in English, which

---

[1] 'Sixteen Wounds of Love': see below.

would therefore encourage people to find out more about Lorca, and perhaps to read originals if they could.

I found, by trying out some of my translations on other poets, that Lorca appeared to leap that language barrier very well. I think this was always because of the images; they come over so clearly and so intensely. So I thought it could be done, though I'm not sure how well I'm doing it. I found that poems could easily be ruined by a poor translation. Although I try to keep very close to Lorca's meaning, or otherwise what is the point, I thought it ought to sound like poetry—not necessarily to rhyme, but to be a poem.

This all mushroomed and I was lucky enough to get a commission from Bloodaxe to write a whole book of Lorca's poems. And then at quite a late stage in the proceedings, I found out about Lorca's eleven sonnets. I had always understood from reading the Penguin edition, that they had been lost in the Civil War—I'd even tried to write a poem myself about the disappearance of the sonnets (it wasn't very good though). Then I found out that they had surfaced in Spain during the 1980s and I managed to get hold of them from the cultural attaché. Though I was at a late stage in the proceedings, faced with these eleven magnificent sonnets, which obviously couldn't be left out since they existed, I had the unenviable task of producing a translation. It seemed obvious to me that these eleven translations would have to rhyme, since they were sonnets. It was quite a struggle.

I think 'Wounds of Love' was probably the most difficult of the sonnets, which is why I've been extremely impressed with what people (many of whom are on the panel today), have done with the sonnet. Especially the third section: I put in line 10 'I try to rally' which is not there in the Spanish text (indeed you get the impression that Lorca didn't try to rally very much—he enjoyed 'dolor' and 'pena' very much indeed).[2] But I wanted something to rhyme with 'valley', so I put it in. And in the final line, instead of 'bitter knowledge', I put in 'bitter fruit' because it sort of rhymed. It was pretty impossible to get conventional, full rhymes in translating Lorca, but that's OK. Right now, British poets are very much experimenting with half-rhyme (which was invented by Wilfred Owen, another poet I'm very keen on). It's what I do myself, very much, when I'm trying to rhyme and so I tried all sorts of interesting variations, like 'round' and 'brand' or 'weight' and 'heart'

[2] See p.277.

or (of all things) 'bed' and 'fruit', which are not even half-rhymes, but which produce slightly similar sounds. That was my apology for a translation, but it had to be done within the boundaries of time.

David Johnston One of the things we'll come back to with Merryn, is the ways in which her own poetic voice and Lorca's play off each other, interpenetrate and so on. So thank you indeed. Gwynne?

Gwynne Edwards I think Nick Round has said some of the things I'm going to say and others will probably repeat them. But the two key questions which might be asked of any translator are probably: why do you translate? and what are you trying to achieve in the translation? The first of these two questions is more difficult to answer. Because to be fascinated by the work of a particular dramatist over a long period of time and to want to embark upon the daunting task of translating it, does not lend itself to easy explanations. My own attraction to Lorca's work may be the affinity of the Celt for an Andalusian. For the powerful feelings and emotions which his work lays bare and for the language in which those emotions are expressed, marked in particular by the strong images and the sheer musicality. It is no accident that my interest in theatre goes hand in hand with my love of music, above all, opera. Lorca is the most operatic of twentieth-century Spanish writers.

What then of the second and more important question—what am I trying to achieve in the translation of Lorca? The one thing I do not have is any theory of translation, much loved by academics, but surely the kiss of death for any genuine translator. For me, the translation of Lorca consists of the transposition of, say, *Blood Wedding* into the kind of English which communicates to a British audience both what Lorca is saying, and secondly, the way in which he is saying it. With regard to what Lorca is saying, it seems to me essential, as Nick has already said, that the translator should have a very good command of the Spanish language. And as well as this, a familiarity with Lorca's world; his cultural background, the traditions and the geography of Andalucía. As to the second point, the way in which he is saying it (his language and his style), the translator has to have an instinctive feeling for Lorca's language, which is something that cannot be taught. Finally, there has to be a desire on the translator's part to serve the original to the best of his ability. This desire to serve the original, however, can result in translation which is strictly literal. This was the basic mistake of the old American translations authorised by the Lorca Estate, in which literal, often word-for-word translation ends in clumsiness. This excessive fidelity to the original, is in fact in a curious way, as much a betrayal as straying too far away from it. For it must be set off against a more important kind of accuracy, to find in English convincing equivalents for the way the characters speak in Spanish. To allow them to speak in the appropriate register, to create a style in English which contains the punch and the vibrancy of Lorca's language, but which, when necessary, moves away from echoing phrases and patterns in Spanish speech, which when slavishly put into English, lead only to clumsiness. Only if the dialogue speaks easily, has the flow of real speech, yet at the same time, captures Lorca's meaning, can it be said to be really true to the original. This is not, however, adaptation, which is an entirely different matter from translation.

The translation of verse in Lorca's plays presents a particular problem. Verse sometimes occurs in the form of songs, such as the famous lullaby in *Blood Wedding*, sometimes in the form of soliloquies, as in the speech of the Moon, and sometimes in the form of dialogue, as in the case of the runaway lovers' exchanges in Act 3 scene 1. The problem with translating is that, more often than not, Lorca employs not rhyme, but assonance (for example, stressed/unstressed vowels in alternate lines, such as 'mojada', 'plata', 'relinchaba', 'garganta' and so on). And as well as that, Lorca's lines are usually of eight syllables. That kind of assonance is easier to achieve in Spanish because the language lends itself to a high degree of conformity in word endings. This cannot be achieved in English translation in any sustained way. My own solution is to use a degree of rhyme, but at the same time to avoid distorting the syntax in a way that trying to find a rhyme at the end of a line sometimes leads to. Lorca's verse retains, in fact, the word order of prose, which I also aim to retain. As far as the 8-syllable line is concerned, it seems to me best not to be restricted by that pattern. The most important thing of all is to achieve the rhythmic and formal qualities of Lorca's original, but not to dilute it.

David Johnston Despite eschewing theory at the start, Gwynne has raised a lot of theoretical issues: the paradox between fidelity and betrayal; the relationship between the translator and the original author and the status of translation as against adaptation. I'm sure that those are all issues that we will come back to. John, please.

John Edmunds I was very interested in what Nick said about the knowledge required in translation. He said that knowledge of one's own language, the language one's translating into, is at least marginally more important than knowledge of the language that one is translating from. I feel relieved about that, because my knowledge of Spanish is certainly not as profound as his. In the collaboration that we embarked on with the *Four Major Plays* for the World's Classics, I felt very much the need for somebody, an academic who was steeped in Spanish literature, to monitor what I had done, because you can think you understand and you can miss things. I translate only for theatre; I don't translate poetry. I undertook this set of translations because I was asked to do them and I found them exceedingly difficult yet enjoyable.

I question the value of doing it the way I did it. The value of translating for theatre, I think, although Lorca's work contains a great deal of poetry, seems to me to be justified, because even if you don't get the poetry right, there is so much more that you can carry over in the theatre. You've got the plot, you've got the structure, you've got the theme, you've got the characters, you've got the journey that the characters travel on and you can certainly keep the imagery at least, even if you do not use it in the same way as Lorca does, which of course works unconsciously on the listener. So it seems to me that translating theatre is something I feel I can do because if I know about anything, I know about theatre, as a director, as someone who has taught theatre in universities and as someone who has analysed many, many texts. So how do I go about it? I don't have a theory of translation. What I do is to try and produce a text which works; I go around the flat acting all the parts, I become all the characters in turn, I become the director; I go through all that process that you go through when you rehearse.

A theatre text is very different from a novel. A theatre text is, by its very nature, elliptical—what is spoken is only the tip of the iceberg. You've got to know where those words come from as an actor, before you can speak them. You've got to know why you say them, what's behind them—are they concealing or revealing? I think that as a translator, I have to go through that process. I've got to know why someone has said something before I can manage to say it in an acceptable way, to make the script jump off the page and give the right material to actors. Different actors playing the same part will find different sources for where the words come from. And that's why performances differ, as well as the personality and character of the actor, which is different in any case. I work out where the words are coming from, but someone else might work out a different subtext.

It seems to me that especially in theatre, if you're translating, you are giving your interpretation of the play, in the same way as an actor or director does. Other people will give a different interpretation of the play and their translations will differ. They will emphasise different things. In one way they will be the same and in other more subtle ways they will be different—when they come to be rehearsed they will be very different. It's a very big undertaking to assume the responsibility of understanding where those words come from, but very exciting and very challenging. I feel that technically it's very important to maintain the rhythms of the original text because that's what you hear. No audience follows every word of every text. When you talk to audiences at the end of a production that you've given your heart to, and ask them details of the plot, they won't have picked them up—it can be very depressing and it's best not to ask. But they will have picked up a tremendous amount unconsciously from the rhythms, from the sounds, from the interaction of the characters, from the situation. It's very important I think, in theatrical dialogue to keep the rhythms and the breathing spaces going. As any actor knows, you need to produce your voice from the diaphragm; it has emotional truth if it comes from here. Where you breathe is vital. Your breathing pattern is like a musical score; I try in my translations (I don't always succeed but I try) to give the English actor who is going to play a part written by Lorca the same breathing pattern, that is to say, the same emotional base, as you would have if you were doing the original text. The best compliment you can have as a translator is to have a compliment from an actor who has played the part in both languages. This happened to me with a Molière, *The School for Wives*—the actor had played the part in French, but was English. He said, 'when I read your translation I felt I could do with it exactly what I did with it when I played it in French. I could breathe in the same way, I could do the same thing with it'. If you can manage that, you're getting close to the life-blood, I think, of the play.

So then you have to think, who has the priority? Who do you owe most loyalty to? Is it to Lorca? Or your potential audience or reader? This is something that weighs on you all the time, because all translation is compromise. My belief is that I have to make it work for an audience *now*, for a theatre *now*. It's no good writing something that is maybe a very good translation, but if it isn't going to work in the theatre, if it isn't going to inspire directors to do good work and communicate something to the audience, then it seems to me a waste of time—it's a purely academic exercise.

There are times when you have cultural things that won't carry across, like those wretched 'migas' which the bride [in *Bodas de sangre*] gets up at first light and cooks for the men before they go out to work. Well I had *migas* in Andalucía a couple of weeks ago because I was very curious to know what they tasted like. They were dried up, with breadcrumbs and pepper. But you can't put 'migas' and you can't say 'fried bread'. So I said 'she gets up in the morning and she fries the bread for the men before they go out to work'—one simply had to leave it out and just say 'she fries the bread'. If you want to put in the original phrase, you put it in a note for the reader, but you've got to make the thing work for yourself as a text for the stage.

As far as the verse is concerned, which Gwynne has spoken about extremely well, it is impossible to do the same things as Lorca does exactly. This is where Nick and I sometimes disagreed in our collaboration. Because I couldn't even rhyme or half-rhyme, I felt it was important to have a rhythm, which at least made Lorca's words verse and took them away from the realm of prose, but that's just a personal feeling that I have. You've got to be aware, of course, of the tremendous shifts of gear in Lorca, which are frequent—you start off absolutely naturalistically and then it will move off and shift gear—and you have to try and capture that. It's an impossible task, but it's great fun trying.

David Johnston Again, all sorts of issues there: page versus stage, the different loyalties that that entails and above all, the process of translation as interrogating the drama from the perspective of a man of the theatre. I can just picture you walking around your flat trying out all the different characters. I would love to see your neighbours' reactions when you translate 'The Public'! Colin Teevan, please.

Colin Teevan I was very interested in what John said when he protested about not having any theory of translation and then went on to give a very clear and very definite theory of translation. I think everyone has a theory of translation—there are people up here with very different views about it. I think knowledge is important. I haven't actually translated a Lorca play, but I've read through a lot of his stuff in both Spanish and

English. I've translated the sonnet ['Wounds of Love'] twice in the programme[3] and I have translated from Ancient Greek, from Italian and from French. Nick talks about knowledge. Now I wouldn't be the expert in any of those languages, but what I found to be the most crucial aspect of translation for the stage anyway, is to have an emotional link with what I'm translating. I don't think it's sufficient to have just knowledge. At least for a text that is going on stage, one has to be able to relate to it.

The plays I have translated from Ancient Greek are plays that have personally appealed to me. I've actually been asked to do others. It was suggested to me to do an *Oedipus* by The Abbey in Dublin, but I couldn't work out a way of getting into it. And although *Oedipus* is considered to be a greater work, I personally felt attracted to the *Iphigenia in Aulis*. I couldn't see how *Oedipus* could fundamentally relate to the culture that I was living in. It's a similar story with the Italian plays that I've translated, written by a close friend of mine; we work in very similar ways and so there's a personal reason for it.

I am repeatedly attracted to the work of Lorca. Since I read him for the first time ten years ago, I have learnt a bit of Spanish. It was wonderful to be asked to come here because it meant I could indulge in going over a lot of his work again. There's something else that John talked about which I think is crucially important (we'll all differ fundamentally about this, but perhaps it's because we're all doing different kinds of translations in different areas): there's a terrible tendency in Ireland, especially with the Greeks, to get a *poet* to do the translations. Similarly with Lorca, Kennelly did a wonderful version linguistically. But theatrically, when directors see verse on the page, they get a lyric poet to do it. Heaney did a translation of Philoctetes; Kennelly has done several classics and Lorca. Some of these have moments of beautiful lyricism. But a knowledge of the stage is fundamentally important for any translation of Lorca.

Lorca had a profound knowledge of the stage. He was a man of the theatre: both opera and drama. He saw the continuation of poetry on the stage and he translated that in physical song which was profound and intricate. Aristotle in the *Poetics*, makes a distinction between the different types of poetry: there's lyric poetry, dramatic poetry and epic poetry. They are different. Just because the words appear in verse form

---

[3] See pp.274-5.

in a play, you can't just say 'oh that's poetry so we'll translate it as poetry'. This is something I would take issue with, with theatre companies. To translate Lorca, you need people who know about the theatre, to translate for the stage. That's different for an actual published text. Again, I agree with John, you have to know who you're going to pitch it at and where it's going to. Are we doing this so that people can read something that is close to the Spanish original, or are we doing this as a text to put on stage?

The weak translations are the ones which try to be a bit of everything. This always struck me about Penguin Classics (particularly some of the older texts); they attempted to be all things to all men, a bit for the stage and a bit for the page. At the same time, they tried to keep line for line and close to the original. I heard a wonderful comment recently: the Lyric Theatre in Belfast, which is our equivalent to Northern Stage, is going through a bit of a renovation and redevelopment period at the moment. They were having consultations with the Board, and the Artistic Director was saying that he wanted to do new versions of the classics and get playwrights from Belfast to work on these. He was talking about one specific Greek play, and a member of the Board said 'why can't you do the original?' and the director replied, 'what, in Greek?', to which she answered, 'no, the Penguin Classic'. It was fixed in her head! The third thing that has struck me about translation is something that David and I have talked of before. I did a translation of *Iphigenia*, called 'Iph', which was performed recently in Belfast. It might come to London, but it was quite interesting in that it was quite local. I found that to translate stuff like classics or Lorca, one has to locate it somewhere in one's own head, whether we use the dialect or not. It's difficult to capture the spirit of Spain and Andalucía in the West of Ireland or Scotland. I think one needs a firm dialect for what one is going into, a language. I think that RP has lost its power. It's part of the problem of Lorca going into RP English because RP is not a located dialect, it is a class dialect. One doesn't get a sense of the world of the play.

This leads me on to why I did two translations of the sonnet in the festival programme. The first version, which appears as a translation, is done in alexandrines, but apart from that, I was trying to capture the rhyming scheme, the formality and clarity of the original. But I felt in my head that it came alive when I found an emotional link to it. When I'd done the first version, I was driving down the Ards Peninsula, which is this extraordinary place south of Belfast. First we drove to this town called Portavogie. We got lost in the back streets and saw, in someone's back yard, hanging on the washing line, besides the knickers and the bras, a bandsman's uniform and the Union Jack. It was such an extraordinary image to see people sprucing up their Union Jack for the season. And as we were driving back along the coast road, we saw this huge piece of graffiti which had apparently been there for years. It said something like: 'We refuse to forsake the blue skies of Ulster for the grey mist of an Irish Republic'. When you see this in the lashing rain it makes you think! Reality is in flux in this country. But it was when I saw that piece of graffiti, that my second translation, 'You put a bomb in my heart', came about. Lorca's poem is about love and hatred. I suppose that in the midst of the run-up to the 'yes' vote and the 'no' vote, people expressed so much hatred. But you also realised that the hatred gave these people living in a backwater of a backwater their definition. When I found a personal reason, I was in the midst of a society so rife with these overwhelming emotions, that's when the poem came alive for me. I have great respect for the work done by my colleagues up here, but that dirty word 'emotion' has not come into the discussion so far.

Nicholas Round   That's a form of knowledge too. Another great voice of twentieth-century Spanish literature (I'm going to get Miguel de Unamuno in here somewhere!) said, 'Siento pensamiento, pienso sentimiento' ('I think feeling, I feel thought'). And if it's not that kind of knowledge, then it is academic in all the wrong senses, and we should be ashamed of it.

David Johnston   It was interesting that the Kennelly version of *Blood Wedding*, done here at Northern Stage, could be read as a meditation on the Northern Ireland peace process. I think you can probably read Colin's version of 'Llagas de Amor' as a meditation on the marching season! Thank you Colin. You're raising some very important points, especially about the emotional link which recreates the energy for the stage. Also you raised something that Nick and I mentioned this morning, that translations should really disappear after a while, rather than be done again, and again and again. Otherwise we enshrine sameness in the way these plays are performed. I'm sorry to leave you to the end, John.

John Clifford There are three stages in translating Lorca. The first one is, as Nick said, knowledge. It's very boring; it's kind of dictionary work—footnotes and trying to understand the text. It's like a square thing; it's very uncomfortable because the English you end up with after that process is horrible; it's really ugly. The second stage has to do with making that square thing erode—finding the emotional connection. Like John, I walk up and down, I become everybody. And you have to try to feel everything; try to overcome your fear of what is going on. It's very like writing an original play, you have to tune into the characters, trust them and listen to what they have to say. Because Lorca was such a wonderful dramatist, these are characters that live on the stage.

It's so important, what John was saying about breathing. I can't even aspire to get the breathing spaces in the same places as Lorca. I know that a character tells me when to breathe. That's how it is, you have to trust the character. It's very similar, it's not very different from me translating that sonnet, which I've never really tried to do before.[4] Because for me poetry is something that is spoken; I can't really cope with poetry on a page; I love poetry that is spoken. So for me a poem is a dramatic thing and it's important to try to tune into the experience of the 'I' that wrote that poem. And then (and I may be wrong), I don't see the necessity to try to keep the rhyme scheme or the sonnet form. I think that experience tells you what the form is and how it's going to be.

And then the final process after trying to find the link within me, within my experience, so that I really understand the work and really live it in my imagination has to be to look at what has come out and to relate it back to the Spanish, because sometimes characters are a bit wicked and they run away with themselves.

It's funny, but your first audience, when you're a playwright, the most important audience, is not these people sitting out there, but the actors. There has to be a way of communicating very directly to the actors and firing their imagination. That's why a read-through is such a scary business. Because if that connection, that piece of communication isn't happening between you and the actors, then there's no chance that it's ever going to come alive on stage.

---

[4] See p.263.

David Johnston I think Lorca had a considerable reputation for the way he spoke his poetry, and he certainly considered his poetry as poetry to be heard, as much as to be read. There are clearly issues of creativity at stake, as John underlined when he talked about translating as being very much like writing a new play. Some of the panel might now like to comment on other points raised. Nick?

Nicholas Round One thing that I think is fundamental, and yet controversial, is that creativity is not the exclusive feif of poets or dramatists or artists or actors or academics or 'creative people'. Creativity is an inherent part of our possession of language; it is something that is in the language. As anybody who has ever written a line worth writing knows, it's like playing an instrument; the tune is in the flute or the fiddle or whatever, and you are just the lucky one who gets it out. Some translators have a bit of luck with language now and again, but it's everybody's patrimony. If we're going to theorise what we do, we must not do it on the grounds that we've got some special gift—like five quid's worth of shares in ICI. It's not like that: it's a commonality. One of the exciting things about Lorca's language is the way in which it flows in and out of the commonality of language. Specialist knowledge and professional know-how has its place but it's not fundamental to creativity.

Colin Teevan It wasn't that I meant that only playwrights should translate plays. There's a practical and a craft side to writing for the theatre. Of the twelve classical Greek plays put on in Ireland over the last ten years, only two have been translated by playwrights. There is a lack of theatrical know-how.

John Clifford What Nick is saying is that creativity is everybody's right; everyone has a right to find ways of expressing that creativity. A terrible thing our society does is to deny that creativity. But at the same time there is a specialised knowledge of the theatre that helps make translation work, as Colin has pointed out.

Question from the floor What exactly is this specialised knowledge that you talk about?

Colin Teevan It's like woodcraft; it's a skill that you learn that keeps growing and evolving. There are different sorts of translations out there: there are ones for the stage and ones that are very good, tight academic ones. I would say that as a playwright, when approached to translate plays for the theatre, I see it as part of my job to make this play work as well for the stage as I can. If it doesn't work for the stage, as in being copied slavishly line for line, then it's wrong. You're taking plays by Lorca that work in Spanish and you're trying to find a way of making them work in English. Translations go out of date much quicker than the originals. This is because each translator is trying to find a way to make it work, often in quite different contexts. Gwynne, you were talking about the American translations, the Penguin Classics. In one sense the context was quite different.

Gwynne Edwards I think one of the problems faced by those translators is that they were hamstrung by the Lorca Estate, which insisted on literal translations, and therefore they got something that was unspeakable.

John Edmunds Translations of plays from the past generally use the language of the translator, don't they? I mean, it's terribly artificial if you try to reproduce seventeenth-century French. This strikes me as being a very interesting point. It reminds me of being a student in Paris and seeing Jean-Louis Barrault playing Gide's prose translation of *Hamlet*. I was very familiar with the text, but because it was in contemporary French, it struck me with the same kind of freshness as it would have struck Shakespeare's original audience. And this of course is how Shakespeare is received all over the world, in their contemporary languages.

Question from the floor How important is it for productions of Lorca to be localised?

David Johnston Are we talking Celtic affinity here? Personally I'm quite opposed to the idea of a Celtic affinity.

Colin Teevan I think it's more of a sociological than a Celtic affinity. Lorca was 'other', he was an outsider in lots of ways. I think that his writing is about being on the edge, so any regional production may appeal more. It's interesting to see all these Celts up here on the panel; he works so well in Scotland and he's produced so much there.

Gwynne Edwards I personally think that Lorca would work very well in a North country accent. Not a terribly exaggerated one, but one that has a certain grit and strength. Whereas it doesn't work in a Southern English accent. This was part of the problem with the West End production of *The House of Bernarda Alba*.

Nicholas Round We've got about three or four overlapping factors here, that I don't think are related to Celtic ethnicity. One is that the areas where Spanish is being taught are areas where it happens to be taught in certain kinds of school. Catholic schools have a tradition of recognising Spanish as a Catholic language, as opposed to German which, for some reason, was recognised as a Protestant language. That has meant that the centres of Spanish teaching have been in places like Glasgow, Belfast and so on. I happened to do Spanish because it was taught at a tiny rural school in Cornwall at the instigation of a headmaster who wanted to give the local hayseeds something that the city slickers hadn't got. So he gave them Spanish and it worked more or less. So there are all sorts of contingencies like that.

Another, slightly more controversial point is that as you move away from metropolitan centres, even in the inner cities, as you move away from the established and élite groups, you move into areas where a spoken-language culture is more vigorous and a written-language culture slightly less so. It's not uniform and there's also cultural deprivation in both types of case, but it does sometimes happen. Lorca's plays, which are predicated on rural communities where speech and interactions with speech are very important, probably have corresponding language possibilities which are a bit more immediate there; it becomes easier, for example, to find the speech-rhythms.

Colin Teevan You also find a mixture of class in a small rural community, whereas in the city they separate.

Nicholas Round There are still people in some cities who are only one generation away from the rural community. People remember. And a final point, if I can sort it out: I think that in certain areas, Ireland being one of them, the response to works that are mythically shaped is more normal because people are living closer to a conscious apprehension of their own myths. It's not that the English don't have this, it's just that they've got to a point where they don't recognise it.

John Edmunds That's interesting, because I felt with *Blood Wedding*, having tried to translate Racine, that I was very close to the same kind of world. And underneath the superficiality of the setting, the impulses driving the characters was very similar to Racine.

David Johnston I think that one of the reasons that Lorca works well in Irish is that the central dislocations of Lorca's world are ours as well: sin, guilt, trying to escape being codified into a particular form of behaviour and so on.

Colin Teevan I also think there's a debate about identity in Lorca's work which is crucial. Irish theatre is based on a continual debate about identity. Maybe in the South East of England there has always been an assumption about identity. Lorca's restlessness during his career made him arrive back to where he was born. These are very marginalised cultures, like Scotland, like Wales, like the North of England; they continue to debate their identity. When you're living in the margins, how do you relate to the power centre? Lorca's plays are not about the power centre.

Question from the floor How do you go about making Lorca's verse sound musical?

Merryn Williams It has to sound good to my ear; not a punchy sort of rhyme which is so discredited in England, but there has to be a rhythm that pleases me before I think it's worthy of translation. I think it's very difficult to translate the 'Gypsy Ballads' because the Spanish poems have all these line endings in 'r' or 'o'. English does not work in the same way, which is why I had to use half-rhyme. Endings like 'moon' and 'June' sound predictable and should be avoided.

Nicholas Round You've got to get the right musicality. The *Gypsy Ballads* are a case in point. It's a snare and a delusion to think you can take things directly into a Scots form. Because Scots ballad metre is built on patterns within the four-line stanza—that's what satisfies you—whereas the Spanish ballad, or *romance*, is continuous—it goes on with a flowing assonance. American translators know more about Lorca than I will ever know. But Andrew Anderson made a terrible mistake by trying to turn the *Gypsy Ballads* into that kind of rhythm, and the result was a real mess. Much better to go for something like a blues rhythm (which also has much shorter lines) so you can get continuity. Find the music. One shouldn't be afraid to go over from a Spanish musicality which is built quite largely around the vowel to an English-language musicality which is built quite substantially around consonants (and very often crunchy, clashing consonants as well). Alliteration is another way of finding out the right music, a way which we often neglect—yet it's been in the English language since before it was English. It's ours, it's wonderful and we do it all the time, even in ordinary speech. It has a place in translating Lorca: it can keep it alive and musical. It links the words, the linguistic 'given' with the identity and physicality of *this* poetry. You're quite right, though, to say that the rhythm is the key—that's where it all happens.

Question from the floor It's purely the rhythm that drives us along—look at the impact of flamenco, for example. But what about if the ambition for rhythm lets the words and the meaning of the words down?

Colin Teevan I went to see one of these *cantaor* [=Flamenco singer] companies in Edinburgh doing a show and they had the misfortune to print a translation of the words that they were actually saying. It was at the interval that I realised the words were there and I'd been really enjoying the first half until I read that. It was such dull rubbish; I don't know if the translation was bad, but it was truly awful. It did look wonderfully mystical and mysterious on stage though, there was no question of that. It was sad to pluck out the heart of the mystery in that way, though.

Nicholas Round It's a question of the whole form. Let's take another example: a Handel opera, which is very nice to watch, pleasant to listen to, and a complete form in itself. But if you translate the words by themselves, the result looks like an old Frankie Howard parody of opera—you know: 'They're coming, they're coming! They're coming, they're coming! They're coming ... ! They ought to be here by now!' But let's get back to Lorca. Lorca is not a flamenco artist. He's an artist who uses flamenco, as he uses a tremendous number of other sources. In the sonnet translated in the festival programme, he uses the Baroque language of the wonderful seventeenth-century sonnet writer, Quevedo; he's referring to Plato and the *Death of Socrates* in the last line. His work is a magpie's nest and this is one of the challenges to the translator, that if you can't enrich your language from all these points, you're producing Lorca-and-water—which, I suppose, you always necessarily are.

Question from the floor Is there any such thing as a universal translation?

Merryn Williams I believe that occasionally you can speak of a universal translation. The first poems I ever came across in translation were those at the end of *Doctor Zhivago*, translated from Russian, a language that I do not know. The first of these is called 'Hamlet' and I still think it's a marvellous poem in English. I remember being very annoyed with a much inferior translation by someone else many years later. But I would say that most of the time it is possible to find a really good translation. Time and time again, a poem strikes sparks in poets' minds differently. Occasionally one does come across a faultless translation, but you'd never get this with a play.

Nicholas Round It's most unlikely that this or that translation will last. If it happens, it won't be done by the translator, it will be done by those who read it, those who respond to it. One can think of poems that have survived a long time in versions that are translations or imitations. Yeats, for example, imitating the French sixteenth-century line: 'When you're old and grey and full of sleep.' I don't think that will fade as a version of that earlier thought for a very, very long time. Or Ronsard taking on the poem about the roses which goes back to late Latin. These things last as works of words. And works of words last for a long time but they don't last forever in the same way. And yet, in the sybilline prophesy at the end of the Icelandic epic cycle—the *Voluspà*, I think it is—when the three survivors of the battle of the end of the world walk out into the morning, and everything is gone—gods, heroes, everything—there's a phrase used: 'Golden chessmen will be found in the grass, which the gods had left in ancient time.' It's a hint that the works of making, or of words, might survive after all. If so, that's not the privilege of the writers of Icelandic books, or of the gods, but of all makers: it's a human privilege.

John Edmunds Is it true that a translation made very close in time to the conception of the original text has more chance of survival? For example, I've just read *Don Quixote* in World's Classics, a version which I thought was brilliant. It was written in the eighteenth century and wasn't very close to the original, but very good. It was a marvellous work in its own right and I would have thought that it should last as long as the *Don Quixote* does in the English-speaking world. Maybe it's true of the authorised version of the Bible. Great works of literature are made from translations. There's a very good translation of Rabelais too—made very, very close to the writing of the original in the sixteenth century, only shortly afterwards. Maybe it's something to do with the length of time that elapses between the writing of the original text and the translation.

Question from the floor How do you feel about people doing things with your translations?

John Clifford When you write something, you give it away, to actors who speak it and so on. There's something about the devotion and skill that somebody has lavished on the work that makes it extraordinary.

Colin Teevan I've got one play translated into French, Portuguese and Italian. It's a comedy and what's really strange is that all the jokes are in different places. What's interesting is what each society laughs at. I've seen it in two of those languages and English. People were just laughing in different places, and I was saying, 'no, no, no, the funny bit isn't that'. Quite often in French, the translation was very close. But despite this proximity of translation, there was quite a cultural difference. There was a different sense of humour in the French; they tended to latch on to the dirty, the bawdy and the scurrilous to a greater extent than the English. It's a really strange experience watching your own stuff in a different language because it's both yours and not yours. I'd never really realised the importance of a good translator up until then. I'd heard it said that *Miss Smilla's Feeling for Snow* [by Peter Hoeg, 1993] was not very successful in Danish but was a very big hit in English because of a very good translation. There's a Northern Irish writer, Robert McLiam Wilson, whose book *Eureka Street* was only moderately successful here, while scooping a place as a top ten bestseller in France. Quite often, a good translation (I'm not saying it's better than the original), can give something a good re-writing. I've often heard it said that if you compare translations of Shakespeare in French and German, Shakespeare seems to go into German much more happily than into French. I was wondering whether Spanish into English is a more difficult leap than maybe German into English or whatever?

Do you think there are languages that translate much better between themselves?

Nicholas Round What you win on the roundabouts you lose on the swings. If the languages are further apart in basic structures, translating is very, very difficult. If the languages lie very close together, such as Spanish and Italian, there's still a problem of translation because you can't establish the carry-over into the other language with that much security. It's not an ideal world: we're stuck with what we're made of. In terms of the range of world languages, the differences between any West European/Indo-European pair of languages are minute anyway, so I don't think that this is a killer obstacle. Though it can be an obstacle in some ways and you generally find yourself working with half-principles and half-truths. Take the widely-held notion that English will prefer concrete and verbal expressions to abstract and noun-based or adjective-based expressions. That's a broad principle that you break seven times in a day, because it doesn't work. (And there are ways of proving that it *can't* work as a reliable way of characterizing the English language.) And yet, because it refers translators to certain particular traditions of English poetry, it can to some extent guide them. But there's a simple fact about English that everybody knows and we've already highlighted its implications: English has a divided vocabulary, part Germanic-Saxon and part French and Latin, while Spanish vocabulary is ninety-five per cent Latin-based. Therefore the direct counterpart in English that looks like the Spanish word, is often a word that has very little emotive charge at all.

John Edmunds Well, some people must think that it's easier to translate from English into Spanish than from French into Spanish. I happily received a cheque one day from the BBC, a repeat fee, and I discovered to my astonishment that my translation of Racine's *Phèdre*, which had been broadcast on Radio 3, had been sold to Argentinian Radio, translated into Spanish and broadcast! You would think that the French would be closer to the Spanish. However, I pocketed the money!

Question from the floor How do you translate context?

David Johnston Do you mean the historical context of the original performance or the cultural context?

Question from the floor Cultural.

Nicholas Round The answer in a sense is that you don't translate context, but you have an option of transposing it, which will affect the detail of your translation. How you try that option depends upon the nature of the materials. If you take *Doña Rosita la soltera*, for instance, clearly the expectations about unmarried women which ultimately destroy Rosita's life are not those of 1990s Britain. But it would be hard to preserve very much of that play, of its tensions, necessities, compulsions—let alone that extraordinary symphony of kitsch cultural references in the second act, which makes such a wonderful comic episode—if you simply replaced those assumptions with the assumptions of present-day Britain, and re-wrote the translation accordingly. Whether you could do another play in another way is another question. This morning we heard about a version of *El público* that had a deliberately atemporal setting, costumes and so forth.[5] I'm sure that play would work extremely well and it could be given a slant as of now, or as of then. But each case is different in the end and we cannot say, 'You're doing it right if you do it this way' or, for that matter, 'You're doing it wrong.'

David Johnston Part of the gender issue in Lorca comes from the honour code, which Lorca was re-working from Golden Age drama. John has a lot of experience in negotiating that code into English.

John Clifford Yes, it's very difficult. It's part of that process of trying to understand for yourself and feel for yourself what it's about. It's all about digging very deep to find out what the underlying question is. If you think about *Yerma*, it's not as scandalous now as it was then. But the main problem, which is to do with misogyny, is very much alive and very much part of our world. I'm interested, Colin, in what you said about finding an emotional link between what you're translating and your own life—if you can relate to it emotionally, you can find a way of somehow conveying the context. But it's making that link, establishing the connection, that's so crucial. It's an internal process and then you have to trust that somehow you'll find a form of words that is necessary to communicate that link.

---

[5] See Maria Delgado's contribution to this volume.

Gwynne Edwards Three of us on this panel have also translated Golden Age plays in which the honour code is very important. The productions in some cases have been taken to task by the critics because they appear not to be able to understand the honour code. It goes back to the influence of Islam; the attitude towards women which found its way into Golden Age plays. The honour code is a persistent problem.

John Clifford If you think of Rosaura in Calderón's *Life is a Dream* who's searching for her honour, it's a difficult idea to communicate in one sense, but at another level, this is a woman who's been betrayed. Even though we might find it hard to relate to the honour code, we do relate to that sense of being betrayed by someone you love—the fury and the rage you feel, the hurt. It's relating at that deep emotional level that I think is important.

Colin Teevan It stops things from going out of date.

John Edmunds Just to come back to *Phèdre*, where it's such a big issue. The love Phèdre feels for Hippolyte was thought of as incest at that time, because he has the same blood as her husband. We no longer think of that as an incestuous relationship. I asked Barbara Jefford, who was rehearsing the part for Radio 3, whether she had a problem with this, the fact that we don't consider the relationship quite as dreadful as Phèdre did. Barbara said that it didn't worry her at all. It was a huge issue for Phèdre, and that was all that mattered to her as an actress, and so she empathised with the character. We can underestimate the capability of actors to empathise with characters. If your actors do it, then I think your audience will too. So I don't find these cultural barriers so difficult. I think we can overestimate them.

Llagas de amor

Esta luz, este fuego que devora.
Este paisaje gris que me rodea.
Este dolor por una sola idea.
Esta angustia de cielo, mundo y hora.

Este llanto de sangre que decora
lira sin pulso ya, lúbrica tea.
Este peso del mar que me golpea.
Este alacrán que por mi pecho mora.

Son guirnalda de amor, cama de herido,
donde sin sueño, sueño tu presencia
entre las ruinas de mi pecho hundido.

Y aunque busco la cumbre de prudencia,
me da tu corazón valle tendido
con cicuta y pasión de amarga ciencia.

Federico García Lorca[1]

---

[1] *Obras completas* (Madrid: Aguilar, 1986), I, 941. Also published in *Sonetos del amor oscuro. Poemas de amor y erotismo. Inéditos de madurez*, ed. Javier Ruiz-Portella (Barcelona: Áltera, 1995), 29.

Scorpion

Even amidst this ashen scene
I am burning, bereft because of one idea.
And all my heavens, world and time
Are now made wretched.

But I gave bloody tears for this.
Even offered lewd illumination
'Til all my strength was gone.
Massive ocean crush of bruising feeling
Made no difference:
The scorpion remained, lodged in my heart.

That was love, my heart's first flowering.
Sick with it, restless, I lay down to die,
Hot-fevered with desire.
Lost then in that dream I had hoped was death
Again I found you:
You, still there, in the ruins of my heart.

Hopeless, then, to hope for wisdom
When you are my life's entire landscape. Poison. Passion.
In the end, for what?
Love's bitter trick of certainty.

Candida Clark

Love Wounds

love wounds with light
love wounds with fire
the fire devours me: greyness surrounds me
love's wound obsesses me
love's wound that I cannot escape
that fills each inch of the sky
each blade of grass each minute of each day

I weep tears of blood which fall
on my poetry and stick
like enamel on a broken guitar
like rancid fat like grease which covers everything
my pulse has a heavy beat
the ocean weighs on me
a small stinging scorpion has taken over my brain

I live like a patient in a hospital bed
love decorates with a fever chart
I pass sleepless nights dreaming you're with me
like an invading army encamped
in the ruins of my chest
where my heart was
I don't want this. I want mountains,
I want to walk on the hills and wear sensible shoes,
but your heart drags me down a dark valley
a valley of bitter knowledge
and of poisoned flowers.

John Clifford

Wounds of Love

This light that consumes, this fire that devours,
This land of grey surrounding me with fear,
This sorrow fathered by a lone idea,
This anguish of sky, world, and dwindling hours,

This blood lament which graces, gives art
To a pulseless lyre, a lusty firebrand,
This heavy ocean pounding me to sand,
This scorpion lurking deep within my heart

Are all love's wreath, a wounded man's bed,
Where without sleep's dreams, I dream your presence
Amidst the ruins of my shattered head.

And though I yearn for the peaks of prudence
Your heart conjures for me a valley spread
With hemlock and passion of harsh science.

Sebastian Doggart

Lacerations of Love

This light, this fire, this quick devouring lime;
This grey and empty landscape that surrounds me;
This torment of one sole idea that hounds me;
This anguish in the heavens, the world and time;

These tears of blood that decorate the strings
Of my mute lyre, bright torch whose flame should light me;
These batterings of a heavy sea that smite me;
This scorpion living in my breast that stings;

These are love's garland, the wounded victim's bed
Where sleepless I dream that with me you remain
Among the ruins of the heart you bled.

I seek the heights of wisdom, but in vain:
Deep in the valley of your heart I'm fed
On hemlock, bitter knowledge bought with pain.

John Edmunds

Wounds of Love

This light, this devouring fire.
This landscape around me, grey forever.
This pain on account of a single idea.
This anguish of sky, of the world, the hour.

This weeping of blood adorning
A lyre now stilled, torch of longing.
This weight of the sea's endless pounding.
This scorpion which makes my heart its dwelling.

They are love's wreaths, a sick man's bed,
Where I, sleepless, dream of your presence
Amongst the ruins of a heart half dead.

And though I seek the heights of prudence,
You offer me only the valley ahead,
And hemlock and longing for bitter experience.

Gwynne Edwards

Stigmata of Love

I'm swallowed by this light, by this fire,
By this grey landscape that's my crime,
By the endless pain of one idea,
By this anguish that's heaven, earth and time,

By the drip drip drip of blood's lament
Across rhythmless strings, thus kindling a flame,
By the maelstrom sea in its torment,
By the scorpion that is my heart's game;

These my garland of love, on which I lie wounded,
And where without dreams, I dream of your presence
Plumbing the depths that my lone heart has sounded.

And though I might crave the summits of prudence
In the vale of your passion such thoughts are dumbfounded
Laid low by hemlock and a lust that's dark science.

James Flint

Wounds of Love

And as the sun dies
on us
and there's nothing we can do
as forever isn't forever any more and this pain in a way feels overdue
feels real ...
What can I do
but silence my mind whilst I lie awake
longing for you?
For all this anger, despair and agony talking
are like wounds
who carry with them a thousand tombs.
Oh, insecurity... I feel imprisoned by your clutch
and burdened by these unbearable moments for loving so
                                            much.
I yearn to be able to make the same sun rise again
and from reliving dreams of our togetherness I try to abstain
and with your body not next to mine
all I can do is sleep so just for a while I don't hear my heart's
                                            pine ...

Paula Guarderas

Wounds of Love

This light, this devouring fire,
This grey landscape encaging me.
This sorrow born of one idea.
This anguished sky, world and hour.

This grieving blood, this dandy art,
Lyre without a pulse now, lascivious torch.
This bull sea goring my flesh.
This scorpion thriving in my heart.

These are love's garland, bed of a wounded man
Where I lie sleepless, dreaming of you
In the ruins of my shattered soul.

And though I'd climb a peak of wisdom
Your heart's valley is a fearsome view
Of hemlock, bitter passion encompassing all.

Brendan Kennelly

The wounds of love

This brilliant light and fire which devour.
This grey expanse by which I am surrounded.
This sorrow which on one idea is founded.
This agony of heaven, world and hour.

These tears of blood with which is dressed
a lyre silent still, a torch of lust.
This sea of which I feel the thrust.
This scorpion which in my heart makes its nest.

They are love's garland, and the wounded's rest,
where, sleepless, I create you in a dream
amongst the ruins of my crushed-in breast;

and though I seek discretion's height supreme
your heart now gives me this vast vale oppressed
by passion's bitter skill, where hemlocks teem.

John Kerr

Your Light—after Lorca

Your light has reached me as a fire
Your light has bled this landscape grey
Your light impales me on desire
Your light is pain in all I see
Your light makes septic every wound
Your light makes knives of catgut strings
Your light's a breeze become monsoon
Your light breeds maggots in my dreams
Your light has shrivelled me to bed
Your light has burnt out all my heart
Your light's left all but needing dead
Your light's left wreckage in my head
By day, I hope that rescue finds me:
Each night I go to you, despite me.

Al Robertson

Wounds of Love

This light, and this consuming flame,
and this grey land on every side,
this grieving for a simple thought,
this agony of earth and sky and time,
these tears of blood that fall like jewels on
my pulseless lyre, now made the torch of lust,
this pounding of me in the heavy seas,
this scorpion that lurks about my breast,
are the rewards love brings: a bed where I
wounded and sleepless, dream that you are here,
among the shattered fragments of my loving,
and though I struggle towards wisdom's height,
your heart has spread a valley at my feet
—hemlock and passion, bred of bitter knowing.

Nicholas Round

Love's Thorns

This light, this fire that devours me,
this landscape that surrounds me,
this sorrow for one idea, and one idea only,
this anguish of sky, world, and extinguishing hours,

this cry of blood that adorns
this dying lyre, this restless pyre,
this ocean weight that sends me down,
this scorpion that ravages my heart,
seeking a place to rest,

aching garland of love, bed of the wounded,
where, sleepless, I dream of your presence
among the ruins of a barren heart.

And though I look for the height of prudence,
your heart only offers
a valley tendered with hemlock
and the bitter passion of science.

Caridad Svich

The Wounds of Love

This light, this unquenchable fire that consumes me,
This scalded black and smoking wasteland all round me,
This one burning obsession that confounds me,
These limits of earth, sky and time which entomb me,

These tears of molten blood which gild and untune me
And my lubricious lyre, a useless tool compounding me
To this barren shore where wave upon wave pounds me,
This scorpion nurtured in my chest which dooms me,

These are thorns in the crown of the love which in bed
I wear through sleepless nights as I dream that you rest,
Amidst the ruins of my heart, your lovely head,

And though wisdom dictates that aloofness is best,
The thought of you drags me down to the dark sea bed
With the bittersweet hemlock of love in my breast.

Colin Teevan

You put a bomb in my heart

First a flash, then a fireball, which like a fash
-ionable new ism, swept all before it before,
Having only itself left to devour, did just that.
The sky, seeing the general distress,
Spat down tears of blood; the earth, for its part,
Through a million ruptured pipes, did its
Damnedest to piss the height of heaven and,
Needless to say, my Apollonian lyre
Was completely banjaxed in the blast.
It was a time for snakes and scorpions.

Yet, though this detritus was the only crop
Gathered from the ruins of our attrition,
And, though I should, in truth, have had more cop
Than to fall for such sweet ammunition,
From the second you blew me all over this shop,
It's been this kamikaze love, that's given me my definition.

Colin Teevan

Love's Wounds

I'm itching all over with Prickly Heat.
I'm trapped within Tupperware Plastic.
An idea lone and neat
Has wounded complete
And Love's Band Aid has lost its elastic.

Tears of blood start to fall on my stringless Les Paul.
I got wiped out whilst surfing The Blue.
My brow is now wringing
And a scorpion stinging
My heart.
Love, I'm sick over you.

Here I lie in dead flowers through the night's sleepless hours
As you bulldoze my derelict dreams.

I would run for the hills
But you offer me pills,
The slough of despond
And dashed schemes.

Mark Westcott

The Wounds of Love

This light, this fire that devours.
This grey landscape that surrounds me.
This obsession that torments me.
Anguish of heaven, world and hours.

This sobbing of the blood, draped round
a broken lyre, a slippery brand.
This sea which pounds me with its weight.
This scorpion dwelling in my heart.

Are all love's garland, and a bed,
where, without sleep, I try to rally,
and dream, amid the ruins, of your presence.

And though I seek the height of prudence
give me your heart, a spread-out valley
of hemlock and desire for bitter fruit.

Merryn Williams[2]

---

[2] Published in Federico García Lorca, *Selected Poems*, trans. Merryn Williams (Newcastle: Bloodaxe, 1992), 209.

Lightning Source UK Ltd.
Milton Keynes UK
UKHW021301201022
410805UK00035B/679